HOLD FAST

HOLD FAST

365 DEVOTIONS FOR MEN BY MEN

Our Daily Bread

Hold Fast: 365 Devotions for Men by Men

The devotional readings collected in this book were previously published over a span of years in *Our Daily Bread* devotional booklets that are distributed around the world in more than fifty languages.

ISBN: 978-1-64070-229-5

Library of Congress Cataloging-in-Publication Data Available

Printed in China
23 24 25 26 27 28 29 30 / 8 7 6 5 4 3 2 1

FOREWORD

The world needs men! Men who are brave, daring, and intentional, men who offer shelter for the weak and vulnerable, men who call out the good in others and fight against sin and evil, men who are willing to sacrifice so others flourish.

I know this in my bones and my heart beats faster as I write these words, but the easy life is tempting, the couch and TV call, and I'm easily distracted. I am like Paul in Romans 7:

> Although I want to do good, evil is right there with me. For in my inner being I delight in God's law; but I see another law at work in me, waging war against the law of my mind and making me a prisoner of the law of sin at work within me. What a wretched man I am! Who will rescue me from this body that is subject to death? (vv. 21–24)

Waging war. The imagery is unavoidable. We are in a battle. Paul reminds us that this battle is not specific to me; it's part of the human condition. It's encouraging to know that we have company. In fact, every man I know, when he's honest, will share about this battle and the shame of his defeats when he's taken the easy route.

So what's the remedy?

Here are three steps to help you in the fight:

1. Find your identity in Christ and not in your successes or failures. The Bible says that when you decided to follow Jesus Christ, you were "crucified with Christ" so that you no longer live for yourself but live by faith in Jesus who loves you and died for you (Galatians 2:20).

2. Hold fast to the Word of God. There are several different Greek words to capture the idea of holding fast that have a range of meanings: to glue, to adhere, to bind, to arrest, to grasp, to possess. These are aggressive words. And the New Testament writers give a list of things we are to hang on to: what is good (Romans 12:9), the gospel (1 Corinthians 15:2), one's wife (Ephesians 5:31), the word of life (Philippians 2:16), Christ (Colossians 2:19), and the confession of our hope (Hebrews 10:23). This is hard work! And how do you do this? It doesn't happen by chance but by being purposeful, and we start to hold fast by reading, reflecting, and responding to the Bible daily.

3. Finally, gather with other men who will encourage you and help you in the battle. These devotions can be the first or ninety-first step in a lifelong journey of knowing and loving God and His people. We were not meant to live this life alone.

If you have read this far, I would like to invite you to take the next step. Start reading daily, but don't stop there. Invite two or three other men to join you and meet or connect weekly to share how God is changing you as you engage the battle. The world needs you, your coworkers need you, your family needs you, other men need you.

And if you do this, we would love to hear your story. Send me or any of the devotional writers in this book an email at books@odb.org. I am pulling for you; we are all pulling for you.

Matt Lucas
President and CEO
Our Daily Bread Ministries

JANUARY 1

Uncharted Waters Ahead

Isaiah 43:1–7

When you pass through the waters, I will be with you. —Isaiah 43:2

The ball drops in New York's Times Square. The crowd counts down to Big Ben chiming. Sydney Harbor erupts in fireworks. However your city marks it, there's something exciting about welcoming in a new year and the fresh start it brings. On New Year's Day we push out into new waters. What friendships and opportunities might we find?

For all its excitement, though, a new year can be unsettling. None of us knows the future or what storms it may hold. Many New Year's traditions reflect this: Fireworks were invented in China to supposedly ward off evil spirits and make a new season prosperous. And New Year's resolutions date back to the Babylonians who made vows to appease their gods. Such acts were an attempt to make an unknown future secure.

When they weren't making vows, the Babylonians were busy conquering people—including Israel. In time, God sent the enslaved Jews this message: "Do not fear. . . . When you pass through the waters, I will be with you" (Isaiah 43:1–2). Later, Jesus said something similar when He and the disciples were caught sailing in a violent storm. "Why are you so afraid?" He told them before commanding the waters to be still (Matthew 8:23–27).

Today we push out from the shore into new, uncharted waters. Whatever we face, our Lord is with us—and He has the power to calm the waves. Only in His power can we stand fast. Sheridan Voysey

Resolutions

Nehemiah 10:28–31

[They] entered into . . . an oath to walk in God's Law, . . . and to observe and do all the commandments of the LORD our Lord. —Nehemiah 10:29 NKJV

In 1722, American theologian Jonathan Edwards drew up a list of seventy resolutions, dedicating himself to live in harmony with God and others. The following resolutions give a picture of the serious purpose with which Edwards approached his relationship with God. He resolved:

- To do whatever is most to God's glory.
- To do my duty, for the good of mankind in general.
- Never to do anything which I should be afraid to do, if it were the last hour of my life.
- To study the Scriptures steadily, constantly, and frequently.
- To ask myself at the end of every day, week, month, and year if I could possibly have done better.
- Until I die, not to act as if I were my own, but entirely and altogether God's.

In Nehemiah 10, God's people made an oath, vowing to follow all the commands, laws, and regulations of the Lord. This oath was so serious that they were willing to accept the curse of God if they failed to keep these commands.

Our resolutions need not be as serious as that. But any resolution to follow God is not a casual promise. Rather, it is a solemn and serious declaration that—with the help of the Holy Spirit—we can renew every day. **Marvin Williams**

How to Hold Fast

Jude 1:24–25

To him who is able to keep you from stumbling. —Jude 1:24

It was a cold, icy winter's day, and my mind was focused on getting from my warm vehicle to a warm building. The next thing I knew I was on the ground, my knees turned inward and my lower legs turned outward. Nothing was broken, but I was in pain. The pain would get worse as time went by, and it would be weeks before I was whole again.

Who among us hasn't taken a spill of some sort? Wouldn't it be nice to have something or someone to keep us on our feet all the time? While there are no guarantees of surefootedness in the physical sense, there is One who stands ready to assist us in our quest to honor Christ in this life and to prepare us to stand joyfully before Him in the next.

Every day we face temptations (and even false teachings) that seek to divert us, confuse us, and entangle us. Yet, it's not ultimately through our own efforts that we remain on our feet as we walk in this world. How assuring to know that when we hold our peace when tempted to speak angrily, to opt for honesty over deceit, to choose love over hate, or to select truth over error—we experience God's power to keep us standing fast (Jude 1:24). And when we appear approved before God when Christ returns, the praise that we offer now for His sustaining grace will echo throughout eternity (v. 25). **Arthur Jackson**

Dying to Live

Matthew 16:21–28

Whoever wants to save their life will lose it, but whoever loses their life for me will find it. —Matthew 16:25

Western Michigan is plagued by snowy winters, requiring that salt be put on road surfaces to make them safer to travel. Here's the problem: salt eats away at a car's metal body. So, unless you own a Corvette, going to a car wash is a frequent winter ritual.

When I lived in Michigan, I was sitting in a car-wash facility near the end of the washing process when the machines began to spray a special liquid all over the car. The sign said it was a "drying agent," but that struck me as odd. Wetting something down to dry it seems contrary to what you'd expect. Yet that is precisely what those chemicals are designed to do. It is counterintuitive thinking—a paradox.

Jesus also dealt in counterintuitive thinking when presenting His kingdom message to His followers. In Matthew 16:25, He said, "Whoever wants to save their life will lose it, but whoever loses their life for me will find it." That doesn't sound right. To save your life, you have to lose it? That seems like saying, "To dry something, you wet it down!" Yet, it is absolutely true. Only as we die to self, entrusting ownership of our lives to Christ, can we learn what it means to really live.

"Dying to live" may seem counterintuitive, but it is the heart of the Christian experience. **Bill Crowder**

Another Chance

Philemon 1:8–19

[You] have put on the new self, which is being renewed in knowledge in the image of its Creator. —Colossians 3:10

For almost one hundred years, a huge piece of flawed Carrara marble lay in the courtyard of a cathedral in Florence, Italy. Then, in 1501, a young sculptor was asked to do something with it. He measured the block and noted its imperfections. In his mind, he envisioned a young shepherd boy.

For three years, he chiseled and shaped the marble skillfully. Finally, when the eighteen-foot towering figure of the biblical David was unveiled, a student of the sculptor—Michelangelo—exclaimed, "Master, it lacks only one thing—speech!"

Onesimus was like that once-flawed marble. He was an unfaithful servant when he fled from his master Philemon. But while on the run he came to know the Jesus, the Master Sculptor. As a changed man, he served God faithfully and was invaluable to Paul's ministry. When Paul sent him back to Philemon, he commended him as one who "was useless to you, but now he has become useful both to you and to me" (Philemon 1:11). He asked Philemon to receive Onesimus back as a brother (v. 16).

Paul knew what it meant to be given another chance after past wrongs (Acts 9:26–28). He knew personally the transformation God can do. Now he saw it in the life of Onesimus. The Lord can chisel His image on our flawed lives and make us beautiful and useful too. **Albert Lee**

JANUARY 6

Tell It!

Mark 5:1–20

The man went away and began to tell . . .
how much Jesus had done for him. —Mark 5:20

The year was 1975 and something significant had just happened to me. I needed to find my friend Francis, with whom I shared a lot of personal matters, and tell him about it. I found him in his apartment hurriedly preparing to go out, but I slowed him down. The way he stared at me, he must have sensed that I had something important to tell him. "What is it?" he asked. So, I told him simply, "Yesterday I surrendered my life to Jesus!"

Francis looked at me, sighed heavily, and said, "I've felt like doing the same for a long time now." He asked me to share what happened, and I told him that the previous day someone had explained the gospel to me—and I had asked Jesus to save me. I still remember the tears in his eyes as he too prayed to receive Jesus's forgiveness. No longer in a hurry, he and I talked and talked about our new relationship with Christ.

After Jesus healed a man with an evil spirit, He told him, "Go home to your own people and tell them how much the Lord has done for you, and how he has had mercy on you" (Mark 5:19). The man didn't need to preach a powerful sermon; he simply needed to share his story.

No matter what our conversion experience is, we can do what that man did: "[He] went away and began to tell . . . how much Jesus had done for him." **Lawrence Darmani**

All Things New

Revelation 21:1–7

If anyone is in Christ, the new creation has come:
The old has gone, the new is here! —2 Corinthians 5:17

Junkyards intrigue me.

I enjoy working on cars, so I frequently make trips to the junkyard near our home. It's a lonely place, where the wind whispers through discarded hulks that were once someone's prized possession. Some were wrecked, some wore out, and others simply outlived their usefulness. As I walk between the rows, a car will sometimes catch my eye, and I'll find myself wondering about the adventures it had during its "lifetime." Like a portal to the past, each has a story to tell—of human hankering after the latest model and the inescapable passage of time.

But I take particular pleasure in finding new life for an old part. Whenever I can take something discarded and give it new life in a restored vehicle, it feels like a small victory against time and decline.

It sometimes makes me think of Jesus's words at the end of the Bible: "I am making everything new!" (Revelation 21:5). These words refer to God's renewal of creation, which includes believers. Already, all who've received Jesus are a "new creation" in Him (2 Corinthians 5:17).

And one day we will enter into His promise of unending days with Him (John 14:3). Age and disease will no longer take their toll, and we will continue the adventure of an eternal lifetime. What stories each of us will have to tell—stories of our Savior's redeeming love and undying faithfulness. **James Banks**

JANUARY 8

The Testing

Genesis 22:1–3, 6–12

Some time later God tested Abraham. —Genesis 22:1

The first time I took my sons to hike a Colorado Fourteener—a mountain with an elevation of a least fourteen thousand feet—they were nervous. Could they make it? Were they up to the challenge? My youngest stopped on the trail for extended breaks. "Dad, I can't go any more," he said repeatedly. But I believed this test would be good for them, and I wanted them to trust me. A mile from the peak, my son who'd insisted he could go no further caught his second wind. He beat us to the summit! He was so glad he trusted me—even amid his fears.

I marvel at the trust Isaac had in his father as they climbed their mountain. Far more, I'm undone by the trust Abraham had in God as he raised his knife over his son (Genesis 22:10). Even with his confused and wrenching heart, Abraham obeyed. Mercifully, an angel stopped him. "Do not lay a hand on the boy," God's messenger declared (v. 12). God never intended for Isaac to die.

As we draw parallels from this unique story to our own with caution, it's crucial to note the opening line: "God tested Abraham" (v. 1). Through his test, Abraham learned how much he trusted God. He discovered His loving heart and profound provision.

In our confusion, darkness, and testing, we learn truths about ourselves and about God. And we may even find that our testing leads to a deeper trust in Him. Winn Collier

Live Wire

Mark 9:2–10

We were eyewitnesses of his majesty. —2 Peter 1:16

"I felt like I had touched a live wire," said Professor Holly Ordway, describing her reaction to John Donne's majestic poem "Holy Sonnet 14." *There's something happening in this poetry*, she thought. *I wonder what it is.* Ordway recalls it as the moment her previously atheistic worldview allowed for the possibility of the supernatural. Eventually she would believe in the transforming reality of the resurrected Christ.

Touching a live wire—that must have been how Peter, James, and John felt on the day Jesus took them to a mountaintop, where they witnessed a dramatic transformation. Christ's "clothes became dazzling white" (Mark 9:3) and Elijah and Moses appeared—an event we know today as the transfiguration.

Descending from the mountain, Jesus told the disciples not to tell anyone what they'd seen until He had risen (v. 9). But they didn't even know what He meant by "rising from the dead" (v. 10).

The disciples' understanding of Jesus was woefully incomplete, because they couldn't conceive of a destiny that included His death and resurrection. But eventually their experiences with their resurrected Lord would transform their lives. Late in his life, Peter described his encounter with Christ's transfiguration as the time when the disciples were first "eyewitnesses of his majesty" (2 Peter 1:16).

When we encounter the power of Jesus we touch a "live wire." There's something happening here. The living Christ beckons us. **Tim Gustafson**

JANUARY 10

Always Alert

Psalm 121

He who watches over Israel will neither slumber nor sleep. —Psalm 121:4

For a man who lives by a code, so to speak, it felt like a major failure. What did I do? Well, I fell asleep.

Our kids have a curfew to meet when they're out for the evening. They're good kids, but my practice is to wait up until I hear their hands turn the front doorknob. I want to know they're home safe. I don't have to do this: I choose to. But one night I awoke to my daughter saying through a smile, "Dad, I'm safe. You should go to bed." Despite our best intentions, sometimes fathers fall asleep at their posts. It was very humbling—and also very human.

But that never happens with God. Psalm 121 is a reassuring song about Him as guardian and protector of His children. The psalmist declares that God who watches over us "will not slumber" (v. 3). And for emphasis, he repeats that truth in verse 4: He "will neither slumber nor sleep."

Can you even imagine? God never falls asleep at His post. He is always keeping watch over us—the sons and daughters and aunts and uncles and mothers, and even fathers. It's not so much that He has to do this, but rather that, out of His great love, He chooses to. Relax. Our God is always alert. **John Blase**

Training for Life

Psalm 66:8–12

For you, God, tested us; you refined us like silver. —Psalm 66:10

My training for the long-distance race was going badly, and the latest run was particularly disappointing. I walked half the time and even had to sit down at one point. It felt like I had failed a mini test.

Then I remembered that this was the whole point of training. It was not a test to pass, nor was there a grade I had to achieve. Rather, it was something I simply had to go through, again and again, to improve my endurance.

Perhaps you feel bad about a trial you are facing. God allows us to undergo these times of testing to toughen our spiritual muscles and endurance. He teaches us to rely on Him, and He purifies us to be holy. It's all part of the process of becoming more like Christ.

No wonder the psalmist could praise God for refining the Israelites through fire and water (Psalm 66:10–12) as they suffered in slavery and exile. God not only preserved them and brought them to a place of great abundance, but He also purified them in the process.

As we go through testing, we can rely on God for strength and perseverance. He is refining us through our toughest moments. Leslie Koh

JANUARY 12

Of Spiders and God's Presence

Ephesians 3:14–19

I pray that out of his glorious riches he may strengthen you with power through his Spirit in your inner being. —Ephesians 3:16

Spiders.

I don't know any kid who likes them. At least not in their rooms . . . at bedtime. But as my daughter was getting ready for bed one evening, she spied one dangerously close to her bed. "Daaaad!!!!! Spiiiderrr!!!!!" she hollered. Despite my determination, I couldn't find the eight-legged interloper. "He's not going to hurt you," I reassured her. She wasn't convinced. It wasn't until I told her I'd stay next to her top bunk and stand guard that she agreed to get in bed.

As my daughter settled in, I held her hand. I told her, "I love you so much. I'm right here. But you know what? God loves you even more than Daddy and Mommy. And He's very close. You can always pray to Him when you're scared." That seemed to comfort her, and peaceful sleep came quickly.

Scripture repeatedly reassures us that God is always near (Psalm 145:18; Romans 8:38–39; James 4:7–8), but sometimes we struggle to believe it. Perhaps that's why Paul prayed for the believers in Ephesus to have *strength* and *power* to grasp that truth (Ephesians 3:16). He knew that when we're frightened, we can lose track of God's proximity. But just as I lovingly held my daughter's hand as she went to sleep that night, so our loving heavenly Father is always as close to us. He is as close as a prayer.

Adam Holz

The Interests of Others

Philippians 2:1–11

Don't look out only for your own interests, but take an interest in others, too. —Philippians 2:4 NLT

My friend Jaime works for a huge international corporation. In his early days with the company, a man came by his desk, struck up a conversation, and asked Jaime what he did there. After telling the man about his work, Jaime asked the man his name. "My name is Rich," he replied.

"Nice to meet you," Jaime answered. "And what do you do around here?"

"Oh, I am the owner."

Jaime suddenly realized that this casual, humble conversation was his introduction to one of the richest men in the world.

In this day of self-glorification and the celebration of "me," this little story can serve as a reminder of Paul's important words in the book of Philippians: "Do nothing out of selfish ambition or vain conceit" (2:3). People who turn their attention to others and not on themselves have the characteristics Paul mentions.

When we "value others above [ourselves]," we demonstrate Christlike humility (v. 3). We mirror Jesus, who came not "to be served, but to serve" (Mark 10:45). When we take "the very nature of a servant" (Philippians 2:7), we have the mindset of Jesus (v. 5).

As we interact with others today, let's not look on our own interests alone but also "to the interests of the others" (v. 4). **Dave Branon**

JANUARY 14

Unbreakable in Jesus

Jeremiah 1:4–10

"Do not be afraid of them, for I am with you and will rescue you," declares the LORD. —Jeremiah 1:8

Louis Zamperini's military plane crashed at sea during World War II, killing eight of the eleven men on board. "Louie" and two others clambered into life rafts. They drifted for two months, fending off sharks, riding out storms, ducking bullets from an enemy plane, and catching and eating raw fish and birds. They finally drifted onto an island and were immediately captured. For two years Louie was beaten, tortured, and worked mercilessly as a prisoner of war. His remarkable story is told in the book *Unbroken.*

Jeremiah is one of the Bible's unbreakable characters. He endured enemy plots (Jeremiah 11:18), was whipped and put in stocks (20:2), was flogged and bound in a dungeon (37:15–16), and was lowered by ropes into the deep mire of a cistern (38:6). He survived because God had promised to stay with him and rescue him (1:8). God makes a similar promise to us: "Never will I leave you; never will I forsake you" (Hebrews 13:5). God didn't promise to save Jeremiah or us from trouble, but He has promised to carry us through trouble.

Louie recognized God's protection, and after the war he gave his life to Jesus. He forgave his captors and led some to Christ. Louie realized that while we can't avoid all problems, we need not suffer them alone. When we face them with Jesus, we become unbreakable. **Mike Wittmer**

Maintain Unity

Ephesians 4:1–6

Make every effort to keep the unity of the Spirit through the bond of peace. —Ephesians 4:3

The story is told about a man who was finally discovered after being stranded by himself on an island. His rescuers were curious about the three huts they saw there. He pointed and said, "This one is my home and that one is my church." When the rescuers asked about the third hut, he responded: "Oh, that was my former church." Though we may laugh at the silliness of this story, it does highlight a concern about unity among believers.

The church of Ephesus during the time of the apostle Paul was comprised of both rich and poor, Jews and Gentiles, men and women, masters and slaves. And where differences exist, so does friction. One concern Paul wrote about was the issue of unity. But observe what Paul said about this issue in Ephesians 4:3. He didn't tell them to be "eager to produce or to organize unity." He told them to endeavor "to keep the unity of the Spirit through the bond of peace." Unity already exists because believers share one body, one Spirit, one hope, one Lord, one faith, one baptism, and one God and Father of all (vv. 4–6).

How do we "keep the unity"? By expressing our different opinions and convictions with lowliness, gentleness, and patience (v. 2). The Spirit will give us the power to react in love toward those with whom we disagree. **Albert Lee**

JANUARY 16

The Boy and the Teenager

1 John 3:1–3

We know that when Christ appears,
we shall be like him. —1 John 3:2

Inside my parents' old photo album is a picture of a young boy. He has a round face, freckles, and straight, light-blond hair. He loves cartoons, hates avocados, and owns just one record, by Abba. Also inside that photo album are pictures of a teenager. His face is long, not round; his hair is wavy, not straight. He has no freckles, likes avocados, watches movies rather than cartoons, and would never admit to owning an Abba record! The boy and the teenager are little alike. According to science they have different skin, teeth, blood, and bones. And yet they are both me. This paradox has baffled philosophers. Since we change throughout our lives, who is the real us?

The Scriptures provide the answer. From the moment God began knitting us together in the womb (Psalm 139:13–14), we've been growing into our unique design. While we can't yet imagine what we'll finally become, we know that if we're children of God we'll ultimately be like Jesus (1 John 3:2)—our body with His nature, our personality but His character, all our gifts glistening, all our sins gone.

Until the day Jesus returns, we're being drawn toward this future self. By His work, step by step, we can reflect His image ever more clearly (2 Corinthians 3:18). We aren't yet who we're meant to be, but as we become like Him, we become our true selves. **Sheridan Voysey**

Correct Gently

Colossians 3:12–17

Clothe yourselves with compassion, kindness, humility, gentleness and patience. Bear with each other. —Colossians 3:12–13

At the end of a conference in Nairobi, Kenya, our group traveled from the conference center to a guesthouse to prepare to fly back home the next morning. When we arrived, one person in our group reported that she had forgotten her luggage back at the conference center. After she left to retrieve it, our group leader (always meticulous on detail) criticized her sharply to us in her absence.

The next morning when we arrived at the airport, the leader discovered to his dismay that he too had left his luggage behind. It and his passport were back at the guesthouse. It was now going to cost us even more to go for his baggage. Later, he apologized and said to all of us, "I'll never criticize so harshly again!"

Because we all have faults and weaknesses, we should bear with one another and forgive each other when things go wrong (Colossians 3:13). We need to be constructive in our criticism and "clothe [our]selves with compassion, kindness, humility, gentleness and patience" (v. 12).

When correction is necessary, it should be done with kindness and love. In that way we become imitators of our Lord Jesus Christ. Lawrence Darmani

JANUARY 18

Flying Machines

Psalm 6

I am worn out from my groaning. All night long I flood my bed with weeping and drench my couch with tears. —Psalm 6:6

Recording artist James Taylor exploded onto the music scene in early 1970 with the song "Fire and Rain." In it, he talked about the disappointments of life, describing them as "sweet dreams and flying machines in pieces on the ground." That was a reference to Taylor's original band Flying Machine, whose attempt at breaking into the recording industry had failed badly, causing him to wonder if his dreams of a musical career would ever come true. The reality of crushed expectations had taken their toll, leaving Taylor with a sense of loss and hopelessness.

The psalmist David also experienced hopeless despair as he struggled with his own failures, the attacks of others, and the disappointments of life. In Psalm 6:6 he said, "I am worn out from my groaning. All night long I flood my bed with weeping and drench my couch with tears." The depth of his sorrow and loss drove him to heartache—but in that grief he turned to the God of all comfort. David's own crushed and broken "flying machines" gave way to the assurance of God's care, prompting him to say, "The Lord has heard my cry for mercy; the Lord accepts my prayer" (v. 9).

In our own seasons of disappointment, we too can find comfort in God, who cares for our broken hearts.

Bill Crowder

That Thing You Do

2 Chronicles 13:10–18

The people of Judah were victorious because they relied on the LORD, the God of their ancestors. —2 Chronicles 13:18

As the convoy waited to roll out, a young Marine rapped urgently on the window of his team leader's vehicle. Irritated, the sergeant rolled down his window.

"What?"

"You gotta do that thing," the Marine said.

"What thing?" asked the sergeant.

"You know, that thing you do," replied the Marine.

Then it dawned on the sergeant. He always prayed for the convoy's safety, but this time he hadn't. So, he dutifully climbed out of the Humvee and prayed for his Marines. The Marine understood the value of his praying leader.

In ancient Judah, Abijah doesn't stand out as a great king. First Kings 15:3 tells us, "His heart was not fully devoted to the LORD his God." But as Judah prepared for war against Israel, outnumbered two to one, Abijah knew this much: Faithful people in his kingdom of Judah had continued worshipping God (2 Chronicles 13:10–12), while the ten tribes of Israel had driven out the priests of God and worshipped pagan gods instead (vv. 8–9). So Abijah turned confidently to the one true God.

Surely Abijah's checkered history had caused grave damage. But he knew where to turn in the crisis, and his army won soundly "because they relied on the LORD, the God of their ancestors" (v. 18). Our God welcomes whoever comes to Him and relies on Him. Tim Gustafson

JANUARY 20

WD-40 and Persistence

Matthew 15:21–28

Jesus said to her, "Woman, you have great faith! Your request is granted." —Matthew 15:28

In 1953, a fledgling business called Rocket Chemical Company and its staff of three set out to create a line of rust-prevention solvents and degreasers for use in the aerospace industry. It took them forty attempts to perfect their formula. The original secret formula for WD-40—which stands for Water Displacement, fortieth attempt—is still in use today. It stands with duct tape as a must-have for every garage. What a story of persistence!

The gospel of Matthew records another story of bold persistence. A Canaanite woman had a daughter who was possessed by a demon. She had no hope for her daughter—until she heard that Jesus was in the region.

This desperate woman came to Jesus with her need because she believed He could help her. She cried out to Him even though everything and everybody seemed to be against her—race, religious background, gender, the disciples, Satan, and seemingly even Jesus (Matthew 15:22–27). Despite all these obstacles, she did not give up. With bold persistence, she pushed her way through the dark corridors of difficulty, desperate need, and rejection. The result? Jesus commended her for her faith and healed her daughter (v. 28).

We too are invited to approach Jesus with bold persistence. As we keep asking, seeking, and knocking, we will find grace and mercy in our time of need. Marvin Williams

Catching Up with Us

Psalm 32:1–3

When I kept silent, my bones wasted away through my groaning. —Psalm 32:3

A pastor told this story on himself in his local newspaper. He was chatting with an older man to whom he had just been introduced. "So, you used to work for a utility company," the pastor said, naming the organization. "Sure did," the man responded. The pastor remarked that when he was a kid the cables from that company ran across his parents' property. "Where did you live?" the man asked. When the pastor told him, the man said, "I remember that property. I had a tough time keeping the cable warning signs up. Kids were always shooting them down." When the pastor's face flushed with embarrassment, the man said, "You were one of the shooters, weren't you?" And indeed he was.

The pastor labeled his confessional story: "Be sure your signs will find you out," a clever play on Moses's words in Numbers 32:23 (NKJV): "Be sure your sin will find you out."

Old wrongs have a way of catching up with us. And old sins that have not been dealt with can lead to serious consequences. As David laments in Psalm 32: "When I kept silent, my bones wasted away." But confessing our wrong restores our fellowship with the Lord: "I acknowledged my sin to you . . . And you forgave the guilt of my sin" (v. 5). Through confession, we can enjoy God's forgiveness. Dave Branon

JANUARY 22

Expect Delays

Proverbs 16:1–3, 9

In their hearts humans plan their course, but the LORD establishes their steps. —Proverbs 16:9

Are you kidding me? I was already late. But the road sign ahead instructed me to adjust my expectations: "Expect Delays," it announced. Traffic was slowing down.

I had to laugh: I expect things to work on my ideal timeline; I don't expect road construction.

On a spiritual level, few of us plan for crises that slow us down or reroute our lives. Yet, if I think about it, I can recall many times when circumstances redirected me—in big ways and small. Delays happen.

Solomon never saw a sign that said, "Expect Delays." But in Proverbs 16, he does contrast our plans with God's providential guidance. *The Message* paraphrases verse 1 as follows: "Mortals make elaborate plans, but GOD has the last word." Solomon restates that idea in verse 9, where he adds that even though we "plan [our] course . . . the LORD establishes [our] steps." In other words, we have ideas about what's supposed to happen, but sometimes God has another path for us.

How do I lose track of this spiritual truth? I make my plans, sometimes forgetting to ask Him what His plans are. I get frustrated when interruptions interfere.

But in place of that worrying, we could, as Solomon teaches, grow in trusting that God guides us, step-by-step, as we prayerfully seek Him, await His leading, and—yes—allow Him to continually redirect us. **Adam Holz**

Live Like Jesus Is Coming

Matthew 25:1–13

Keep watch, because you do not know the day or the hour. —Matthew 25:13

I'm inspired by country singer Tim McGraw's song "Live Like You Were Dying." In it he describes some of the exciting "bucket list" things a man did after receiving bad news about his health. He also chose to love and forgive people more freely—speaking to them more tenderly. The song recommends that we live well, as if knowing our lives will end soon.

This song reminds us that our time is limited. It's important for us to not put off for tomorrow what we can do today, because one day we'll run out of tomorrows. This is particularly urgent for believers in Jesus, who know that Jesus may return at any moment (perhaps in the very second you're reading this sentence!). Jesus urges us to be ready, not living like the five "foolish" virgins who were caught unprepared when the bridegroom returned (Matthew 25:6–10).

But McGraw's song doesn't tell the whole story. We who love Jesus will never truly run out of tomorrows. Jesus said, "I am the resurrection and the life. The one who believes in me will live, even though they die; and whoever lives by believing in me will never die" (John 11:25–26). Our life in Him never ends.

So don't live like you're dying. Because you're not. Rather, live like Jesus is coming. Because He is! Mike Wittmer

Only Trust

1 Kings 17:8–16

So there was food every day for Elijah and for the woman and her family. —1 Kings 17:15

Three hundred children were dressed and seated for breakfast, and a prayer of thanks was offered for the food. But there was no food!

Situations like this were not unusual for British orphanage director and missionary George Mueller (1805–1898). Here was yet another opportunity to see how God would provide. Within minutes of Mueller's prayer, a baker who couldn't sleep the night before showed up at the door. Sensing that the orphanage could use the bread, he had made three batches. Not long afterward, the town milkman appeared. His cart had broken down in front of the orphanage. Not wanting the milk to spoil, he offered it to Mueller.

It's normal to experience bouts of worry, anxiety, and self-pity when we lack resources essential to our well-being—food, shelter, health, finances, friendships. First Kings 17:8–16 reminds us that God's help can come through unexpected sources like a needy widow. "I don't have any bread—only a handful of flour in a jar and a little olive oil in a jug" (v. 12). Earlier it was a raven that provided for Elijah (vv. 4–6).

Concerns for our needs to be met can send us searching in many directions. A clear vision of God as our Provider who has promised to supply our needs can be liberating. Before we seek solutions, let's be careful to seek Him first. Doing so can save us time, energy, and frustration.

Arthur Jackson

The Last Word

1 Corinthians 15:12–19

If only for this life we have hope in Christ, we are of all people most to be pitied. —1 Corinthians 15:19

Her name was Saralyn, and I sort of had a crush on her back in our school days. She had the most wonderful laugh. I'm not sure whether she knew about my crush, but I suspect she did. After graduation I lost track of her. Our lives went in different directions, as lives often do.

I keep up with my graduating class in some online forums, and I was intensely sad when I heard that Saralyn died. I found myself wondering about the direction her life had taken over the years. This is happening more and more the older I grow—this experience of losing friends and family. But many of us tend to avoid talking about it.

While we still sorrow, the certain hope that the apostle Paul talks about is this: Death doesn't have the final say (1 Corinthians 15:54–55). There is something that follows—another word: resurrection. Paul bases that hope in the reality of the resurrection of Christ (v. 12), and he says, "if Christ has not been raised, our preaching is useless and so is your faith" (v. 14). If our hope as believers is limited to this world only, that's just a pity (v. 19).

We will one day see those again who have "fallen asleep in Christ" (v. 18)—grandparents and parents, friends and neighbors, or perhaps even old schoolyard crushes.

Death doesn't get the last word. Resurrection does.
John Blase

JANUARY 26

Guiding the Children

2 Timothy 3:10–15

Continue in what you have learned . . . how from infancy you have known the Holy Scriptures. —2 Timothy 3:14–15

An outspoken atheist believes it's immoral for parents to teach their children religion as though it were actually true. He even claims that parents who pass along their faith to their children are committing child abuse. Though these views are extreme, I do hear from parents who are hesitant to boldly encourage their children toward faith. While most of us readily hope to influence our children with our view of politics or nutrition or sports, for some reason some of us treat our convictions about God differently.

In contrast, Paul wrote of how Timothy had been taught "from infancy . . . the Holy Scriptures, which are able to make you wise for salvation through faith in Christ Jesus" (2 Timothy 3:15). Timothy didn't arrive at faith as an adult through the power of his own, unaided reason. Rather, his mother nurtured his heart toward God; then he continued in what he had learned (v. 14). If God is life and the source of true wisdom (and He is!), then it's vital for us to tenderly cultivate a love for God in our families.

There are many belief systems influencing our children. TV shows, movies, music, teachers, friends, social media—each of these carry assumptions (either obvious or under the radar) about faith, and they exert real influence. We can't be silent. The beauty and grace we've experienced in Jesus compels us to guide our children toward God. Winn Collier

And Seven Others

James 2:1–4

Believers in our glorious LORD Jesus Christ must not show favoritism. —James 2:1

Tragedy struck near Los Angeles in January 2020 when nine people died in a helicopter crash. Most news stories began something like this, "NBA superstar Kobe Bryant, his daughter Gianna ("Gigi"), and seven others lost their lives in the accident."

It's natural and understandable to focus on the well-known people involved in a horrible situation like this—and the deaths of Kobe and his precious teenager Gigi are heartbreaking beyond description. But we must keep in mind that in life's big picture there's no dividing line that makes the "seven others" (Payton, Sarah, Christina, Alyssa, John, Keri, and Ara) any less significant.

Sometimes we need to be reminded that each human is important in God's eyes. Society shines bright lights on the rich and famous. Yet fame doesn't make a person any more important than your next-door neighbor, the noisy kids who play in your street, the down-on-his-luck guy at the city mission, or you.

Every person on earth is created in God's image (Genesis 1:27), whether rich or poor (Proverbs 22:2). No one is favored more than another in His eyes (Romans 2:11), and each needs a Savior (3:23).

We glorify our great God when we refuse to show favoritism—whether in the church (James 2:1–4) or in society at large. Dave Branon

JANUARY 28

Treasures in Heaven

Matthew 6:19–24

Store up for yourselves treasures in heaven, where moths and vermin do not destroy, and where thieves do not break in and steal. —Matthew 6:20

Poorly installed electric wiring caused a fire that burned down our newly built home. The flames leveled our house within an hour, leaving nothing but rubble. Another time, we returned home from church one Sunday to find our house had been broken into, and some of our possessions were stolen.

In our imperfect world, loss of material wealth is all too common—vehicles are stolen or crashed, ships sink, buildings crumble, homes are flooded, and personal belongings are stolen. This makes Jesus's admonition not to put our trust in earthly wealth even more powerful (Matthew 6:19).

Jesus told a story of a man who accumulated abundant treasures and decided to store up everything for himself (Luke 12:16–21). "Take life easy," the man told himself; "eat, drink and be merry" (v. 19). But that night he lost everything, including his life. In conclusion, Jesus said, "This is how it will be with whoever stores up things for themselves but is not rich toward God" (v. 21).

Material wealth is temporary. Nothing lasts forever—except what our God enables us to do for others. Giving of our time and resources to spread the good news, visiting those who are lonely, and helping those in need are just some of the many ways to store up treasure in heaven (Matthew 6:20). **Lawrence Darmani**

Waiting in Hope

Luke 2:25–35

Simeon . . . was righteous and devout. He was waiting for the consolation of Israel, and the Holy Spirit was on him. —Luke 2:25

In the movie *Hachi: A Dog's Tale*, a college professor befriended a stray Akita puppy named Hachi. The dog expressed his loyalty by waiting at the train station each day for the professor to return from work. One day, the professor suffered a fatal stroke. Hachi waited hours at the train station that day, and for the next ten years he returned each day—awaiting his loving master.

Luke tells the story of a man named Simeon, who patiently waited for the coming of his Master (Luke 2:25). The Holy Spirit revealed to Simeon that he would not see death until he saw the Messiah (v. 26). As a result, Simeon kept waiting for the One who would provide "salvation" for God's people (v. 30). When Mary and Joseph entered the temple with Jesus, the Holy Spirit whispered to Simeon that He was the One! The wait was finally over! Simeon held Jesus in his arms—the hope, salvation, and comfort for all people (vv. 28–32).

If we find ourselves in a season of waiting, may we hear the words of the prophet Isaiah with fresh ears: "Those who hope in the Lord will renew their strength. They will soar on wings like eagles; they will run and not grow weary, they will walk and not be faint" (Isaiah 40:31). As we await Jesus's return, He provides the hope and strength we need for each new day. **Marvin Williams**

JANUARY 30

Growing a Servant's Heart

Luke 22:24–30

I am among you as
one who serves. —Luke 22:27

It was a long day at work. But when I got home, it was time to resume my "other" job—being a good dad. Greetings from my wife and kids soon became, "Dad, what's for dinner?" "Dad, can you get me some water?" "Dad, can we play soccer?"

I just wanted to sit down. And even though *part* of me really wanted to be a good dad, I didn't *feel* like serving my family's needs. That's when I saw it: a thank-you card my wife had received from someone at church. It pictured a bowl of water, a towel, and dirty sandals. Across the bottom were these words from Luke 22:27: "I am among you as one who serves."

That statement of Jesus's mission, to serve those He came to seek and save (Luke 19:10), was *exactly* what I needed. If Jesus was willing to do the dirtiest of jobs for His followers—like scrubbing His followers' sandy, filthy feet (John 13:1–17)—I could get my son a cup of water without grumbling about it. In that moment, I was reminded that my family's requests to serve them weren't merely an *obligation* but an *opportunity* to reflect Jesus's servant heart and His love to them. When requests are made of us, they are opportunities to become more like the One who served His followers by laying down His life for us. Adam Holz

Out of Breath

Deuteronomy 5:12–15

Six days you shall labor and do all your work, but the seventh day is a sabbath to the Lord your God. —Deuteronomy 5:13–14

There's a home-improvement store near me that has a big green button in one of its departments. If no assistant is present, you push the button, which starts a timer. If you're not served within a minute, you get a discount on your purchase.

In this scenario, we like being the customer who enjoys the speedy service. But the demand for fast service often takes a toll when we're the ones expected to deliver it. So many of us today feel rushed doing our jobs, working long hours, checking email multiple times a day, and feeling pressured to meet tighter and tighter deadlines. The customer service tactics of the home-improvement store have seeped into all our lives, creating a culture of rush.

When God told the Israelites to keep a Sabbath, He added an important reason: "Remember that you were slaves in Egypt" (Deuteronomy 5:15). There they'd been forced to work ceaselessly under Pharaoh's excessive time constraints (Exodus 5:6–9). Now freed, they were to give themselves a whole day each week to ensure that they and those who served them could rest (Deuteronomy 5:14). Under God's rule, there were to be no flush-faced, out-of-breath people.

How often do you work to the point of exhaustion or get impatient with people who keep you waiting? Let's give ourselves and each other a break. A culture of rush is Pharaoh's doing, not God's. Sheridan Voysey

FEBRUARY 1

Jesus Restores Us

Genesis 3:17–24

The Lord God made garments of skin for Adam and his wife and clothed them. —Genesis 3:21

Although Sam had done nothing wrong, he lost his job on the assembly line. Carelessness in another division led to problems in cars they built. After several crashes made the news, wary customers stopped buying their brand. The company had to downsize, leaving Sam out of work. He's collateral damage, and it isn't fair. It never is.

History's first collateral damage occurred immediately after the first sin. Adam and Eve were ashamed of their nakedness, so God graciously clothed them with "garments of skin" (Genesis 3:21). It's painful to imagine, but one or more animals that had always been safe in the garden were now slaughtered and skinned.

There was more to come. God told Israel, "Every day you are to provide a year-old lamb without defect for a burnt offering to the Lord; morning by morning you shall provide it" (Ezekiel 46:13). Every. Single. Day. How many thousands of animals have been sacrificed because of human sin?

Their death was necessary to cover our sin until Jesus, the Lamb of God, came to remove it (John 1:29). Call this "collateral repair." As Adam's sin kills us, so the Last Adam's (Christ's) obedience restores all who believe in Him (Romans 5:17–19). Collateral repair isn't fair—it cost Jesus's life—but it's free. Reach out to Jesus in belief and receive the salvation He offers, and His righteous life will count for you. **Mike Wittmer**

Beat Again

Judges 5:19–21

March on, my soul; be strong! —Judges 5:21

The song "Tell Your Heart to Beat Again" by Phillips, Craig and Dean was inspired by the true story of a heart surgeon. After removing a patient's heart to repair it, the surgeon returned it to the chest and began gently massaging it back to life. But the heart wouldn't restart. More intense measures followed, but the heart still wouldn't beat. Finally, the surgeon knelt next to the unconscious patient and spoke to her: "Mrs. Johnson," he said, "this is your surgeon. The operation went perfectly. Your heart has been repaired. Now tell your heart to beat again." Her heart began to beat.

The idea that we could tell our physical heart to do something might seem strange, but it has spiritual parallels. "Why, my soul, are you downcast?" the psalmist says to himself. "Put your hope in God" (Psalm 42:5). "Return to your rest, my soul," says another, "for the LORD has been good to you" (116:7). After beating Israel's enemies in war, Deborah, a judge, revealed that she too had spoken to her heart during battle. "March on, my soul," she told it, "be strong" (Judges 5:21), because the Lord had promised victory (4:6–7).

Our capable Surgeon has mended our heart (Psalm 103:3). So, when fear, depression, or condemnation come, perhaps we too should address our souls and say: March on! Be strong! Feeble heart, beat again. **Sheridan Voysey**

FEBRUARY 3

Take Another Look at Jesus!

Hebrews 3:1–6

But Christ is faithful as the Son over God's house. And we are his house, if indeed we hold firmly to our confidence and the hope in which we glory. —Hebrews 3:6

If there ever was a faithful person, it was Brother Justice. He was committed to his marriage, dedicated to his job as a postal worker, and each Sunday stood at his post as a leader in our local church. I visited my childhood church recently, and I noticed that perched on the upright piano was the same bell Brother Justice rang to notify us that the time for Bible study was about to end. The bell has endured the test of time. And although Brother Justice has been with the Lord for years, his legacy of faithfulness also endures.

Hebrews 3 brings a faithful servant (Moses) and a faithful Son (Jesus) to the reader's attention. Though the faithfulness of Moses as God's "servant" is undeniable, Jesus is the one that believers are taught to focus on. "Therefore, holy brothers and sisters, . . . fix your thoughts on Jesus" (v. 1). Such was the encouragement to everyone who faces temptation (2:18). A legacy of hope and joy come only from following Jesus, the faithful one.

What do you do when the winds of temptation are swirling all around you? When you are weary and worn and want to quit? The text invites us to, as one paraphrase renders it, "Take a good hard look at Jesus" (3:1 MSG). Look at Him again—and again and again. As we reexamine Jesus, we find the trustworthy Son of God who gives us courage to live in His family. **Arthur Jackson**

Remember When

Psalm 71:19–24

Your righteousness, God, reaches to the heavens,
you who have done great things. —Psalm 71:19

Our son wrestled with drug addiction for seven years, and during that time my wife and I experienced many difficult days. As we prayed and waited for his recovery, we learned to celebrate small victories. If nothing bad happened in a twenty-four-hour period, we would tell each other, "Today was a good day." That short sentence became a reminder to be thankful for God's help with the smallest things.

Tucked away in Psalm 71 is an even better reminder of God's tender mercies and what they ultimately mean for us: "Your righteousness, God, reaches to the heavens, you who have done great things" (v. 19). What a great verse to take to heart as we remember Jesus's compassion for us on the cross! The difficulties of any given day cannot change the truth that, come what may, our Lord has already shown us unfathomable kindness and "His love endures forever" (Psalm 136:1).

When we have lived through a difficult circumstance and discovered that God was faithful, keeping that in mind helps greatly the next time life's waters turn rough. We may not know how God will get us through our circumstances, but His kindness to us in the past helps us trust that He will. James Banks

FEBRUARY 5

Seeds of Grace

Mark 4:26–29

The seed sprouts and grows, though he does not know how. —Mark 4:27

For nearly four decades, a man in India has worked to bring a scorched, sandy wasteland back to life. Seeing how erosion and changing ecosystems had destroyed the river island he loved, he began to plant one tree at a time—bamboo, then cotton. Now lush forests and abundant wildlife fill more than 1,300 acres.

The man, however, insists that the rebirth was not something he made happen. Acknowledging the amazing way the natural world is designed, he marvels at how seeds are carried to fertile ground by the wind. Birds and animals participate in sowing them as well, and rivers also contribute in helping plants and trees flourish.

Creation works in ways we can't comprehend or control. According to Jesus, this same principle applies to the kingdom of God. "This is what the kingdom of God is like," Jesus said. "A man scatters seed on the ground. . . . The seed sprouts and grows, though he does not know how" (Mark 4:26–27). God brings life and healing into the world as pure gifts, without our manipulation. We do whatever God asks of us, and then we watch life emerge. We know that everything flows from His grace.

It's tempting to believe that we are responsible to change someone's heart or ensure results for our faithful efforts. However, we need not live under that exhausting pressure. God makes all our seeds grow. It's all Him. It's all grace.

Winn Collier

The Thinking Christian

2 Corinthians 10:1–11

We demolish arguments and . . . take captive every thought to make it obedient to Christ. —2 Corinthians 10:5

David McCullough's biography of John Adams, one of America's founding fathers and early presidents, describes him as "both a devout Christian and an independent thinker, and he saw no conflict in that." I am struck by that statement, for it carries a note of surprise, suggesting that Christians are somehow naïve or unenlightened, and that the idea of a "thinking Christian" is a contradiction.

Nothing could be further from the truth. One of the great benefits of salvation is that it causes the believer's mind to be guarded by the peace of God (Philippians 4:7), which can foster clear thinking, discernment, and wisdom. Paul described this in his second letter to Corinth when he wrote that in Christ we are equipped for "demolish[ing] arguments and every pretension that sets itself up against the knowledge of God, and we take captive every thought to make it obedient to Christ" (2 Corinthians 10:5).

To sift through an argument wisely, to embrace the clarity of the knowledge of God, and to align our thinking with the mind of Christ are valuable skills when living in a world lacking in discernment. These skills enable us to use our minds to represent Christ. Every Christian should be a thinking Christian. Are you? **Bill Crowder**

He Carried Our Burden

1 Peter 1:18–25

"He himself bore our sins" in his body on the cross, so that we might die to sins and live for righteousness; "by his wounds you have been healed." —1 Peter 2:24

It's not unusual for utility bills to be surprisingly high. But Kieran Healy of North Carolina received a water bill that would make your heart stop. The notification said that he owed $100,000,000! Confident he hadn't used that much water the previous month, Healy jokingly asked if he could pay the bill in installments.

Owing a $100,000,000 debt would be an overwhelming burden, but that pales in comparison to the real—and immeasurable—burden sin causes us to carry. Attempting to carry the burden and consequences of our own sins ultimately leaves us feeling tired and riddled with guilt and shame. The truth is, we are incapable of carrying this load.

And we were never meant to. As Peter reminded believers, only Jesus, the sinless Son of God, could carry the heavy burden of our sin and its weighty consequences (1 Peter 2:24). In His death on the cross, Jesus took all our wrongdoing on himself and offered us His forgiveness. Because He carried our burden, we don't have to suffer the punishment we deserve.

Instead of living in fear or guilt, the "empty way of life handed down to" us (1:18), we can enjoy a new life of love and freedom (vv. 22–23). Marvin Williams

Privileged Access

Hebrews 12:18–24

You have come . . . to the church of the firstborn. —Hebrews 12:22–23

Even though it was just a replica, the tabernacle set up in southern Israel was awe-inspiring. Built life-size and as close as possible to the specifications laid out in Exodus 25–27 (without actual gold and acacia wood, of course), it stood tall in the Negev desert.

When our tour group was taken through the "Holy Place" and into the "Most Holy Place" to see the "ark," some of us hesitated. Wasn't this the holiest place, where only the high priest was allowed to enter? How could we enter it so casually?

I can imagine how fearful the Israelites must have felt as they approached the real-life tent of meeting with their sacrifices each time, knowing that they were coming into the presence of the Almighty God. Think of the wonder they must have felt each time God had a message for them—delivered through Moses.

Today, you and I can come straight to God with confidence, knowing that Jesus's sacrifice has torn down the barrier between us and God (Hebrews 12:22–23). Each of us can talk to God any time we want, and we can hear from Him directly when we read His Word. We enjoy direct access that the Israelites could only dream of. May we never take it for granted. Let's appreciate this awesome privilege of coming to the Father as His beloved children every day. **Leslie Koh**

FEBRUARY 9

The Power of Influence

Matthew 5:1–16

You are the salt of the earth. But if the salt loses its saltiness, how can it be made salty again? —Matthew 5:13

On February 9, 1964, the Beatles appeared on *The Ed Sullivan Show* and captivated the youth of America. After hearing their music and seeing their "look," I did what millions of young American boys did—I begged my parents to let me grow my hair. Then, along with my best friend Tommy, I started a garage band. The Beatles' performance had such an impact on us that we intentionally tried to be like them. It was a significant introduction to the power of influence.

Years later, the power of influence came to mean something far more significant to me as I began my journey as a believer in Jesus Christ. I had the desire to live under His influence, but I also wanted to be an influencer of others by pointing them to the Savior.

In part, this is what Jesus was challenging us to understand in Matthew 5:13–16. Salt and light are influential factors in a dark and corrupting world, and Christ, who is the Light of the world, calls us to be lights of influence as well. The Master who modeled perfect purity calls us to be salt that adds flavor and prevents corruption.

May we not only be influenced by Christ but also influencers for Christ in a needy world. **Bill Crowder**

"Wah Gwan"

Acts 17:22–32

As I walked around and looked carefully at your objects of worship, I even found an altar with this inscription: *TO AN UNKNOWN GOD.* —Acts 17:23

I stood before the gathering at a small Jamaican church and said in my best local dialect, "Wah Gwan, Jamaica?" The reaction was better than I expected, as smiles and applause greeted me.

In reality, all I had said was the standard greeting, "What's going on?" in Patois [pa-twa], but to their ears I was saying, "I care enough to speak your language." Of course, I did not yet know enough Patois to continue without truly embarrassing myself, but a door had been opened.

When the apostle Paul stood before the people of Athens, he let them know that he knew their culture. He told them that he had noticed their altar "TO AN UNKNOWN GOD," and he quoted one of their poets. Of course, not everyone believed Paul's message about Jesus's resurrection, but some said, "We want to hear you again on this subject" (Acts 17:32).

As we interact with others about Jesus and the salvation He offers, the lessons of Scripture show us to invest ourselves in others—to learn their language, as it were—as a way to open the door to telling them the good news (see also 1 Corinthians 9:20–23).

As we find out "Wah Gwan?" in others' lives, it will be easier to share what God has done in ours. **Dave Branon**

Our Singing Father

Zephaniah 3:14–20

The LORD your God is with you, the Mighty Warrior who saves.
He will take great delight in you; in his love he will . . .
rejoice over you with singing. —Zephaniah 3:17

No one told me before my wife and I had children how important singing would be. My children are now in or nearing their teen years. But all three had problems sleeping early on. Each night, my wife and I took turns rocking our little ones, praying they'd nod off quickly. I spent hundreds of hours rocking them, desperately crooning lullabies to (hopefully!) speed up the process. But as I sang over our children night after night, something amazing happened: It deepened my bond of love and delight for them in ways I had never dreamed.

Did you know that Scripture describes our heavenly Father singing over His children too? Just as I sought to soothe my children with song, so Zephaniah concludes with a portrait of our heavenly Father singing over His people: "He will take great delight in you; in his love he will . . . rejoice over you with singing" (3:17).

Much of Zephaniah's prophetic book warns of a coming time of judgment for those who reject God. Yet that's not where it ends. Zephaniah concludes not with judgment but with a description of God not only rescuing His people from all their suffering (vv. 19–20) but also tenderly loving and rejoicing over them with song (v. 17).

Our God is not only a "Mighty Warrior who saves" and restores (v. 17) but also a loving Father who tenderly sings songs of love over us. **Adam Holz**

Deeper Love

1 Peter 4:7–11

God demonstrates his own love for us in this: While we were still sinners, Christ died for us. —Romans 5:8

When they first met, Edwin Stanton snubbed US president Abraham Lincoln personally and professionally—even referring to him as a "long-armed creature." But Lincoln appreciated Stanton's abilities and chose to forgive him, eventually appointing Stanton to a vital cabinet position during the Civil War. Stanton later grew to love Lincoln as a friend. It was Stanton who sat by Lincoln's bed throughout the night after the president was shot at Ford's Theatre and whispered through tears on his passing, "Now he belongs to the ages."

Reconciliation is an amazing thing. The apostle Peter pointed followers of Jesus there when he wrote, "Above all, love each other deeply, because love covers over a multitude of sins" (1 Peter 4:8). Peter's words cause me to wonder if he was thinking of his own denial of Jesus (Luke 22:54–62) and the forgiveness Jesus offered him (and us) through the cross.

The deep love Jesus demonstrated through His death on the cross frees us from the debt for our sins and opens the way for our reconciliation with God (Colossians 1:19–20). His forgiveness empowers us to forgive others as we realize we can't forgive in our own strength, so we ask Him to help us. When we love others because our Savior loves them and forgive because He has forgiven us, God gives us strength. He helps us let go of the past and walk forward with Him into spectacular new places of grace. **James Banks**

FEBRUARY 13

Good for You?

Psalm 119:65–72

You are good, and what you do is good;
teach me your decrees. —Psalm 119:68

Because I like dark chocolate, I once Googled "Is dark chocolate good for you?" I got a variety of results—some good, some bad. You can do the same for almost any food product. Is milk good for you? Is coffee good for you? Is rice good for you? There is a dizzying array of answers to these questions, so you have to be aware that the search itself may not be good for you. It may give you a headache!

But if you're looking for something that's 100 percent good for you all the time, can I recommend the Word of God? Listen to what it can do for the follower of Jesus who is seeking to build a relationship with God.

It can keep you pure (Psalm 119:9, 11).
It blesses you (Luke 11:28).
It makes you wise (Matthew 7:24).
It gives light and understanding (Psalm 119:130).
It helps you grow spiritually (1 Peter 2:2).

Our God is good: "The Lord is good to all," says Psalm 145:9. And in His goodness, He has provided those who love Him with a guide that helps us see how to enhance our relationship with Him. As we try to decide how to live in a world full of choices, praise God that He's told us in Scripture what's good for us.

Let's say with the psalm-writer: "How sweet are your words to my taste, sweeter than honey to my mouth!" (Psalm 119:103). **Dave Branon**

Marriage Before Love

Genesis 24:61–67

Enjoy life with your wife, whom you love. —Ecclesiastes 9:9

A man went to his pastor for counseling. In his hands were pages of complaints against his wife. After an extended period of uninterrupted listening, the pastor couldn't help but ask, "If she is that bad, why did you marry her?" Immediately the man shot back, "She wasn't like this at first!" The pastor, unable to hold back his thoughts, asked, "So, are you saying that she is like this because she's been married to you?"

Whether or not this story is true, it does suggest an important lesson to be learned. At times, feelings toward a spouse may grow cold. But love is much more than feelings—it's a lifelong commitment.

Although most people choose to marry because of love, in some cultures people still get married through matchmaking. In the lives of Isaac and Rebekah recorded in the book of Genesis, love came after marriage. It says in chapter 24 that Isaac married Rebekah and then he loved her (v. 67).

Biblical love is about our willingness to do what is good for another. Husbands are instructed to "love their wives as their own bodies" (Ephesians 5:28).

So, walking in obedience to the Lord, let's keep our marriage vows to love "till death do us part." **Albert Lee**

Trying to Impress

Matthew 15:1–11, 16–20

Out of the heart come evil thoughts. . . .
These are what defile a person. —Matthew 15:19–20

When a college class went on a cultural field trip, the instructor almost didn't recognize one of his star pupils. In the classroom she had concealed six-inch heels beneath her pant legs. But in her walking boots she was less than five feet tall. "My heels are how I want to be," she said with a laugh. "But my boots are how I really am."

Our physical appearance doesn't define who we are; it's our heart that matters. Jesus had strong words for those masters of appearances—the super religious "Pharisees and teachers of the law." They asked Jesus why His disciples didn't wash their hands before eating, as their religious traditions dictated (Matthew 15:1–2). Jesus asked, "Why do you break the command of God for the sake of your tradition?" (v. 3). Then He pointed out how they had invented a legal loophole to keep their wealth instead of caring for their parents (vv. 4–6), thus dishonoring them and violating the fifth commandment (Exodus 20:12).

If we obsess over appearances while looking for loopholes in God's clear commands, we're violating the spirit of His law. Jesus said that "out of the heart come evil thoughts—murder, adultery, sexual immorality," and the like (Matthew 15:19). Only God, through the righteousness of His Son Jesus, can give us a clean heart. **Tim Gustafson**

When to Walk Away

Genesis 39:1–12

God is faithful; he will not let you be tempted beyond what you can bear. —1 Corinthians 10:13

When my father became a Christian in his old age, he fascinated me with his plan for overcoming temptation. Sometimes he just walked away! For example, whenever a disagreement between him and a neighbor began to degenerate into a quarrel, my father just walked away rather than be tempted to advance the quarrel.

One day he met with some friends who ordered *pito* (a locally brewed alcoholic beer). My father had formerly struggled with alcohol and had decided he was better off without it. So, he simply stood up, said his goodbyes, and left the gathering of old friends for another day.

In Genesis, we read how Potiphar's wife tempted Joseph. He immediately recognized that giving in would cause him to "sin against God," so he fled (Genesis 39:9–12).

Temptation knocks often at our door. Sometimes it comes from our own desires; other times it comes through the situations and people we encounter. As Paul told the Corinthians, "No temptation has overtaken you except what is common to mankind" (1 Corinthians 10:13). But then he said, "God is faithful; he will not let you be tempted beyond what you can bear. But when you are tempted, he will also provide a way out so that you can endure it."

The "way out" may include removing the objects of temptation or fleeing from them. Our best course of action may be to simply walk away. **Lawrence Darmani**

FEBRUARY 17

Serving the Least

Matthew 25:31–40

The King will reply, "Truly I tell you, whatever you did for one of the least of these brothers and sisters of mine, you did for me." —Matthew 25:40

His name is Spencer. But everybody calls him "Spence." He was a state track champion in high school. Then he went on to attend a prestigious university on a full academic scholarship. He lives now in one of America's largest cities and is highly respected in the field of chemical engineering. But if you were to ask Spence his greatest achievements to date, he wouldn't mention any of those things. He would excitedly tell you about the trips he makes to Nicaragua every few months to check in on the kids and teachers in the tutoring program he helped establish in one of the poorest areas of that country. And he'd tell you how enriched his life has been by serving them.

"The least of these." It's a phrase people use in a variety of ways, yet Jesus used it to describe those who, according to the world's standards, have little or nothing to offer us in return for our service. They are the men and women and children the world often overlooks—if not forgets completely. Yet it's exactly those people Jesus elevates to such a beautiful status by saying, "Whatever you did for [them], you did for me" (Matthew 25:40).

You don't have to have a degree from a prestigious university to understand Christ's meaning: serving "the least" is the same as serving Him. All it really takes is a willing heart. **John Blase**

Ready for Restoration

Psalm 85

Will you not revive us again, that your people may rejoice in you? —Psalm 85:6

While stationed in Germany in the army, I purchased a brand-new 1969 Volkswagen Beetle. The car was a beauty! The dark green exterior complemented the brown leatherette interior. But as the years took their toll, stuff began to happen, including an accident that ruined the running board and destroyed one of the doors. With more imagination, I could have thought, *My classic car was a perfect candidate for restoration!* And with more money, I could have pulled it off. But that didn't happen.

Thankfully the God of perfect vision and unlimited resources doesn't give up so easily on battered and broken people. Psalm 85 describes both the people who were perfect candidates for restoration and the God who is able to restore them. The setting is likely after the Israelites had returned from seventy years of exile (their punishment for rebellion against God). Looking back, they were able to see His favor—including His forgiveness (vv. 1–3). They were motivated to ask God for His help (vv. 4–7) and to expect good things from Him (vv. 8–13).

Who among us doesn't occasionally feel battered, bruised, and broken? Sometimes it's because of something we've done to ourselves. But because the Lord is the God of restoration and forgiveness, those who humbly come to Him are never without hope. With open arms He welcomes those who turn to Him. Those who do, find safety in His arms. **Arthur Jackson**

FEBRUARY 19

Stay on the Way

John 14:1–7

LORD, we don't know where you are going, so how can we know the way? —John 14:5

Dusk fell as I followed Li Bao along the tops of terraced walls cut into the mountains of central China. I had never been this way before, and I couldn't see more than one step ahead or how steep the ground dropped off to our left. I gulped and stuck close to Li. I didn't know where we were going or how long it would take to get there, but I trusted my friend.

I was in the same position as Thomas, the disciple who always seemed to need reassurance. Jesus told His disciples that He must leave to prepare a place for them and that they knew "the way to the place where [He was] going" (John 14:4). Thomas asked a logical follow-up question: "Lord, we don't know where you are going, so how can we know the way?" (v. 5).

Jesus didn't quench Thomas's doubt by explaining where He was taking them. He simply assured His disciple that He was the way there. And that was enough.

We too have questions about our future. None of us knows the details of what lies ahead. Life is full of twists we don't see coming. That's okay. It's enough to know Jesus, who is "the way and the truth and the life" (v. 6).

Jesus knows what's next. He only asks that we walk close to Him along the way. Mike Wittmer

When to Sacrifice

Galatians 5:22–26

But the fruit of the Spirit is love, joy, peace, forbearance, kindness, goodness, faithfulness, gentleness and self-control. —Galatians 5:22–23

In February 2020, as the COVID-19 crisis was just beginning, a newspaper columnist's concerns struck me. Would we willingly self-isolate, she wondered, changing our work, travel, and shopping habits so others wouldn't get sick? "This isn't just a test of clinical resources," she wrote, "but of our willingness to put ourselves out for others." Suddenly, the need for virtue was front-page news.

It can be hard to consider others' needs while we're anxious about our own. Thankfully, we're not left with willpower alone to meet the need. We can ask the Holy Spirit to give us love to replace our indifference, joy to counter sadness, peace to replace our anxiety, forbearance (patience) to push out our impulsiveness, kindness to care about others, goodness to see to their needs, faithfulness to keep our promises, gentleness instead of harshness, and self-control to lift us beyond self-centeredness (Galatians 5:22–23). While we won't be perfect at all of this, we're called to seek the Spirit's gifts of virtue regularly (Ephesians 5:18).

Author Richard Foster once described holiness as the ability to do what needs to be done when it needs to be done. And such holiness is needed every day, not just in a pandemic. Do we have the capacity to make sacrifices for the sake of others? Holy Spirit, fill us with the power to do what needs to be done. Sheridan Voysey

FEBRUARY 21

God's Guidance

Psalm 1:1–3

Blessed is the one who does not walk in step with the wicked or stand in the way that sinners take or sit in the company of mockers. —Psalm 1:1

When their bank accidentally deposited $120,000 into their account, a couple went on a shopping spree. They purchased an SUV, a camper, and two four-wheelers in addition to paying off bills. Discovering the deposit error, the bank told the couple to return the money. When they couldn't, they were then charged with felony theft. When the couple arrived at the local court, the husband said to a reporter, "We took some bad legal advice." The two learned that following bad advice could lead to making a mess of their lives.

In contrast, the psalmist shared wise advice that can help us avoid messing up in life. He wrote that those who find genuine fulfillment—who are "blessed"—refuse to be influenced by the advice of those who don't serve God (Psalm 1:1).

They know that unwise, ungodly counsel can lead to unseen dangers and costly consequences. They're motivated by (find "delight" in) and preoccupied with ("meditate on") the timeless, unshakable truths of Scripture (v. 2). They've found that submitting to God's guidance leads to stability and fruitfulness (v. 3).

When we're making decisions, big or small, about our careers, money, relationships, and more, we should seek God's wisdom found in the Bible, godly counsel from godly friends, and the leading of the Holy Spirit. **Marvin Williams**

It's Good to Ask

Psalm 143:4–11

Show me the way I should go. —Psalm 143:8

My father has always had a directional sense I've envied. He just instinctively knew where north, south, east, and west are. It's like he was born with that sense. And he's always been right.

Until the night he wasn't.

That was the night my father got lost. He and my mother attended an event in an unfamiliar town and left after dark. He was convinced he knew the way back to the highway, but he didn't. He got turned around, then confused, and ultimately frustrated. My mother reassured him, "I know it's hard, but ask your phone for directions. It's okay."

For the first time in his life that I'm aware of, my seventy-six-year-old father asked for directions. From his phone.

The psalmist David was a man with a wealth of life experience. But the psalms reveal moments when it appears he felt lost spiritually and emotionally. Psalm 143 contains one of those times. The great king's heart was dismayed (v. 4). He was in trouble (v. 11). So, he paused and prayed, "Show me the way I should go" (v. 8). And far from counting on a phone, the psalmist cried out to the Lord, "for to you I entrust my life" (v. 8).

If the "man after [God's] own heart" (1 Samuel 13:14) felt lost from time to time, it's a given that we too will need to turn to God for His direction. **John Blase**

Doing Right

James 2:1–13

If you really keep the royal law found in Scripture, "Love your neighbor as yourself," you are doing right. —James 2:8

In the book *Flags of Our Fathers*, James Bradley recounts the World War II battle of Iwo Jima and its famous flag-raising on Mount Suribachi. Bradley's father, John, was one of the flag-raisers. But more important, he was a Navy corpsman—a medic.

In the heat of battle, facing a barrage of bullets from both sides, Bradley exposed himself to danger so he could care for the wounded and dying. This self-sacrifice showed his willingness and determination to care for others, even though it meant placing himself at great personal risk.

Doc Bradley won the Navy Cross for his heroism and valor, but he never spoke of it to his family. In fact, it was only after his death that they learned of his military decorations. To Doc, it wasn't about winning medals; it was about caring for his buddies.

In James 2:8 we read: "If you really keep the royal law found in Scripture, 'Love your neighbor as yourself,' you are doing right." By intentionally seeking to care for others in the way that we would hope to be treated, James says we are "doing right."

Selflessly "doing right" expresses the heart of God, and it fulfills His law of love. **Bill Crowder**

Freed from Our Cage

Psalm 18:3–6, 16–19

He brought me out into a spacious place. —Psalm 18:19

While out taking walks, writer Martin Laird would often encounter a man with four Kerry Blue Terriers. Three of the dogs ran wild through the open fields, but one stayed near its owner, running in tight circles. When Laird finally stopped and asked about this odd behavior, the owner explained that it was a rescue dog that had spent most of his life locked in a cage. The terrier continued to run in circles as though contained inside a confined box.

The Scriptures reveal that we're trapped and hopeless unless God rescues us. The psalmist spoke of being afflicted by an enemy, entrapped by "the snares of death" with the "cords of death . . . coiled around" him (Psalm 18:4–5). Enclosed and shackled, he cried to God for help (v. 6). And with thundering power, the Lord "reached down . . . and took hold" of him (v. 16).

God can do the same for us. He can break the chains and release us from our confining cages. He can set us free and carry us "out into a spacious place" (v. 19). How sad it is, then, when we keep running in small circles, as if we're still confined in our old prisons. In His strength, may we no longer be bound by fear, shame, or oppression. God has rescued us from those cages of death. We can run free. Winn Collier

Snow Muse

Job 36:26–29; 37:5–7

He says to the snow, "Fall on the earth,"
and to the rain shower, "Be a mighty downpour." —Job 37:6

Named for a tough blue-collar neighborhood in Cincinnati, Ohio, the grassroots musical group Over the Rhine sings about a transformation that took place each year in the city. "Whenever we'd get our first real snowfall of the year, it felt like something sacred was happening," explains band cofounder Linford Detweiler. "Like a little bit of a fresh start. The city would slow down and grow quiet."

If you've experienced a heavy snowfall, you understand how it can inspire a song. A magical quietness drapes the world as snow conceals grime and grayness. For a few moments, winter's bleakness brightens, inviting our reflection and delight.

Elihu, the one friend of Job's who may have had a helpful view of God, noted how creation commands our attention. "God's voice thunders in marvelous ways," he said (Job 37:5). "He says to the snow, 'Fall on the earth,' and to the rain shower, 'Be a mighty downpour.'" Such splendor can interrupt our lives, demanding a sacred pause. "So that everyone he has made may know his work, he stops all people from their labor," Elihu observed (vv. 6–7).

Nature sometimes seizes our attention in ways we don't like. Regardless of what happens to us or what we observe around us, each moment—magnificent, menacing, or mundane—can inspire our worship. The poet's heart within us craves the holy hush. **Tim Gustafson**

Working Off Bad Information

Proverbs 23:9–12

Apply your heart to instruction and your ears to words of knowledge. —Proverbs 23:12

On a trip to New York City, my wife and I wanted to brave a snowy evening and hire a taxi for a three-mile ride from our hotel to a Cuban restaurant. After entering the details into the taxi service's app, I gulped hard when the screen revealed the price for our short jaunt: $1,547.26. After recovering from the shock, I realized I had mistakenly requested a ride to our home—several hundred miles away!

If you're working with the wrong information, you're going to end up with disastrous results. Always. This is why Proverbs encourages us to "apply [our] heart to instruction and [our] ears to words of knowledge," namely, God's wisdom (23:12). If we instead seek advice from those who are foolish, those who pretend to know more than they do and who have turned their back on God, we'll be in trouble. They "scorn . . . prudent words" and can lead us astray with unhelpful, misguided, or even deceptive advice (v. 9).

Instead, we can bend our "ears to words of knowledge" (v. 12). We can open our heart and receive God's liberating instruction—words of clarity and hope. When we listen to those who know the deep ways of God, we discover that they can help us receive and follow divine wisdom. God's wisdom will never lead us astray; it always encourages us and leads us toward life and wholeness. Winn Collier

FEBRUARY 27

When Things Don't Go Well

Romans 8:28–30

We know that in all things God works for the good to those who love him. —Romans 8:28

The first words that many people like to quote when misfortune hits are: "We know that in all things God works for the good of those who love him, who have been called according to his purpose" (Romans 8:28). But that's hard to believe in hard times. I once sat with a man who had lost his third son in a row, and I listened as he lamented, "How can this tragedy work for my good?" I had no answer but to sit silently and mourn with him. Several months later, he was thankful as he said, "My sorrow is drawing me closer to God."

As tough as Romans 8:28 may be to understand, countless testimonies give credence to the truth of it. The story of hymn writer Fanny Crosby is a classic example. The world is the beneficiary of her memorable hymns, yet what worked together for good was born of her personal tragedy, for she became blind when she was an infant. At only age eight, she began to write poetry and hymns. Writing over eight thousand sacred songs and hymns, she blessed the world with such popular songs as "Blessed Assurance," "Safe in the Arms of Jesus," and "Pass Me Not, O Gentle Savior." God used her difficulties to bring good for her and us—and glory for Him.

When tragedy befalls us, it's hard to understand how anything good can come from it, and we won't always see it in this life. But God has good purposes and always remains with us. Lawrence Darmani

Lost but Found

Luke 15:1–9

Rejoice with me; I have found my lost sheep. —Luke 15:6

When we discovered that my mother-in-law had gone missing while shopping with a relative, my wife and I were frantic. Mom suffered from memory loss and confusion, and there was no telling what she might do. Would she wander the area, or hop onto any bus thinking it would take her home? Worst-case scenarios spun through our minds as we began to search for her, crying out to God, "Please find her."

Hours later, my mother-in-law was spotted stumbling along a road, miles away. How God blessed us in being able to find her! Several months later, He blessed her: at eighty years of age, my mother-in-law turned to Jesus Christ for salvation.

Jesus, comparing humans to lost sheep, gives us this illustration: "Suppose [a shepherd] has a hundred sheep and loses one of them. Doesn't he leave the ninety-nine in the open country and go after the lost sheep until he finds it? And when he finds it, . . . he calls his friends and neighbors together and says, 'Rejoice with me; I have found my lost sheep'" (Luke 15:4–6).

Shepherds counted their sheep to make sure every one of them was where it should be. In the same way, Jesus, who is the Good Shepherd (John 10:11), values each of us, young and old. When we are wandering in life, searching, confused about our purpose, it's never too late to turn to Christ. He is looking for us to return to Him so we can enjoy His love and blessings. Leslie Koh

FEBRUARY 29

Undigested Knowledge

John 8:39–47

If you hold to my teaching, you are really my disciples. —John 8:31

In his book on language, British diplomat Lancelot Oliphant (1881–1965) observed that many students give correct answers on tests but fail to put those lessons into practice. "Such undigested knowledge is of little use," declared Oliphant.

Author Barnabas Piper noticed a parallel in his own life: "I thought I was close to God because I knew all the answers," he said, "but I had fooled myself into thinking that was the same as *relationship* with Jesus."

At the temple one day, Jesus encountered people who thought they had all the right answers. They were proudly proclaiming their status as Abraham's descendants yet refused to believe in God's Son.

"If you were Abraham's children," said Jesus, "then you would do what Abraham did" (John 8:39). And what was that? Abraham "believed the LORD, and he credited it to him as righteousness" (Genesis 15:6). Still, Jesus's hearers refused to believe. "The only Father we have is God himself," they said (John 8:41). Jesus replied, "Whoever belongs to God hears what God says. The reason you do not hear is that you do not belong to God" (v. 47).

Piper recalls how things "fell apart" for him before he "encountered God's grace and the person of Jesus in a profound way." When we allow God's truth to transform our lives, we gain much more than the right answer. We introduce the world to Jesus. Tim Gustafson

MARCH 1

The Definitive Choice

Joshua 24:15–24

We will serve the LORD! —Joshua 24:21

Coming from someone who used to value ancestral gods, my ninety-year-old father's statement near the end of his life was remarkable: "When I die," he spoke laboriously, "nobody should do anything other than what the church will do. No soothsaying, no ancestral sacrifices, no rituals. As my life is in the hands of Jesus Christ, so shall my death be!"

My father chose the path of Christ in his old age when he invited Jesus into his life as Savior. His contemporaries mocked him: "An old man like you shouldn't be going to church!" But my father's choice to follow and worship the one true God was definite, like the people Joshua addressed.

"Choose for yourselves this day whom you will serve," Joshua challenged them. "But as for me and my household, we will serve the LORD," he concluded (24:15). Their response was resolute—they chose to worship the Lord. Even after Joshua warned them to count the cost (vv. 19–20), they still resolved to follow the Lord, recalling His deliverance, provision, and protection (vv. 16–17, 21).

Such a confident choice, however, calls for equally confident actions, as Joshua strongly reminded them: "Throw away the foreign gods . . . and yield your hearts to the LORD" (v. 23). Have you made a choice to live for God and God alone? Lawrence Darmani

MARCH 2

The Greatest Rescue Mission

Luke 19:1–10

The Son of Man came to seek and to save the lost. —Luke 19:10

On February 18, 1952, a massive storm split the *SS Pendleton*, a tanker ship, into two pieces about ten miles off the Massachusetts coast. More than forty sailors were trapped inside the ship's sinking stern amid fierce winds and violent waves.

When word of the disaster reached the Coast Guard station in Chatham, Massachusetts, Boatswain's Mate First Class Bernie Webber took three men on a lifeboat to try to save the stranded crew against nearly impossible odds—and brought thirty-two of the seemingly doomed sailors to safety. Their courageous feat was deemed one of the greatest rescues in United States Coast Guard history and was the subject of the 2016 movie *The Finest Hours*.

In Luke 19:10, Jesus declared His own rescue mission when He said, "The Son of Man came to seek and to save the lost." The cross and the resurrection became the ultimate expression of that rescue, as Jesus took upon himself our sins and restored to the Father all who trust Him. For two thousand years, people have embraced His offer of abundant life now and eternal life with Him. Rescued!

As followers of Jesus, we have the privilege—with the Holy Spirit's help—to join our Savior in the greatest rescue mission of all. Who in your life needs His rescuing love? **Bill Crowder**

Diamond Dust

Isaiah 1:18–20

Wash me, and I will be whiter than snow. —Psalm 51:7

During a bitterly frigid winter in our part of Michigan, there were many mixed emotions about the weather. As the snowy winter season pressed on into March, most people had long before fallen out of love with snow and were bemoaning long-range forecasts of low temperatures.

Yet the majestic beauty of the snow continued to amaze me. Even as I threw endless shovelfuls of it from my driveway onto the over-my-head snowbanks, I was enthralled with the white stuff. One particular day, ice crystals filtered down from the sky to fall atop old snow. As my wife and I took a walk through this sparkling scene, it looked as if diamond dust had been sprinkled across the landscape.

In Scripture, snow seems to have varied purposes. God sends it as an indicator of His creative greatness (Job 37:6; 38:22–23). Snowcapped mountains irrigate the arid valleys below. But more significantly, God gives snow as a picture of our forgiveness. The gospel of Jesus provides a way for us to be cleansed of our sins and for our hearts to be made much "whiter than snow" (Psalm 51:7; Isaiah 1:18).

The next time you see snow—in life or in photos—thank God for the forgiveness and the freedom from sin's penalties that this beautiful, natural gift pictures for all who have put their trust in our Savior. **Dave Branon**

MARCH 4

Getting What We Want

1 Kings 1:5, 32–37

Adonijah . . . put himself forward and said, "I will be king." —1 Kings 1:5

Aaron Burr anxiously awaited the result of the tie-breaking vote from the US House of Representatives. Deadlocked with Thomas Jefferson in the 1800 race for the presidency, Burr had reason to believe that the House would declare him the winner. But he lost. Nurturing grievances against Alexander Hamilton for not supporting his candidacy, Burr killed Hamilton in a gun duel less than four years later. Outraged by the killing, his country turned its back on him, and Burr died a dour old man.

Political power plays are a tragic part of history. When King David was nearing death, his son Adonijah recruited David's commander and a leading priest to make himself king (1 Kings 1:5–8). But David had chosen Solomon to be the next king (v. 17). With the help of the prophet Nathan, the rebellion was put down (vv. 11–53). Despite his reprieve, Adonijah plotted a second time to steal the throne. Solomon had him executed (2:13–25).

How human of us to want what's not rightfully ours! No matter how hard we pursue power, prestige, or possessions, it's never quite enough. We always want something more. How unlike Jesus, who "humbled himself by becoming obedient to death—even death on a cross"! (Philippians 2:8).

Ironically, selfishly pursuing our own ambitions never brings us our truest, deepest longings. Leaving the outcome to God is the only path to peace and joy. Tim Gustafson

False Places of Safety

Mark 1:9–15

The kingdom of God has come near.
Repent and believe the good news! —Mark 1:15

When our dog Rupert was a puppy, he was so afraid of going outside I'd have to drag him to the park. After getting him there one day, I foolishly let him off his leash. He sprinted home—back to his place of safety.

That experience reminded me of a man I met on a plane. He began apologizing to me as we taxied down the runway. "I'm going to get drunk on this flight," he said. "It sounds like you don't want to," I replied. "I don't," he said, "but I always run back to the wine." He got drunk, and the saddest part was watching his wife embrace him when he got off the plane, smell his breath, then push him away. Drink was his place of safety, but it was no safe place at all.

Jesus began His mission with the words, "The kingdom of God has come near. Repent and believe the good news!" (Mark 1:15). *Repent* means "to reverse direction." *The kingdom of God* is "His loving rule over our lives." Jesus is saying that instead of running to places that entrap us or being ruled by fears and addictions, we can be ruled by God himself, who lovingly leads us to new life and freedom.

Today Rupert runs to the park barking with joy. I pray that the man on the plane finds joy and freedom in Christ, leaving behind his false place of safety. **Sheridan Voysey**

MARCH 6

That Smiling Man

Colossians 3:18–23

Whatever you do, work at it with all your heart, as working for the LORD, not for human masters. —Colossians 3:23

Going to the grocery store isn't something I particularly enjoy. It's just a mundane part of life—something that must be done.

But there's one part of this task I've unexpectedly come to look forward to: checking out in Fred's lane. Fred, you see, turns checkout into show time. He's amazingly fast, always has a big smile, and even dances (and sometimes sings!) as he acrobatically flips (unbreakable) purchases into a plastic bag. Fred clearly enjoys a job that could be seen as one of the most tedious around. And for just a moment, his cheerful spirit brightens the lives of people in his checkout lane.

The way Fred does his job has won my respect and admiration. His cheerful attitude, desire to serve, and attention to detail all line up well with the apostle Paul's Colossians 3:23 description of how we are to work: "Whatever you do, work at it with all your heart, as working for the Lord."

When we're in relationship with Jesus, any job we have to do gives us an opportunity to reflect His presence in our lives. No task is too small . . . or too big! Tackling our responsibilities—whatever they may be—with joy, creativity, and excellence gives us an opportunity to influence those around us, no matter our job. Adam Holz

Serving the Smallest

Luke 14:15–23

God chose the lowly things of this world and the despised things. —1 Corinthians 1:28

The video showed a man kneeling beside a busy freeway during an out-of-control brush fire. He was clapping his hands and pleading with something to come to him. What was it? A dog? Moments later a bunny hopped into the picture. The man scooped up the scared rabbit and sprinted to safety.

How did the rescue of such a small thing make national news? Because there's something endearing about compassion shown to something so tiny and helpless. It takes a big heart to make room for the smallest creature.

Jesus said the kingdom of God is like a man who gave a banquet and made room for everyone who was willing to come. Not just the movers and shakers but also "the poor, the crippled, the blind and the lame" (Luke 14:21). I'm thankful that God targets the weak and the seemingly insignificant, because otherwise I'd have no shot. Paul said, "God chose the weak things of the world to shame the strong. God chose the lowly things of this world and the despised things . . . so that no one may boast before him" (1 Corinthians 1:27–29).

How big must God's heart be to save a small person like me! In response, how large has my heart grown to be? I can easily tell—not by how I please the "important people," but by how I serve the ones society might deem the least important. Mike Wittmer

The Primary Actor

Psalm 118:6–9, 21–25

The LORD has done this. —Psalm 118:23

I once heard about a student taking a class in preaching at a prominent seminary. The student, a young man who was a bit full of himself, delivered his sermon with eloquence and evident passion. He sat down self-satisfied, and the professor paused a moment before responding. "That was a powerful sermon," he said. "It was well organized and moving. Here's the problem: God was not the subject of a single one of your sentences."

The professor highlighted a problem all of us struggle with at times: We can talk as if we're the primary actor (emphasizing what we do, what we say) when in truth God is the primary actor in life. We often profess that God is somehow generally "in charge," but we act as if all the outcomes depend on us.

The Scriptures insist that God is the true subject of our lives, the true force. Even our necessary acts of faith are done "in the name of the LORD"—in the Lord's power (Psalm 118:10–11). God enacts our salvation. God rescues us. God tends to our needs. "The LORD has done this" (v. 23).

So, the pressure's off. We don't need to fret, compare, work with compulsive energy, or feed our many anxieties. God is in charge. We need only trust Him and follow His lead in obedience and with diligence. Winn Collier

Not Fatherless

Matthew 6:5–13

His Spirit joins with our spirit to affirm that we are God's children. —Romans 8:16 NLT

In his book *Fatherless Generation*, John Sowers writes that "No generation has seen as much voluntary father absence as this one with twenty-five million kids growing up in single-parent homes." In my own experience, if I'd bumped into my father on the street, I wouldn't have known him. My parents were divorced when I was very young, and all the photos of my dad were burned. For years, I felt fatherless. Then at age thirteen, I heard the Lord's Prayer (Matthew 6:9–13) and thought to myself, *You may not have an earthly father, but now you have God as your heavenly Father.*

In Matthew 6:9 we're taught to pray, "Our Father in heaven, hallowed be your name." Previously verse 7 says not to "keep on babbling" when praying, and we may wonder how these verses are connected. I realized that because God remembers, we don't need to repeat. He truly understands, so we don't need to explain. He has a compassionate heart, so we don't need to be uncertain of His goodness. And because He knows the end from the beginning, we know His timing is perfect.

Because God is our Father, we don't need to use "many words" (v. 7) to move Him. Through prayer, we're talking with a Father who loves and cares for us and made us His children through Jesus. Albert Lee

MARCH 10

We Bow Down

Psalm 95

Come, let us bow down in worship; let us kneel before the LORD our Maker. —Psalm 95:6

The ancient Greeks and Romans rejected kneeling as a part of their worship. They said that kneeling was unworthy of a free man, unsuitable for the culture of Greece, and appropriate only for barbarians. The scholars Plutarch and Theophrastus regarded kneeling as an expression of superstition. Aristotle called it a barbaric form of behavior. This belief, however, was never held by God's people.

In Psalm 95:6, the psalmist indicated that kneeling expressed a deep reverence for God. In this single verse he used three different Hebrew words to express what the attitude and position of the worshipper should be.

First, he used the word *worship*, which means "to fall prostrate as a sign of honor to the Lord," with an associated meaning of allegiance to Him. The second word he used was *bow*. This means "to sink down to one's knees, giving respect and worship to the Lord." The psalmist then used the word *kneel*, which means "to be on one's knees giving praise to God."

According to the psalmist, kneeling in God's presence is a sign of reverence rather than a barbaric form of behavior. The important thing, however, is not just our physical position but a humble posture of the heart.

Marvin Williams

Are You There?

Exodus 3:11–14

I will be with you. —Exodus 3:12

When his wife contracted a terminal illness, Michael longed for her to experience the peace he had through his relationship with God. He had shared his faith with her, but she wasn't interested. One day, as he walked through a local bookstore, a title caught his eye: *God, Are You There?* Unsure how his wife would respond to the book, he walked in and out of the store several times before finally buying it. To his surprise, she accepted it.

The book touched her, and she began to read the Bible too. Two weeks later, Michael's wife passed away—at peace with God and resting in the assurance that He would never leave or forsake her.

When God called Moses to lead His people out of Egypt, He didn't promise him power. Instead, He promised His presence: "I will be with you" (Exodus 3:12). In Jesus's last words to His disciples before His crucifixion, He also promised God's eternal presence, which they would receive through the Holy Spirit (John 15:26).

There are many things God could give us to help us through life's challenges, such as material comfort, healing, or immediate solutions to our problems. Sometimes He does. But the best gift He gives is himself. This is the greatest comfort we have: whatever happens in life, He will be with us; He will never leave us nor forsake us.

Leslie Koh

MARCH 12

Straight Ahead

2 Kings 22:1–2, 8–13

He did what was right in the eyes of the LORD . . . , not turning aside to the right or to the left. —2 Kings 22:2

It used to take the steady eye and the firm hand of a farmer to drive a tractor or a combine down straight rows. But even the best eyes would overlap rows, and by the end of the day even the strongest hands would be fatigued. But now there's autosteer—a GPS-based technology that allows for accuracy to within one inch when planting, cultivating, and spraying. It's incredibly efficient and hands-free. Just imagine sitting in a mammoth combine and instead of gripping the wheel, you're gripping a roast beef sandwich. Autosteer is an amazing tool to keep you moving straight ahead.

You may recall the name Josiah. He was crowned king when he was only "eight years old" (2 Kings 22:1). Years later, when Josiah was in his mid-twenties, Hilkiah the high priest found "the Book of the Law in the temple" (v. 8). It was then read to the young king, who tore his robes in sorrow due to his ancestors' disobedience to God. Josiah set about to do what was "right in the eyes of the LORD" (v. 2). The book became a tool to steer the people so there would be no turning to the right or left. God's instructions were there to set things straight.

Allowing the Scriptures to guide us day by day keeps our lives in line with knowing God and His will. The Bible is an amazing tool that, if followed, keeps us moving straight ahead. **John Blase**

The Gift and the Giver

Luke 1:67–79

Because of God's tender mercy, the morning light from heaven is about to break upon us. —Luke 1:78 NLT

It's only a key chain. Five little blocks held together by a shoelace. My daughter gave it to me years ago when she was seven. Today the lace is frayed, and the blocks are chipped, but they spell a message that never grows old: "I ♥ DAD."

The most precious gifts are determined not by what went into them but by who they're from. Ask any parent who ever received a bouquet of dandelions from a chubby hand. The best gifts are valued not in money but in love.

Zechariah understood that. We hear it in his prophetic song as he praised God for giving him and his wife, Elizabeth, their son, John, when they were well past their childbearing years (Luke 1:67–79). Zechariah rejoiced because John was to be a prophet who would proclaim God's greatest gift to all people—the coming Messiah: "Because of God's tender mercy, the morning light from heaven is about to break upon us" (Luke 1:78 NLT). Those words point to a gift given with so much love that it will even "shine on those living in darkness and in the shadow of death" (1:79).

The sweetest gift we can receive is God's tender mercy—the forgiveness of our sins through Jesus. That gift cost Him dearly at the cross, but He offers it freely out of His deep love for us. James Banks

Set Free

Galatians 5:1, 4–14

It is for freedom that Christ has set us free. —Galatians 5:1

When I was young, a classmate gave my family a registered collie that had become too old to breed puppies. We soon learned this beautiful dog had, sadly, spent much of her life inside a small pen. She couldn't fetch or run in a straight line. And even with a large yard in which to play, she thought she was fenced in.

The first Christians, many who were Jews, were accustomed to being fenced in by the Mosaic law. Though the law was good and had been given by God to convict them of sin and lead them to Jesus (Galatians 3:19–25), it was time to live out their new faith based in God's grace and the freedom of Christ. But they hesitated. After all this time, were they really free?

We may have the same problem. Perhaps we grew up in churches with rigid rules that fenced us in. Or we were raised in permissive homes and are now desperate for the security of rules. Either way, it's time to embrace our freedom in Christ (Galatians 5:1). Jesus has freed us to obey Him out of love (John 14:21) and to "serve one another humbly in love" (Galatians 5:13). An entire field of joy and love is open for those who realize that "if the Son sets you free, you will be free indeed" (John 8:36).

Mike Wittmer

God-Sized Love

Matthew 5:43–48

If you love those who love you, what reward will you get? —Matthew 5:46

I once visited an impoverished neighborhood of Santo Domingo in the Dominican Republic. Homes were made of corrugated iron, and electrical wires dangled live above them. There I had the privilege of interviewing families and hearing how churches were helping to combat unemployment, drug use, and crime.

In one alleyway I climbed a rickety ladder to a small room to interview a mother and her son. But just a moment later someone rushed up, saying, "We must leave now." A machete-wielding gang leader was apparently gathering a mob to ambush us.

We visited a second neighborhood, but there we had no problem. Later I discovered why. As I visited each home, a gang leader stood outside guarding us. It turned out his daughter was being fed and educated by the church, and because believers were standing by her, he stood by us.

Jesus presented a standard of love that's beyond comparison. This kind of love embraces not just the "worthy" but the undeserving as well (Matthew 5:43–45), reaching beyond family and friends to touch those who can't or won't love us back (vv. 46–47). This is God-sized love (v. 48)—the kind that blesses everyone.

As believers in Santo Domingo live out this love, neighborhoods are starting to change. Tough hearts are warming to their cause. That's what happens when God-sized love comes to town. **Sheridan Voysey**

MARCH 16

Promise Keeper

Hebrews 6:13–20

After waiting patiently, Abraham received what was promised. —Hebrews 6:15

Jonathan found himself stumbling as he repeated his wedding vows. He thought, *How can I make these promises and not believe they're possible to keep?* He made it through the ceremony, but the weight of his commitments remained. After the reception, Jonathan led his wife to the chapel where he prayed—for more than two hours—that God would help him keep his promise to love and care for LaShonne.

Jonathan's wedding-day fears were based on the recognition of his human frailties. But God, who promised to bless the nations through Abraham's offspring (Galatians 3:16), has no such limitations. To challenge his Jewish Christian audience to perseverance and patience to continue in their faith in Jesus, the writer of Hebrews recalled God's promises to Abraham, the patriarch's patient waiting, and the fulfillment of what had been promised (Hebrews 6:13–15). Abraham and Sarah's status as senior citizens was no barrier to the fulfillment of God's promise to give Abraham "many descendants" (v. 14).

Are you challenged to trust God despite being weak, frail, and human? Are you struggling to keep your commitments, to fulfill your pledges and vows? In 2 Corinthians 12:9, God promises to help us: "My grace is sufficient for you, for my power is made perfect in weakness." For nearly forty years God has helped Jonathan and LaShonne to remain committed to their vows. Why not trust Him to help you? **Arthur Jackson**

Hang in There

Isaiah 41:8–13

I will strengthen you and help you; I will uphold you with my righteous right hand. —Isaiah 41:10

When my father-in-law celebrated a recent birthday, during our family gathering to honor him, someone asked him, "What's the most important thing you've learned in your life so far?" His answer? "Hang in there."

Hang in there. It might be tempting to dismiss those words as simplistic. But my father-in-law wasn't promoting blind optimism or positive thinking. He's endured tough things in his nearly eight decades. His determination to press on wasn't grounded in some vague hope that things might get better but in Christ's work in his life.

"Hanging in there"—the Bible calls it *perseverance*—isn't possible through mere willpower. We persevere because God promised, over and over, that He is with us, that He will give us strength, and that He will accomplish His purposes in our lives. That's the message He spoke to the Israelites through Isaiah: "So do not fear, for I am with you; do not be dismayed, for I am your God. I will strengthen you and help you; I will uphold you with my righteous right hand" (Isaiah 41:10).

What does it take to "hang in there"? According to Isaiah, the foundation for hope is God's character. Knowing God's goodness allows us to release our grip on fear so we can cling to the Father and His promise that He will provide what we need each day: strength, help, and God's comforting, empowering, and upholding presence.

Adam Holz

MARCH 18

A Beginner's Guide to Life

Romans 6:16–23

The wages of sin is death, but the gift of God is eternal life in Christ Jesus our LORD. —Romans 6:23

After my mother's sudden death, I was motivated to start blogging. I wanted to write posts that would inspire people to use their minutes on earth to create significant life moments. So, I turned to a beginner's guide to blogging. I learned what platform to use, how to choose titles, and how to craft compelling posts. And soon, my first blog post was born.

Paul wrote a "beginner's guide" that explains how to obtain eternal life. In Romans 6:16–18, he contrasts the fact that we're all born in rebellion to God (sinners) with the truth that Jesus can help us be "set free from [our] sin" (v. 18). Paul then describes the difference between being a slave to sin and a slave to God and His life-giving ways (vv. 19–20). He continues by stating that "the wages of sin is death, but the gift of God is eternal life" (v. 23). *Death* means "being separated from God forever." This is the devastating outcome we face when we reject Christ. But God has offered us a gift in Jesus—new life. It's the kind of life that begins on earth and continues forever in heaven with Him.

Paul's beginner's guide to eternal life leaves us with two choices—choosing sin, which leads to death, or choosing Jesus's gift, which leads to eternal life. Receive His gift of life, and if you've already accepted Christ, why not share this gift with others today! **Marvin Williams**

Pure Worship

Mark 11:15–18

My house will be called a house of prayer. —Mark 11:17

Jose pastored a church known for its programs and theatrical productions. They were well done, yet he worried that the church's busyness had slipped into a business. Was the church growing for the right reasons or because of its activities? Jose wanted to find out, so he canceled all extra church events for one year. His congregation would focus on being a living temple where people worshipped God.

Jose's decision seems extreme, until you notice what Jesus did when He entered the temple's outer courts. The holy space that should have been full of simple prayers had become a flurry of worship business. "Get your doves here! Lily white, as God requires!" Jesus overturned the merchant's tables and stopped those who bought their merchandise. Furious at what they were doing, He quoted Isaiah 56 and Jeremiah 7: "'My house will be called a house of prayer for all nations.' But you have made it 'a den of robbers'" (Mark 11:17). The court of the gentiles, the place for outsiders to worship God, had been turned into a mundane marketplace for making money.

There's nothing wrong with business or staying busy. But that's not the point of church. We're the living temple of God, and our main task is to worship Jesus. We likely won't need to flip over any tables as Jesus did, but He may be calling us to do something equally drastic so we can concentrate on true worship, sincere prayer, and the preaching of the Word. Mike Wittmer

The Joy of Giving

1 Thessalonians 5:12–24

Encourage the disheartened, help the weak, be patient with everyone. —1 Thessalonians 5:14

It was a dreary week. I had been feeling lethargic and listless, although I couldn't figure out why.

Near the end of the week, I found out that an aunt had kidney failure. I knew I had to visit her—but to be honest, I felt like postponing the visit. Still, I made my way to her place, where we had dinner, chatted, and prayed together. An hour later, I left her home feeling upbeat for the first time in days. Focusing on someone else rather than myself had somehow improved my mood.

Psychologists have found that the act of giving can produce satisfaction, which comes when the giver sees the recipient's gratitude. Some experts even believe that humans are wired to be generous!

Perhaps that's why Paul, when encouraging the church in Thessalonica to build up their faith community, urged them to "help the weak" (1 Thessalonians 5:14). Earlier, he had also cited Jesus's words, "It is more blessed to give than to receive" (Acts 20:35). While this was said in the context of giving financially, it applies as well to the giving of time and effort.

When we give, we get an insight into how God feels. We understand why He's so delighted to give us His love, and we share in His joy and the satisfaction of blessing others. I think I'll be visiting my aunt again soon. **Leslie Koh**

Legal versus Right

Acts 5:17–29

Peter and the other apostles replied: "We must obey God rather than human beings!" —Acts 5:29

In his powerful book *Unspeakable*, Os Guinness wrestles with the problem of evil in the world. In one section, he focuses on the Nuremberg trials that followed World War II. The Nazis stood charged with crimes against humanity, and their mantra of defense was simple: "I was merely following orders." The verdict, however, was that the soldiers had a moral obligation to defy orders that, though legal, were clearly wrong.

In a much different context, Peter and the disciples were arrested for presenting the message of the risen Christ and brought before the religious rulers in Jerusalem. Rather than allowing themselves to be shaped by the mood of the mob, the disciples declared their intention to continue preaching Christ.

The orders of the religious establishment may have been legal, but they were wrong. When the disciples chose to obey God rather than the godless religious leaders, they raised a standard of conviction that rose above the opinions of the rulers of this world.

The trials we face may test our commitment. But we will find opportunities to exalt the King if we trust Him for the strength to go beyond the words of the crowd-pleasers and do right as He defines it in His Word. Bill Crowder

Mirrors and Hearers

James 1:16–27

Whoever looks intently into the perfect law that gives freedom, and continues in it . . . will be blessed in what they do. —James 1:25

When I emerged from my hotel in Kampala, Uganda, my hostess, who had come to pick me up for our seminar, looked at me with an amused grin. "What's so funny?" I inquired. She laughed and asked, "Did you comb your hair?" It was my turn to laugh, for I had indeed forgotten to comb my hair. I had looked at my reflection in the hotel mirror. Why had I not noticed what I saw?

In a practical analogy, James gives us a useful dimension to make our study of Scripture more beneficial. We look in the mirror to examine ourselves to see if anything needs correction—hair combed, face washed, shirt properly buttoned. Like a mirror, the Bible helps us to examine our character, attitude, thoughts, and behavior (James 1:23–24). This enables us to align our lives according to the principles God has revealed. We will "keep a tight rein" on our tongues (v. 26) and "look after orphans and widows" (v. 27). We will pay heed to God's Holy Spirit within us and keep ourselves "from being polluted by the world" (v. 27).

When we look attentively into "the perfect law that gives freedom" and apply it to our lives, we will be blessed in what we do (v. 25). As we look into the mirror of Scripture, we can "humbly accept the word planted in [us]" (v. 21).

Lawrence Darmani

Forever Perfect

Hebrews 10:8–18

By one sacrifice he has made perfect forever those who are being made holy. —Hebrews 10:14

When I first heard of Sara Lee cakes, the name brand caught my attention because one of the most common Asian family names is "Lee." Being a Chinese Lee myself, I wondered if Sara was Chinese or Korean.

Then I learned that Charlie Lubin, an American bakery entrepreneur, had named his cheesecakes after his daughter Sara Lee. Sara said her father wanted this product to be "perfect because he was naming it after me."

Perfection is a standard that none of us could ever hope to attain. Yet we learn from the book of Hebrews that Jesus, through His one supreme sacrifice for our sins, "has made perfect forever those who are being made holy" (10:14).

The continual sacrifices made by the priests since the time of Moses could never change anyone's sinful standing before God (Hebrews 10:1–4). But the onetime sacrifice of Christ on the cross—the sinless one dying for the sinful—perfected us forever in the eyes of God. Jesus's once-for-all payment for our sins was sufficient. The writer to the Hebrews paraphrased Jeremiah 31:34, "Their sins and lawless acts I will remember no more" (Hebrews 10:17).

We are perfected forever to stand before God because of the perfect work accomplished by Jesus on the cross. This is the assurance of our salvation. Albert Lee

MARCH 24

Borrowed Blessings

1 Chronicles 29:6–16

The earth is the LORD's, and everything in it. —Psalm 24:1

As we bowed our heads over lunch, my friend Jeff prayed: "Father, thank you for letting us breathe your air and eat your food." Jeff had just been through a difficult job loss, so his heartfelt trust in God and recognition that everything belongs to Him profoundly moved me. I found myself thinking: *Do I honestly understand that even the most basic, everyday things in my life are really God's, and He's simply letting me use them?*

When King David received offerings from the people of Israel for building the temple in Jerusalem, he prayed, "But who am I, and who are my people, that we should be able to give as generously as this? Everything comes from you, and we have given you only what comes from your hand." Then he added, "All of it belongs to you" (1 Chronicles 29:14, 16).

Scripture tells us that even "the ability to produce wealth" and earn a living come from Him (Deuteronomy 8:18). When we understand that everything we have is borrowed, we are encouraged to loosen our grip on the stuff of this world and live with open hands and hearts—sharing freely because we're deeply thankful for the kindnesses we receive daily.

God is a generous giver. He is so loving that He even gave up His Son "for us all" (Romans 8:32). Because we have been given so much, may we give Him our heartfelt thanks for blessings small and large. James Banks

The Cyrus Cylinder

Ezra 1:1–4

The LORD moved the heart of Cyrus king of Persia. —Ezra 1:1

In 1879, archaeologists discovered a remarkable little item in an area now known as Iraq (biblical Babylon). Just nine inches long, the Cyrus Cylinder records something that King Cyrus of Persia did 2,500 years ago. It says that Cyrus allowed a group of people to return to their homeland and rebuild their "holy cities."

It's the same story told in Ezra 1. There we read that "the LORD moved the heart of Cyrus king of Persia" to make a proclamation (v. 1). Cyrus said he was releasing the captives in Babylon to go home to Jerusalem, reestablish their homes, and rebuild their temple (vv. 2–5).

But there's more to the story. Daniel confessed his sins and his people's sins and pleaded with God to end the Babylonian captivity (Daniel 9). In response, God sent an angel to speak to Daniel (v. 21). Later He moved Cyrus to release the Hebrews. (See also Jeremiah 25:11–12; 29:10.)

Together, the Cyrus Cylinder and God's Word combine to show us that the king's heart was changed, and he allowed the exiled Hebrews to go home and worship.

This story has great implications for us today. In a world that seems out of control, we can rest assured that God can move the hearts of leaders. We read in Proverbs 21:1 that "the king's heart is in the hand of the LORD" (NKJV). And Romans 13:1 says that "there is no authority except that which God has established."

The Lord, who is able to change our own hearts as well as the hearts of our leaders, is in control. **Dave Branon**

MARCH 26

We Are Dust

Psalm 103:8–14

He remembers that we are dust. —Psalm 103:14

The young father was at the end of his rope. "Ice cream! Ice cream!" his toddler screamed again. The meltdown in the middle of the crowded mall began drawing the attention of shoppers nearby. "Fine, but we just need to do something for mommy first, okay?" the father said. "Nooooo! Ice cream!"

And then she approached them: a small, well-dressed woman with shoes that matched her handbag. "He's having a big fit," the father said. The woman smiled and responded, "Actually, it looks like a big fit is having your little boy. Don't forget he's so small. He needs you to be patient and stay close." The situation didn't magically resolve itself, but it was just the kind of pause the father and son needed in the moment.

The wise woman's words sound like echoes from Psalm 103. David writes of the Lord, who is "compassionate and gracious, slow to anger, abounding in love" (v. 8). He then continues by invoking the image of an earthly father who "has compassion on his children," and even more so "the Lord has compassion on those who fear him" (v. 13). God our Father "knows how we are formed, he remembers that we are dust" (v. 14). He knows we're small and fragile.

We often fail and are overwhelmed by what this big world hands us. What an amazing assurance to know of our Father's patient, ever-present, abounding love.

John Blase

All Too Human

Romans 7:14–25

The trouble is with me, for I am all too human. —Romans 7:14 NLT

British writer Evelyn Waugh (1903–1966) wielded his words in a way that accentuated his character flaws. Eventually the novelist converted to Christianity, yet he still struggled with his inadequacies. One day a woman asked him, "Mr. Waugh, how can you behave as you do and still call yourself a Christian?" He replied, "Madam, I may be as bad as you say. But believe me, were it not for my religion, I would scarcely be a human being."

Waugh was waging the internal battle the apostle Paul describes: "I want to do what is right, but I can't" (Romans 7:18 NLT). He also says, "The trouble is not with the law . . . [It] is with me, for I am all too human" (v. 14 NLT). He further explains, "In my inner being I delight in God's law; but I see another law at work in me. . . . Who will rescue me from this body that is subject to death?" (vv. 22–24). And then the exultant answer: "Thanks be to God, who delivers me through Jesus Christ our Lord!" (v. 25).

When we come in faith to Christ, admitting our wrongdoing and need of a Savior, we immediately become a new creation. But our spiritual formation remains a lifelong journey. As John the disciple observed: "Now we are children of God, and what we will be has not yet been made known. But . . . when Christ appears, we shall be like him, for we shall see him as he is" (1 John 3:2). Tim Gustafson

MARCH 28

A Wide, Sweeping, Grace

Isaiah 44:21–23

I have swept away your offenses. —Isaiah 44:22

Alexa, Amazon's voice-controlled device, has an interesting feature: it can erase everything you say. Whatever you've asked Alexa to do, whatever information you've asked Alexa to retrieve, one simple sentence ("Delete everything I said today") sweeps it all clean, as if it never happened.

It's too bad the rest of our life doesn't have this capability. Every misspoken word, every disgraceful act, every moment we wish we could erase—we'd just speak the command, and the entire mess would disappear.

There's good news, though. God does offer each of us a clean start. Only, He goes far deeper than merely deleting our mistakes or bad behavior. God provides redemption, a deep healing that transforms us and makes us new. "Return to me," He says, "I have redeemed you" (Isaiah 44:22). Even though Israel rebelled and disobeyed, God reached out to them with lavish mercy. He "swept away [their] offenses like a cloud, [their] sins like the morning mist" (v. 22). He gathered all their shame and failures and washed them away with His wide, sweeping grace.

God will do the same with our sin and blunders. There's no mistake He can't mend, no wound He can't heal. God's mercy heals and redeems the most painful places in our soul—even the ones we've hidden for so very long. His mercy sweeps away all our guilt, washes away every regret. That is one joyful result of our salvation in Jesus—His wide, sweeping grace. Winn Collier

Facing Fear

Psalm 56:3–11

When I am afraid, I put my trust in you. —Psalm 56:3

Warren moved to a small town to pastor a church. After his ministry had some initial success, one of the locals turned on him. Concocting a story accusing Warren of horrendous acts, the man took the story to the local newspaper and even printed his accusations on pamphlets to distribute to local residents by mail. Warren and his wife started praying hard. If the lie was believed, their lives would be upended.

King David once experienced something similar. He faced an attack of slander by an enemy. "All day long they twist my words," he said, "all their schemes are for my ruin" (Psalm 56:5). This sustained assault left him fearful and tearful (v. 8). But in the midst of the battle, he prayed this powerful prayer: "When I am afraid, I put my trust in you. . . . What can mere mortals do to me?" (vv. 3–4).

David's prayer can be a model for us today. "When I am afraid"—in times of fear or accusation, we turn to God. "I put my trust in you"—we place our battle in God's powerful hands. "What can mere mortals do to me?"—facing the situation with Him, we remember how limited the powers against us really are.

The newspaper ignored the story about Warren. For some reason, the pamphlets were never distributed. What battle do you fear today? Talk to God. He's willing to fight it with you. Sheridan Voysey

Bridge Builders

Acts 9:17–27

Barnabas took him and brought him to the apostles. —Acts 9:27

A new believer in Jesus recently attended a worship service at our church. He had long, multicolored, spiked hair. He was dressed in dark clothes and had many piercings and tattoos. Some gaped, and others just gave him that "It's good to see you in church, but please don't sit next to me" smile. Yet there were some during the greeting time who went out of their way to welcome and accept him. They were bridge builders.

Barnabas was that bridge builder for Saul (later called Paul). When Saul arrived in Jerusalem three years after his conversion, many disciples were afraid of him and doubted his transformation (Acts 9:26). He didn't receive a warm welcome from the Jerusalem church greeters for good reason. Saul had a terrible reputation for persecuting Christians! But Barnabas, a Jewish convert, believed God's work of grace in Saul's life and became a bridge between him and the apostles (v. 27).

Saul needed someone to come alongside him to encourage, teach him, and introduce him to other believers. Barnabas was that bridge. As a result, Saul was brought into deeper fellowship with the disciples in Jerusalem and was able to preach the gospel there freely and boldly.

New believers need a Barnabas in their lives. Find ways to be a bridge in the lives of others. Marvin Williams

His Scars

John 20:24–29

He was pierced for our transgressions, . . .
and by his wounds we are healed. —Isaiah 53:5

After my conversation with Grady, it occurred to me why his preferred greeting was a "fist bump" not a handshake. A handshake would've exposed the scars on his wrist—the result of his attempts to do himself harm. It's not uncommon for us to hide our wounds—external or internal—caused by others or self-inflicted.

In the wake of my interaction with Grady, I thought about Jesus's physical scars, the wounds caused by nails pounded into His hands and feet and a spear thrust into His side. Rather than hiding His scars, Christ called attention to them.

After Thomas initially doubted that Jesus had risen from the dead, He said to him, "Put your finger here; see my hands. Reach out your hand and put it into my side. Stop doubting and believe" (John 20:27). When Thomas saw those scars for himself and heard Christ's amazing words, he was convinced that it was Jesus. He exclaimed in belief, "My Lord and my God!" (v. 28). Jesus then pronounced a special blessing for those who haven't seen Him or His physical wounds but still believe in Him: "Blessed are those who have not seen and yet have believed" (v. 29).

The best news ever is that His scars were for our sins—our sins against others or ourselves. The death of Jesus is for the forgiveness of the sins of all who believe in Him and confess with Thomas, "My Lord and my God!"
Arthur Jackson

APRIL 1

Just What I Need

2 Corinthians 1:3–7

[God] comforts us in our troubles, so that we can comfort those in any trouble. —2 Corinthians 1:4

As I stood in the back of the room at a senior citizens' center in Palmer, Alaska, listening to my daughter's high school chorale sing "It Is Well with My Soul," I wondered why she, the choir director, had chosen that song. It had been played at her sister Melissa's funeral, and Lisa knew it was always tough for me to hear it without having an emotional response.

My musings were interrupted when a man sidled up next to me and said, "This is just what I need to hear." I asked why he needed this song. "I lost my son Cameron last week in a motorcycle accident," he said.

Wow! I had been so focused on myself that I never considered the needs of others, and God was busy using that song exactly where He wanted it to be used. I took my new friend Mac, who worked at the center, aside, and we talked about God's care in this toughest time in his life.

All around us are people in need, and sometimes we have to set aside our own feelings and agendas to help them. One way we can do that is to remember how God has comforted us in our trials and troubles "so that we can comfort those in any trouble with the comfort we ourselves receive from God" (2 Corinthians 1:4).

How easy it is to be so engrossed in our own concerns that we forget that someone right next to us might need a prayer, a word of comfort, a hug, or gift of mercy in Jesus's name. **Dave Branon**

Different Goals

1 Corinthians 1:18–31

God has chosen the foolish things of the world to put to shame the wise. —1 Corinthians 1:27 NKJV

In 1945, professional golfer Byron Nelson had an unimaginable season. Of the thirty tournaments he entered, he won an amazing eighteen times—including eleven in a row. Had he chosen to, he could have continued his career and perhaps become the greatest of all time. But that was not his goal. His goal was to earn enough money playing golf to buy a ranch and spend his life doing what he really loved. So, instead of continuing on at the peak of his career, Nelson retired at age thirty-four to become a rancher. He had different goals.

The world may find that kind of thinking to be foolish. It doesn't really understand the heart that looks beyond trying to gain more wealth or fame and instead seeks real satisfaction and contentment. This is especially true when it comes to our choice to live for Christ. But it is in the world's perception of our alleged foolishness that we might best represent the Master's different goals to this world. Paul wrote, "But God chose the foolish things of the world to shame the wise; God chose the weak things of the world to shame the strong" (1 Corinthians 1:27).

A commitment to living according to kingdom values might brand us as foolish in the eyes of the world, but it can bring honor to our God. And that is truly what is important. Bill Crowder

When We Know Who Wins

Revelation 21:1–5

There will be no more death or mourning or crying or pain. —Revelation 21:4

My supervisor is a huge fan of a certain college basketball team. One year, they won the national championship, so another coworker texted him congratulations. One problem: my boss had not yet had a chance to watch the final game!

He was frustrated, he said, knowing the outcome beforehand. But, he admitted, at least when he watched the game he wasn't nervous when the score stayed close to the end. He knew who won!

We never really know what tomorrow will hold. Some days can feel mundane and tedious, while other days are filled with joy. Still other times, life can be grueling, agonizing even, for long periods of time.

But despite life's unpredictable ups and downs, we can still be securely grounded in God's peace. Because, like my supervisor, we know the end of the story. We know who "wins."

Revelation, the Bible's final book, lifts the curtain on that spectacular finale. After the final defeat of death and evil (20:10, 14), John say, there will be a beautiful victory scene (21:1–3) where God makes His home with His people (v. 3) and wipes "every tear from their eyes" in a world with "no more death or mourning or crying or pain" (v. 4).

On difficult days, we can cling to this promise. No more loss or weeping. No more what-ifs or broken hearts. Instead, we'll spend eternity together with our Savior. What a glorious celebration that will be! Adam Holz

Still the King

Psalm 74:4–8, 12–23

Rise up, O God, and defend your cause. —Psalm 74:22

One news report called it "the single deadliest day for Christians in decades." The pair of attacks on Palm Sunday worshippers in April 2017 defies our understanding. We simply don't have a category to describe bloodshed in a house of worship. But we can find some help from others who know this kind of pain well.

Most of the people of Jerusalem were in exile or had been slain when Asaph wrote Psalm 74. Pouring out his heart's anguish, he described the destruction of the temple at the hands of ruthless invaders. "Your foes roared in the place where you met with us," Asaph said (v. 4). "They burned your sanctuary to the ground; they defiled the dwelling place of your Name" (v. 7).

Yet the psalmist found a place to stand despite the awful reality—providing encouragement that we can do so too. "But God is my King from long ago," Asaph resolved. "He brings salvation on the earth" (v. 12). This truth enabled Asaph to praise God's mighty power even though His salvation seemed absent in the moment. "Have regard for your covenant," Asaph prayed. "Do not let the oppressed retreat in disgrace; may the poor and needy praise your name" (vv. 20–21).

When justice and mercy seem absent, God's love and power are in no way diminished. With Asaph, we can confidently say, "But God is my King." Tim Gustafson

APRIL 5

Learning from Little Ones

Matthew 21:8–17

From the lips of children and infants you, LORD, have called forth your praise. —Matthew 21:16

When a friend and I rode into one of the slums in Nairobi, Kenya, our hearts were deeply humbled by the poverty we witnessed. In that same setting, however, different emotions—like fresh waters—were stirred in us as we witnessed young children running and shouting, "Mchungaji, Mchungaji!" (Swahili for "pastor"). Such was their joy-filled response upon seeing their spiritual leader in the vehicle with us. With these tender shouts, the little ones welcomed the one known for his care and concern for them.

As Jesus arrived in Jerusalem riding on a donkey, joyful children were among those who celebrated Him. "Blessed is he who comes in the name of the Lord! . . . Hosanna to the Son of David" (Matthew 21:9, 15). But praises for Jesus were not the only sounds in the air. One can imagine the noisiness of scurrying, money making merchants who were put to flight by Jesus (vv. 12–13). Furthermore, religious leaders who had witnessed His kindness in action "were indignant" (vv. 14–15). They voiced their displeasure with the children's praises (v. 16) and thereby exposed the poverty of their own hearts.

We can learn from the faith of children of God of all ages and places who recognize Jesus as the Savior of the world. He's the one who hears our praises and our cries, and He cares for and rescues us when we come to Him with childlike trust. **Arthur Jackson**

Dad at the Dentist

Matthew 26:36–39

My Father, if it is possible, may this cup be taken from me. Yet not as I will, but as you will. —Matthew 26:39

I didn't expect a profound lesson about God's heart at the dentist's office—but I got one. I was there with my ten-year-old son. He had an adult tooth coming in under a baby tooth that hadn't fallen out yet. It had to come out. There was no other way.

My son, in tears, pleaded with me: "Dad, isn't there another way? Can't we just wait and see? Please, Dad, I don't want to have this tooth pulled!" It just about broke my heart, but I told him, "Son, it's got to come out. I'm sorry. There's no other way." And I held his hand as he wriggled and writhed while the dentist removed that stubborn molar, tears in my eyes too. I couldn't take his pain away; the best I could offer was to be present with him in it.

In that moment, I remembered Jesus in the garden of Gethsemane, asking His Father for a different way. How it must have broken the Father's heart to see His beloved Son in such agony! Yet there was no other way to save His people.

In our lives, we sometimes face unavoidable yet painful moments—just like my son did. But because of Jesus's work for us through His Spirit, even in our darkest moments our loving heavenly Father is always present with us (Matthew 28:20). Adam Holz

Death Row Joy

1 Peter 1:3–9

Though you do not see him now, you believe in him and are filled with an inexpressible and glorious joy. —1 Peter 1:8

In 1985 Anthony Ray Hinton was charged with the murders of two restaurant managers. It was a setup—he'd been miles away when the crimes happened—but he was found guilty and sentenced to death. At the trial, Ray forgave those who lied about him, adding that he still had joy despite this injustice. "After my death, I'm going to heaven," he said. "Where are you going?"

Life on death row was hard for Ray. Prison lights flickered whenever the electric chair was used for others, a grim reminder of what lay ahead. Ray passed a lie detector test, but the results were ignored—one of many injustices he faced while trying to get his case reheard.

Finally, in early 2015, Ray's conviction was overturned by the US Supreme Court. He'd been on death row for nearly thirty years. His life is a testament to the reality of God. Because of his faith in Jesus, Ray had a hope beyond his trials (1 Peter 1:3–5), and he experienced supernatural joy in the face of injustice (v. 8). "This joy that I have," Ray said after his release, "they couldn't ever take that away in prison." Such joy proved his faith to be genuine (vv. 7–8).

Death row joy? That's hard to fabricate. It points us to a God who exists even though He's unseen. He is ready to sustain us in our ordeals. Sheridan Voysey

Interrupted Fellowship

Matthew 27:32–50

My God, my God, why have you forsaken me? —Matthew 27:46

The loud, sorrowful cry pierced the dark afternoon air. I can imagine it drowning out the sound of mourning from friends and loved ones gathered at Jesus's feet. It must have overwhelmed the moans of the dying criminals who flanked Jesus on both sides. And surely it startled all who heard it.

"Eli, Eli, lema sabachthani?" Jesus cried out in Aramaic, voicing His agony and utter despondency as He hung on that cross of shame on Golgotha. "My God, my God, why have you forsaken me?" (Matthew 27:45–46).

I cannot think of more heart-wrenching words. Throughout eternity, Jesus had been in perfect fellowship with God the Father. Together they had created the universe, had fashioned mankind in their image, and planned salvation. Never in the eons past had they not been in total fellowship with each other.

And now, as the anguish of the cross continued to bring devastating pain on Jesus—He for the first time lost the awareness of God's presence as He carried the burden of the sins of the world.

It was the only way. Only through this time of interrupted fellowship could our salvation be provided for. And it was only because Jesus was willing to experience this sense of being forsaken on the cross that we humans can gain fellowship with God.

Thank you, Jesus, for experiencing such pain so we could be forgiven. Dave Branon

APRIL 9

The Torn Curtain

Matthew 27:51–54

We have confidence to enter the Most Holy Place by the blood of Jesus, by a new and living way opened for us through the curtain, that is, his body. —Hebrews 10:19–20

It was a dark and somber day on the outskirts of Jerusalem. On a hill just outside the city walls, a Man who'd been attracting crowds of eager followers for the past three years hung in disgrace and pain on a rough wooden cross. Mourners wept and wailed in sorrow. The light of the sun no longer brightened the afternoon sky. And the intense suffering of the Man on the cross ended when He cried out in a loud voice, "It is finished" (Matthew 27:50; John 19:30).

At that very moment, another sound came from the great temple across town—the sound of ripping fabric. Miraculously, without human intervention, the huge, thick curtain that separated the outer temple from the Holy of Holies tore in two from top to bottom (Matthew 27:51).

That torn curtain symbolized the reality of the cross: a new way was now open to God! Jesus, the Man on the cross, had shed His blood as the last sacrifice—the one true and sufficient sacrifice (Hebrews 10:10)—which allows all who believe in Him to enjoy forgiveness and enter into a relationship with God (Romans 5:6–11).

Amidst the darkness of that original Good Friday, we received the best news ever—Jesus opened a way for us to be saved from our sins and to experience fellowship with God forever (Hebrews 10:19–22). Thank God for the message of the torn curtain! **Dave Branon**

Running the Race

1 Corinthians 9:19–27

Do you not know that in a race all the runners run, but only one gets the prize? Run in such a way as to get the prize. —1 Corinthians 9:24

Spyridon Louis isn't well known around the world, but he is in Greece. That's because of what happened in 1896 when the Olympic Games were revived in Athens.

During the competition that year, the Greeks did quite well—winning the most medals of any nation. But the event that became a source of true Greek pride was the first-ever marathon. Seventeen athletes competed in this race of 40 kilometers (24.8 miles), but it was won by Louis—a common laborer. For his efforts, Louis was honored by king and country, and he became a national hero.

The apostle Paul used running a race as a picture of the Christian life. In 1 Corinthians 9:24, he challenged us not just to run but to run to win, saying, "Do you not know that in a race all the runners run, but only one gets the prize? Run in such a way as to get the prize." Not only did Paul teach this but he also lived it out. In his final epistle, he said, "I have fought the good fight, I have finished the race, I have kept the faith" (2 Timothy 4:7). Having finished his race, Paul joyfully anticipated receiving the victory crown from the King of heaven.

Like Paul, run your earthly race to win—and to please your King. Bill Crowder

GAD or God?

1 Peter 5:6–11

Cast all your anxiety on him because he cares for you. —1 Peter 5:7

Are you a chronic worrier? Do you worry about bills, the future, health, debt, marriage issues? Has worry so consumed you that you have become "a fret machine"? If this describes you, perhaps you have *generalized anxiety disorder*, or GAD—a condition marked by a perpetual state of worry about most aspects of life. According to David Barlow, professor of psychology at Boston University, "The key psychological feature of GAD is a state of chronic, uncontrollable worry." A little anxiety is normal, but constant worry is not.

Overwhelmed by suffering and persecution, the first-century Christians were driven out of Jerusalem and scattered throughout Asia (1 Peter 1:1–7). Many of these Jesus-followers were experiencing feelings of distress because of possible danger or misfortune. Peter encouraged these believers not to be filled with anxiety but to cast all their worries upon God (5:7). He wanted them to realize that it made very little sense for them to carry their worries when they could cast them on God, who cared deeply about what happened to them.

Are you a chronic worrier? Let God be responsible for your anxieties. When you start to worry, turn your thoughts to trusting Him completely. Why suffer from GAD when you can trust God? Marvin Williams

Listening to Your Brother

Matthew 18:15–20

Whoever turns a sinner from the error of their way will save them from death and cover over a multitude of sins. —James 5:20

"You need to listen to me, I'm your brother!" The plea came from a concerned older brother in my neighborhood and was directed to a younger sibling who was moving farther away from him than the older child was comfortable with. Clearly the older child was better able to judge what was best in the situation.

How many of us have resisted the wise counsel of a brother or sister? If you've had to face the consequences of resisting the good advice of someone more mature, you're not alone.

One of the greatest resources we can have as believers in Jesus is a family—those who are spiritually related because of a common faith in Him. This family includes mature men and women who love God and each other. Like the little brother in my neighborhood, we sometimes need a word of caution or correction to get us back on track. This is particularly true when we offend someone, or someone offends us. Doing what's right can be difficult. Yet Jesus's words in Matthew 18:15–20 show us what to do when offenses happen within our spiritual family.

Thankfully, our gracious heavenly Father places in our lives people who are prepared to help us honor Him and others. When we listen, things go better in the family (v. 15). Arthur Jackson

Don't Stop Building

Ezra 5:1–5

The eye of their God was watching over [them] . . . and they were not stopped. —Ezra 5:5

When Simon received an opportunity to take on a new role at work, he thought it was a godsend. After praying over the decision and seeking counsel, he felt that God was giving him this opportunity to take on bigger responsibilities. Everything fell into place, and his boss supported his move. Then things began to go wrong. Some colleagues resented his promotion and refused to cooperate. He began to wonder if he should give up.

When the Israelites returned from Babylon to Jerusalem to rebuild the temple, enemies sought to frighten and discourage them (Ezra 4:4). The Israelites stopped at first, but they continued their work after God encouraged them through the prophets Haggai and Zechariah (4:24–5:2).

Later, enemies hassled them again. This time the Israelites persevered, knowing that "the eye of their God was watching over [them]" (5:5). They followed God's instructions and trusted Him to carry them through. Sure enough, God moved the Persian king to support the temple's completion (vv. 13–15).

Similarly, Simon sought God's wisdom to discern whether he should stay or find a new position. Sensing God calling him to remain, he relied on God's strength to persevere. Over time, he slowly gained his colleagues' acceptance.

As we seek to follow God—wherever He places us—we may face opposition. That's when we need to keep following Him. He will guide us and carry us through. Leslie Koh

Photobombing Jesus

John 3:26–36

He must become greater; I must become less. —John 3:30

When the teacher asked our Sunday school class a difficult question about the life of Jesus, my hand shot up. I had just read the story, so I knew this one. And I wanted the others in the room to know that I knew it too. After all, I'm a Bible teacher. How embarrassing it would be to be stumped in front of them! Now I was embarrassed by my fear of embarrassment. So I lowered my hand. Am I this insecure?

John the Baptist shows a better way. When his disciples complained that people were beginning to leave him and follow Jesus, John said he was glad to hear it. He was merely the messenger. "I am not the Messiah but am sent ahead of him. . . . He must become greater; I must become less" (3:28, 30). John realized that the point of his existence was Jesus. He is "the one who comes from heaven" and "is above all" (v. 31)—the divine Son who gave His life for us. He must receive all the glory and fame.

Any attention drawn to ourselves distracts from our Lord. And since He is our only Savior and the only hope for the world, any credit we steal from Him ends up hurting us.

Let's resolve to step out of the picture—to stop photobombing Jesus. It's best for Him, for the world, and for us. Mike Wittmer

APRIL 15

Listening Matters

Psalm 85

I will listen to what God the LORD says. —Psalm 85:8

"Come at once. We have struck a berg." Those were the first words Harold Cottam, the wireless operator on the *RMS Carpathia*, received from the sinking *RMS Titanic* at 12:25 a.m. on April 15, 1912. The *Carpathia* would be the first ship to the disaster scene, saving 706 lives.

In the US Senate hearings days later, the *Carpathia*'s captain Arthur Rostron testified, "The whole thing was absolutely providential. . . . The wireless operator was in his cabin at the time, not on official business at all, but just simply listening as he was undressing. . . . In ten minutes maybe he would have been in bed, and we would not have heard the message."

Listening matters—especially listening to God. The writers of Psalm 85, the sons of Korah, urged attentive obedience when they wrote, "I will listen to what God the LORD says; he promises peace to his people, his faithful servants—but let them not turn to folly. Surely his salvation is near those who fear him" (vv. 8–9). Their admonition is especially poignant because their ancestor Korah had rebelled against God and had perished in the wilderness (Numbers 16:1–35).

The night the *Titanic* sank, another ship was much closer, but its wireless operator had gone to bed. Had he heard the distress signal, perhaps more lives would have been saved. When we listen to God by obeying His teaching, He'll help us navigate even life's most troubled waters. **James Banks**

Obey the Call

Mark 1:16–20

At once they left their nets and followed him. —Mark 1:18

I read about Captain Ray Baker, who flew for the Strategic Air Command during the Vietnam War. The Air Force trained him, along with the other pilots, to run out of their barracks to their planes at the sound of a buzzer. Many times during dinner he had to drop his utensils and bolt to his bomber. He had been trained to respond to the call with immediate obedience. He was so well-trained that one day while on furlough, he ran out of a restaurant when he heard a buzzer.

When Jesus called His first followers, they had an immediacy in their response to His call. The call of these fishermen was abrupt. "At once they left their nets and followed him" (Mark 1:18). The author of this account, Mark, may have wanted to impress upon his readers the authority of Jesus. When He extended the call, these men jumped to obey because helping people enter the kingdom of God was a more compelling adventure and a grander vision than catching fish.

When Jesus issues a call to follow Him, He doesn't want us to delay. He expects immediate obedience when it comes to telling others the good news. Take the story of salvation to someone today! Marvin Williams

APRIL 17

The Snake and the Trike

Luke 1:1–4

I myself have carefully investigated everything from the beginning. —Luke 1:3

For years, I had retold a story from a time when my brother and I were toddlers and our family was living in Ghana. As I recalled the story, I said that he had parked our old iron tricycle on a small cobra. The trike was too heavy for the snake, which remained trapped under the front wheel.

But after my aunt and my mother had both passed away, we discovered a long-lost letter from Mom recounting the incident. In reality, I was the one who had left the tricycle on the snake, and my brother had run to tell Mom. Her eyewitness account, written close to the actual event, revealed the reality.

The historian Luke understood the importance of accurate records. He explained how the story of Jesus was "handed down to us by those who from the first were eyewitnesses" (Luke 1:2). "I too decided to write an orderly account for you," he wrote to Theophilus, "so that you may know the certainty of the things you have been taught" (vv. 3–4). The result was the gospel of Luke. Then, in his introduction to the book of Acts, Luke said of Jesus, "After his suffering, he presented himself to them and gave many convincing proofs that he was alive" (Acts 1:3).

Our faith is not based on hearsay or wishful thinking. It is rooted in the well-documented, historically true life of Jesus, who came to give us peace with God. His Story stands. Tim Gustafson

The Contents of Lincoln's Pockets

Romans 15:1–13

Each of us should please our neighbors for their good, to build them up. —Romans 15:2

On the night in 1865 when US president Abraham Lincoln was shot at Ford's Theater, his pockets contained the following: two spectacles, a lens polisher, a pocketknife, a watch fob, a handkerchief, a leather wallet containing a five-dollar Confederate bill, and eight newspaper clippings, including several that praised him and his policies.

I wonder what the Confederate money was doing in the president's pocket, but I have little doubt about the glowing news stories. Everyone needs encouragement, even a great leader like Lincoln! Can you see him, in the moments before the fateful play began, perhaps reading them to his wife?

Who do you know who needs encouragement? Everyone! Look around you. There isn't one person in your line of vision who is as confident as they seem. We're all one failure, snide comment, or bad hair day away from self-doubt.

What if we all obeyed God's command in Romans 15:2 to "please our neighbors for their good, to build them up"? What if we determined only to speak "gracious words" that are "sweet to the soul and healing to the bones"? (Proverbs 16:24). What if we wrote these words down, so friends could reread and savor them? Then we'd all have notes in our pockets (or on our phones!). And we'd be more like Jesus, who "did not please himself" but lived for others (Romans 15:3). Mike Wittmer

APRIL 19

An Eternal Perspective

Colossians 3:1–7

Set your mind on things above,
not on earthly things. —Colossians 3:2

In the movie *Gladiator*, General Maximus Decimus Meridius seeks to stir his cavalry to fight well in the coming battle against Germania. Addressing his troops, he challenges them to give their very best. He makes this profound statement: "What we do in life echoes in eternity."

These words from a fictional military leader convey a powerful concept that is of particular significance to believers in Christ. We are not just taking up time and space on a rock that's floating through the universe. We are here with the opportunity to make an eternal difference with our lives.

Jesus himself said, "Store up for yourselves treasures in heaven, where moths and vermin do not destroy, and where thieves do not break in and steal" (Matthew 6:20). Having the perspective of living for eternity can make all the difference in this world.

How can we learn to set our minds "on things above" (Colossians 3:2)? A good way to begin is to discover what our eternal God values. Throughout the pages of the Bible, He reminds us that He values people above possessions and our character above our performance. Those are the truths that last forever. Embracing them can bring an eternal perspective to our daily living. **Bill Crowder**

Finding Treasure

Matthew 13:44–46

The kingdom of heaven is like treasure hidden in a field. —Matthew 13:44

John and Mary were walking their dog on their property when they stumbled on a rusty can partially unearthed by recent rains. When they took the can home and opened it, they discovered a cache of gold coins more than a century old! The couple returned to the spot and located seven more cans containing 1,427 coins in all. Then they protected their treasure by reburying it elsewhere.

That cache of coins (valued at $10 million) is called the Saddle Ridge Hoard, the largest find of its kind in US history. The story is strikingly reminiscent of a parable Jesus told: "The kingdom of heaven is like treasure hidden in a field. When a man found it, he hid it again, and then in his joy went and sold all he had and bought that field" (Matthew 13:44).

Tales of buried treasure have captured imaginations for centuries, though such discoveries rarely happen. But Jesus tells of a treasure accessible to all who confess their sins and receive and follow Him (John 1:12).

We'll never come to an end of that treasure. As we leave our old lives and pursue God and His purposes, we encounter His worth. Through "the incomparable riches of his grace, expressed in his kindness to us in Christ Jesus" (Ephesians 2:7), God offers us treasure beyond imagination—new life as His sons and daughters, new purpose on earth, and the incomprehensible joy of eternity with Him. James Banks

APRIL 21

Family Privilege

John 1:6–14

To all who did receive him, to those who believed in his name, he gave the right to become children of God. —John 1:12

When I was in primary school in Ghana, I had to live with a loving and caring family away from my parents. One day, all the children assembled for a special family meeting. The first part involved all of us sharing individual experiences. But next, when only children who legally belonged to the parents were required to be present, I was politely excluded. Then the stark reality hit me: I was not a "child of the house." Despite their love for me, the family required that I should be excused because I was only living with them; I was not adopted or born into their family.

This incident reminds me of John 1:11–12. The Son of God came to His own people, and they rejected Him. Those who received Him then and receive Him now are given the right to become God's children. When we are adopted into His family, "the Spirit himself bears witness with our spirit that we are children of God" (Romans 8:16 ESV).

Jesus doesn't exclude anybody who is adopted by the Father. Rather, He welcomes us as a permanent part of His family. "To all who did receive him, to those who believed in his name, he gave the right to become children of God" (John 1:12). **Lawrence Darmani**

A Devastating Cycle

Proverbs 7:10–27

Her house is a highway to the grave, leading down to the chambers of death. —Proverbs 7:27

Heroin addiction is poignantly tragic. Users build tolerance, so larger hits are required for the same high. Soon the dosage they seek is more than enough to kill them. When addicts hear someone has died from an exceptionally strong batch, their first thought may not be fear but "Where can I get that?"

C. S. Lewis warned of this downward spiral in *Screwtape Letters*, his imaginative look at a demon's explanation of the art of temptation. Start with some pleasure—if possible one of God's good pleasures—and offer it in a way God has forbidden. Once the person bites, give less of it while enticing him to want more. Provide "an ever-increasing craving for an ever-diminishing pleasure," until finally we "get the man's soul and give him nothing in return."

Proverbs 7 illustrates this devastating cycle with the temptation of sexual sin. Sex is God's good gift, but when we seek its enjoyment outside of marriage we're "like an ox going to the slaughter" (v. 22). People stronger than us have destroyed themselves by pursuing highs that are harmful, so "pay attention" and "do not let your heart turn to [wrongful] ways" (vv. 24–25). Sin can be alluring and addicting, but it always ends in death (v. 27). By avoiding—in God's strength—the temptation to sin, we can find true joy and fulfillment in Him. **Mike Wittmer**

APRIL 23

Confident Prayer

Luke 11:5–13

Which of you fathers, if your son asks for a fish, will give him a snake instead? —Luke 11:11

Having tried for years to have a child, Richard and Susan were elated when Susan became pregnant. Her health problems, however, posed a risk to the baby, and so Richard lay awake each night praying for his wife and child. One night, Richard sensed he didn't need to pray so hard, that God had promised to take care of things. But a week later Susan miscarried. Richard was devastated. He wondered, *Had they lost the baby because he hadn't prayed hard enough?*

On first reading, we might think today's parable suggests so. In the story, a neighbor (sometimes thought to represent God) only gets out of bed to help the friend because of the friend's annoying persistence (Luke 11:5–8). Read this way, the parable suggests that God will give us what we need only if we badger Him. And if we don't pray hard enough, maybe God won't help us.

But biblical commentators like Klyne Snodgrass believe this misunderstands the parable—its real point is that if neighbors might help us for selfish reasons, how much more will our unselfish Father help us. We can therefore ask confidently (vv. 9–10), knowing that God is greater than flawed human beings (vv. 11–13). He isn't the neighbor in the parable but the opposite of him.

"I don't know why you lost your baby," I told Richard, "but I know it wasn't because you didn't pray 'hard' enough. God isn't like that." **Sheridan Voysey**

We Need Our Church Community

Hebrews 10:19–25

[Let us] not [give] up meeting together, as some are in the habit of doing, but [encourage] one another. —Hebrews 10:25

I grew up the firstborn son of a Southern Baptist preacher. Every Sunday the expectation was clear: I was to be in church. Possible exceptions? Maybe if I had a significant fever. But the truth is, I absolutely loved going, and I even went a few times feverish. But the world has changed, and the numbers for regular church attendance are not what they used to be. Of course, the quick question is why? The answers are many and varied. Author Kathleen Norris counters those answers with a response she received from a pastor to the question, "Why do we go to church?" He said, "We go to church for other people. Because someone may need you there."

Now by no means is that the only reason we go to church, but his response does resonate with the heartbeat of the writer to the Hebrews. He urged the believers to persevere in the faith, and to achieve that goal he stressed "not giving up meeting together" (Hebrews 10:25). Why? Because something vital would be missed in our absence: "encouraging one another" (v. 25). We need that mutual encouragement to "spur one another on toward love and good deeds" (v. 24).

Brothers and sisters, keep meeting together, because someone may need you there. And the corresponding truth is that you may need them as well. John Blase

APRIL 25

Is Faithfulness Enough?

Isaiah 6:8–13

I heard the voice of the LORD, saying: "Whom shall I send? And who will go for us? —Isaiah 6:8

A young missionary in Central America was tempted to give up. He wrote to friends and family, "I go about on fishing boats through the day. At night I sleep on piles of hides on the deck. The people do not seem to be interested in the gospel message I bring. Sometimes the adversary tempts me to discouragement in the face of seeming lack of success." But then he added, "I take courage and press on anew as I remember that God does not hold me responsible for success but for faithfulness."

The prophet Isaiah also may have been tempted to give up his difficult assignment. The Lord told him that the result of his efforts would be that the people would hear but not understand, and they would see but not perceive (Isaiah 6:9). Their hearts would be dull, their ears heavy, and their eyes shut (v. 10).

Put yourself in the shoes of Isaiah or that missionary. Would you have pressed on or given up? Is faithfulness enough, or do you think your work must be recognized as successful before you feel satisfied in serving the Lord?

The prophet and the missionary did what God asked them to do. They preached God's Word and trusted in His purposes. You too can be a faithful servant. Do your best and leave the results in the Lord's hands. **Albert Lee**

That Is Mine!

Ezekiel 29:1–9

I am the LORD; that is my name! —Isaiah 42:8

The Nile River of Africa, which spans more than 4,100 miles and flows northward across several northeastern African countries, is the world's longest river. Over the centuries, the Nile has provided sustenance and livelihood for millions of citizens in the countries it passes through. Currently, Ethiopia is building what will become Africa's largest hydro-power dam on the Nile. It will be a great resource for Ethiopia.

Pharaoh, the king of Egypt, claimed to be the Nile's owner and originator. He and all Egypt boasted, "The Nile belongs to me; I made it for myself" (Ezekiel 29:3; see v. 9). The Pharaoh and the people failed to acknowledge that God alone provides natural resources. As a result, God promised to punish the nation (vv. 8–9).

We are to care for God's creation and not forget that everything we have comes from the Lord. Romans 11:36 says, "For from him and through him and for him are all things. To him be the glory forever!" God is the one who also endows humanity with the ability to manufacture and invent man-made resources.

Whenever we talk about a good thing that has come to us or that we have accomplished, we need to remember what God says in Isaiah 42:8, "I am the LORD; that is my name! I will not yield my glory to another." Lawrence Darmani

APRIL 27

An Open, Generous Heart

1 Timothy 6:17–19

Be generous and willing to share. —1 Timothy 6:18

After Vicki's old car broke down with no option for repair, she started scraping together money for another vehicle. Chris, a frequent customer at the restaurant where Vicki works the drive-thru window, one day heard her mention she needed a car. "I couldn't stop thinking about it," Chris said. "I [had] to do something." So he bought his son's used car (his son had just put it up for sale), shined it up, and handed Vicki the keys. Vicki was shocked. "Who does that?" she said in amazement and gratitude.

The Scriptures call us to live with open hands, giving freely as we can—providing what's truly best for those in need. As Paul says: "Command [those who are rich] to do good, to be rich in good deeds" (1 Timothy 6:18). We don't merely perform a benevolent act here or there, but rather we live out a cheerful spirit of giving. Bigheartedness is our normal way of life. "Be generous and willing to share," we're told (v. 18).

As we live with an open, generous heart, we don't need to fear running out of what we need. Rather, the Bible tells us that in our compassionate generosity, we're taking "hold of the life that is truly life" (v. 19). With God, genuine living means loosening our grip on what we have and giving freely to others. Winn Collier

Slapton Sands

1 Peter 5:1–11

Be alert and of sober mind. Your enemy the devil prowls around like a roaring lion looking for someone to devour. —1 Peter 5:8

On the southern shores of England is Slapton Sands. This beautiful beach area carries a tragic memory from its past.

On April 28, 1944, during World War II, Allied soldiers were engaged in Operation Tiger, a training exercise in amphibious beach landings in preparation for the D-Day invasion of Normandy. Suddenly, enemy gunboats appeared and killed over seven hundred American servicemen in a surprise attack. Today, a monument stands on Slapton Sands to commemorate the sacrifice of those young men who died while training for a battle they would not live to fight.

This tragedy is a metaphor that warns the believer in Christ. We too are involved in combat with an enemy who is powerful and deceptive. That is why the apostle Peter warned: "Be alert and of sober mind. Your enemy the devil prowls around like a roaring lion looking for someone to devour" (1 Peter 5:8).

Like the soldiers on Slapton Sands, we face an enemy who desires our undoing. In the service of our King, we must be on the alert. The call to be effective in battle (2 Timothy 2:3–4) challenges us to be ready for the surprise attacks of our spiritual enemy—so that we can endure to serve another day. Bill Crowder

APRIL 29

Spending Time with God

Luke 5:12–16

Jesus often withdrew to lonely places and prayed. —Luke 5:16

A River Runs Through It is Norman Maclean's masterful story of two boys growing up in western Montana with their father, a Presbyterian minister. On Sunday mornings, Norman and his brother, Paul, went to church where they heard their father preach. Once Sunday evening rolled around, there was another service, and their father would preach again. But between those two services, they were free to walk the hills and streams with him "while he unwound between services." It was an intentional withdrawing on their father's part to "restore his soul and be filled again to overflowing for the evening sermon."

Throughout the Gospels, Jesus is seen teaching multitudes on hillsides and cities, and healing the sick and diseased who were brought to Him. All this interaction was in line with the Son of Man's mission "to seek and to save the lost" (Luke 19:10). But it's also noted that He "often withdrew to lonely places" (5:16). His time there was spent communing with the Father—being renewed and restored to step back once more into His mission.

In our faithful efforts to serve, it's good for us to remember that Jesus "often" withdrew. If this practice was important for Jesus, how much more so for us? May we regularly spend time with our Father, who can fill us again to overflowing. **John Blase**

Our Children Are Watching

Deuteronomy 6:1–9

Love the LORD your God with all your heart and with all your soul and with all your strength. —Deuteronomy 6:5

It can be disturbing to realize that our children often mirror the way we speak and act. I remember being concerned about the way my son angrily lashed out at his sister when she was annoying him. My wife gently pointed out to me that his behavior was a reflection of mine.

A few weeks later, I caught myself lashing out at my son when I was frustrated. Through my wife's encouragement, I apologized to him for my behavior and told him I would learn to treat him with more respect. In the months that followed, I noticed that my son's attitude toward his sister also improved.

Children do not learn to love and obey God only by what we say. They also learn by watching what we do. We are to teach them constantly about God and His Word as we "sit at home and when [we] walk along the road, when [we] lie down and when [we] get up" (Deuteronomy 6:7). Along with what we say to our children, we need to set an example by our love and obedience to the Lord.

We can't be perfect parents, but our children must see our desire to please the Lord. And when we fall short, they need to see our repentance. We teach them by both what we say and what we do. **Albert Lee**

Debt Eraser

Revelation 1:4–7

[Jesus Christ] loves us and has freed us from our sins by his blood. —Revelation 1:5

Stunned is just one word that described the response of the crowd at the 2019 graduation ceremony at Morehouse College in Atlanta, Georgia. The commencement speaker announced that he and his family would be donating millions of dollars to erase the student debt of the entire graduating class. One student, who had $100,000 in loans, was among the overwhelmed graduates expressing their joys with tears and shouts.

Most of us have experienced indebtedness in some form—having to pay for homes, vehicles, education, medical expenses, or other things. But we've also known the amazing relief of a bill being stamped "PAID"!

After declaring Jesus as "the faithful witness, the firstborn from the dead, and the ruler of the kings of the earth," John worshipfully acknowledged His debt-erasing work: "To him who loves us and has freed us from our sins by his blood" (Revelation 1:5). This statement is simple, but its meaning is profound. Better than the surprise announcement the Morehouse graduating class heard is the good news that the death of Jesus (the shedding of His blood on the cross) frees us from the penalty that our sinful attitudes, desires, and deeds deserve. Because that debt has been satisfied, those who believe in Jesus are forgiven and become a part of God's kingdom family (v. 6). That is the best news of all! **Arthur Jackson**

Revival

2 Kings 22:11–23:3

The king stood by the pillar and renewed the covenant in the presence of the LORD. . . . All the people pledged themselves to the covenant. —2 Kings 23:3

In May of 2001, English evangelist J. John spoke in Liverpool, England, on the eighth commandment: "You shall not steal" (Exodus 20:15; Deuteronomy 5:19). The results of his preaching were dramatic.

People's hearts were changed. One author reported that large amounts of stolen goods were returned, including hotel towels, hospital crutches, library books, cash, and more. One man, who later went into the ministry, even returned towels he had taken from the Wimbledon tennis championships years earlier when he worked there.

Something similar happened with King Josiah in the eighteenth year of his reign over Judah. Because of the long line of evil kings before him, the record of God's laws had been lost. So, when Hilkiah found God's law and the temple secretary Shaphan read it to King Josiah, the king tore his clothes in grief and immediately began making religious reforms in his own life and throughout the nation. With just one reading of God's Word, he changed the course of the nation (2 Kings 22:8–23:25)

Today, many of us own Bibles, but are we changed by the truths found there? We are called to read, hear, and obey His Word. It should cause us, like Josiah, to take immediate action to bring our lives into harmony with God's desires. Marvin Williams

It's What We Do

Psalm 112

Whoever fears the LORD has a secure fortress, and for their children it will be a refuge. —Proverbs 14:26

My father was critically injured when he took a bullet in the leg as a second lieutenant leading his men on Hill 609 in North Africa during World War II. Dad was never again 100 percent physically. I was born several years after this, and when I was young I didn't even know he had been wounded. I found out later when someone told me. Although he felt constant pain in his leg, my dad never complained about it, and he never used it as an excuse for not providing for our family.

My parents loved the Savior and raised us to love, trust, and serve Him. Through good times and bad, they simply trusted God, worked hard, and loved us unconditionally. Proverbs 14:26 says that "Whoever fears the LORD has a secure fortress, and for their children it will be a refuge." My dad did that for our family. No matter what difficulties he faced, he provided a safe place for us spiritually, emotionally, and physically.

If you're a dad, you can provide a safe haven for your family with the help of our perfect heavenly Father, whose love for His children is deep and eternal. **Dave Branon**

Growing to Know

Philippians 4:10–13

I can do all this through him who gives me strength. —Philippians 4:13

"You're going to be an exchange student!" I was seventeen and thrilled to hear I was approved to study in Germany. But it was only three months before my departure, and I had never taken a class in German.

The days that followed found me cramming—studying for hours and even writing words on my hands to memorize them.

Months later I was in a classroom in Germany, discouraged because I didn't know more of the language. That day a teacher gave me wise advice. "Learning a language is like climbing a sand dune. Sometimes you feel like you're not getting anywhere. But just keep going and you will."

Sometimes I reflect on that insight when I consider what it means to grow as a follower of Jesus. The apostle Paul recalled, "I have learned the secret of being content in any and every situation" (Philippians 4:12). Even for Paul, personal peace didn't happen overnight. It was something he learned—he grew into. Paul shares the secret of spiritual progress, specifically contentment: "I can do all this through him who gives me strength" (4:13).

Life has its challenges. But as we turn to the One who has "overcome the world" (John 16:33), we discover not only that He's faithful to get us through but also that nothing matters more than closeness to Him. He gives us His peace, helps us trust, and empowers us to go the distance as we walk with Him. James Banks

Leave a Little Behind

Leviticus 23:15–22

Leave them for the poor and for the foreigner residing among you. —Leviticus 23:22

Pennies, nickels, dimes, quarters, and occasionally a half-dollar. That's what you'd find on the nightstand beside his bed. He'd empty his pockets each evening and leave the contents there, for he knew eventually they'd come to visit—"they" being his grandchildren. Over the years the kids learned to visit his nightstand as soon as they arrived. He could have put all that spare change in a coin bank or even stored it away in a savings account. But he didn't. He delighted in leaving it there for the little ones, the precious guests in his home.

A similar mindset is what's expressed in Leviticus 23 when it comes to bringing in the harvest from the land. God, via Moses, told the people something quite counterintuitive: not to "reap to the very edges of your field or gather the gleanings of your harvest" (v. 22). Essentially, He said, "Leave a little behind." This instruction reminded the people that God was responsible for the harvest in the first place, and that He used His people to provide for those of little account (the strangers in the land).

Such thinking is definitely not the norm in our world. But it's exactly the kind of mindset that will characterize grateful sons and daughters of God. He delights in a generous heart. And that often comes through you and me.

John Blase

In It Together

Romans 12:9–16

Rejoice with those who rejoice;
mourn with those who mourn. —Romans 12:15

During a two-month period in 1994, as many as one million Tutsis were slain in Rwanda by Hutu tribe members bent on killing their fellow countrymen. In the wake of this horrific genocide, Bishop Geoffrey Rwubusisi approached his wife about reaching out to women whose loved ones had been slain. Mary's reply was, "All I want to do is cry." She too had lost members of her family. The bishop's response was that of a wise leader and caring husband: "Mary, gather the women together and cry with them." He knew his wife's pain had prepared her to uniquely share in the pain of others.

The church, the family of God, is where all of life can be shared—the good and the not-so-good. The New Testament words "one another" are used to capture our interdependence. "Be devoted to one another in love. Honor one another above yourselves. . . . Live in harmony with one another" (Romans 12:10, 16). The extent of our connectedness is expressed in verse 15: "Rejoice with those who rejoice; mourn with those who mourn."

While the depth and scope of our pain may pale in comparison with those affected by genocide, it's nonetheless personal and real. And, as with the pain of Mary Rwubusisi, because of what God has done for us it can be embraced and shared for the comfort and good of others.

Arthur Jackson

Flight Simulator

John 16:25–33

I have told you these things, so that in me you may have peace. —John 16:33

When airplane pilots are training, they spend many hours in flight simulators. These simulators give the students a chance to experience the challenges and dangers of flying an aircraft—but without the risk. The pilots don't have to leave the ground, and if they crash in the simulation, they can calmly walk away.

Simulators are tremendous teaching tools—helpful in preparing the aspiring pilot to take command of an actual aircraft. The devices, however, have a shortcoming. They create an artificial experience in which the full-blown pressures of handling a real cockpit cannot be fully replicated.

Real life is like that, isn't it? It can't be simulated. There is no risk-free environment in which we can experience life's ups and downs unharmed. The risks and dangers of living in a broken world are inescapable. That's why the words of Jesus are reassuring. He said, "I have told you these things, so that in me you may have peace. In this world you will have trouble. But take heart! I have overcome the world" (John 16:33).

Although we can't avoid the dangers of life in a fallen world, we can have peace through a relationship with Jesus. He has secured our ultimate victory. **Bill Crowder**

True Greatness

Mark 9:33–37

Anyone who wants to be first must be the very last, and the servant of all. —Mark 9:35

Cuthbert is a much-loved figure in northern England. Responsible for evangelizing much of the area in the seventh century, Cuthbert counseled monarchs and influenced state affairs; and after his death, the city of Durham was built in his honor. But Cuthbert's legacy is great in more ways than these.

After a plague ravaged the region, Cuthbert once toured affected towns offering solace. As he prepared to leave one village, he saw a woman, clutching a child. She had already lost one son, and the child she held was nearing death too. Cuthbert took the fevered boy in his arms, prayed for him, and kissed his forehead. "Do not fear," he told her, "for no one else of your household will die." The boy reportedly lived.

Jesus once took a small boy into his arms to give a lesson on greatness, saying, "Whoever welcomes one of these little children in my name welcomes me" (Mark 9:37). To "welcome" someone in Jewish culture meant to serve them, the way a host welcomes a guest. The idea must've been shocking. Jesus's point? True greatness resides in serving the smallest and lowliest (v. 35).

A counselor to monarchs. An influencer of history. A city built in his honor. But perhaps heaven records Cuthbert's legacy more like this: A mother noticed. A forehead kissed. A humble life reflecting his Master. **Sheridan Voysey**

Raise Praise

Psalm 48

Your praise reaches to the ends of the earth. —Psalm 48:10

We all tend to think our home is the center of the world, so if we were to draw a map, we would probably put a dot in the middle (representing our home) and sketch out from there. Nearby towns might be fifty miles to the north or half a day's drive to the south, but all would be described in relation to where we are. The Psalms draw their "map" from God's earthly home in the Old Testament, so the center of biblical geography is Jerusalem.

Psalm 48 is one of many psalms that praise Jerusalem. This "city of our God, his holy mountain" is "beautiful in its loftiness, the joy of the whole earth" (vv. 1–2). Because "God is in her citadels," He "makes her secure forever" (vv. 3, 8). God's fame begins in Jerusalem's temple and spreads outward to "the ends of the earth" (vv. 9–10).

Unless you're reading this in Jerusalem, your home is not in the center of the biblical world. Yet your region matters immensely, because God will not rest until His praise reaches "to the ends of the earth" (v.10). Would you like to be part of the way God reaches His goal? Worship each week with God's people, and openly live each day for His glory. God's fame extends "to the ends of the earth" when we devote all that we are and have to Him.

Mike Wittmer

What Motivates Us?

1 Thessalonians 2:3–9

We speak as those approved by God. . . . We are not trying to please people but God, who tests our hearts. —1 Thessalonians 2:4

My wife and I received a notice that we had won a prize of either $1,000 dollars in cash or $250 in vouchers. When we arrived at the collection site, we were told that to be eligible, we would have to sit through a ninety-minute presentation.

As we listened, we learned that we could receive vacation accommodations for twenty-five years at today's prices, which would amount to about $15,000 in savings. But to enjoy this privilege, we had to pay a membership fee of $5,200. We declined the offer but were given some discount vouchers, which we realized we'd probably never use.

Reflecting on that experience, my wife and I wondered why we had endured what had become a three-hour presentation. What had motivated us? We wanted to be polite, but we also had to admit we were partly motivated by greed.

Wrong motives can even slip into our service for the Lord. Paul wrote to the believers at Thessalonica: "You remember, brothers and sisters, our toil and hardship; we worked night and day in order not to be a burden to anyone" (1 Thessalonians 2:9). He had the right to receive financial help from them, but he didn't want to be accused of unworthy motives.

What motivates us? Let's learn from Paul's example, remembering that God tests our hearts. **Albert Lee**

Good Works Prepared

Ephesians 2:6–10

For we are . . . created in Christ Jesus to do good works, which God prepared in advance for us to do. —Ephesians 2:10

We were traveling overseas when a burly stranger approached my wife and me on a street. We shrank back in fear. Our vacation had already been going badly; we had been yelled at, cheated, and extorted from several times. Were we going to be shaken down again?

To our surprise, the man just wanted to show us where to get the best view of his city. Then he gave us a chocolate bar, smiled, and left. That little gesture made our day—and saved the whole trip. It made us grateful—both to the man and to God for cheering us up.

What had made the man reach out to two strangers? Had he gone around with a chocolate bar the entire day, looking to bless someone with it? We'll never know, but we were reminded how the smallest action can bring the biggest smile—and possibly, direct someone to God. The Bible stresses the importance of doing good works (James 2:17, 24). If that sounds challenging, we have the assurance that God not only enables us to do these works but has also "prepared [them] in advance for us to do" (Ephesians 2:10).

Perhaps God has arranged for us to "bump into" someone who needs a word of encouragement today, or maybe He will give us an opportunity to offer someone a helping hand. All we have to do is respond in obedience.

Leslie Koh

When God Fills Us

Psalm 16:5–11

You make known to me the path of life; you will fill me with joy in your presence, with eternal pleasures at your right hand. —Psalm 16:11

What had I done? It should have been one of the most exciting times of my life. Instead, it was one of the loneliest. I'd just gotten my first "real" job after college, in a city hundreds of miles from where I grew up. But the thrill of that big step quickly faded. I had a tiny apartment with no furniture. I didn't know the city. I didn't know *anyone*. The job was interesting, but the loneliness felt *crushing*.

One night, I sat at home with my back against the wall. I opened my Bible and stumbled onto Psalm 16, where verse 11 promises God will fill us. "Lord," I prayed, "I thought this job was the right thing, but I feel so alone. Please fill me with a sense of your nearness." I offered variants of that plaintive plea for weeks. Some nights, my sense of loneliness eased, and I had a deep experience of God's presence. Other nights, I still felt achingly isolated.

But as I returned to that verse, anchoring my heart in it night by night, God gradually deepened my faith. I experienced His faithfulness in a way I never had before. And I learned that my task was simple: Pour out my heart to Him . . . and humbly await His faithful response—trusting His promise to fill me with His Spirit. Adam Holz

MAY 13

I Am with You

Jeremiah 1:1–10

I am with you always. —Matthew 28:20

When I served as an intern for a Christian magazine, I wrote a story about a person who had become a Christian. In a dramatic change, he said goodbye to his former life and embraced his Savior: Jesus. A few days after the magazine hit the street, an anonymous caller threatened, "Be careful, Darmani. We are watching you! Your life is in danger in this country if you write such stories."

That was not the only time I have been threatened for pointing people to Christ. On one occasion a man told me to vanish with the tract I was giving him or else! In both cases, I cowered. But these were only verbal threats. Many Christians have had threats carried out against them. In some cases, simply living a godly lifestyle attracts mistreatment from people.

The Lord told Jeremiah, "You must go to everyone I send you to and say whatever I command you" (Jeremiah 1:7), and Jesus told His disciples, "I am sending you out like sheep among wolves" (Matthew 10:16). Yes, we may encounter threats, hardships, and even pain. But God assures us of His presence. "I am with you," He told Jeremiah (Jeremiah 1:8), and Jesus assured His followers, "I am with you always" (Matthew 28:20).

Whatever struggles we face in our attempt to live for the Lord, we can take comfort in the Lord's presence. **Lawrence Darmani**

Officer Miglio's Heart

Matthew 18:1–10

See that you do not despise one of these little ones. For I tell you that their angels in heaven always see the face of my Father in heaven. —Matthew 18:10

Back at the police station, Officer Miglio slumped wearily against a wall. A domestic violence call had just consumed half his shift. Its aftermath left a boyfriend in custody, a young daughter in the emergency room, and a shaken mother wondering how it had come to this. This call would wear on the young officer for a long time.

"Nothing you could do, Vic," said his sergeant sympathetically. But the words rang hollow. Some police officers seem able to leave their work at work. Not Vic Miglio. Not tough cases like this one.

Officer Miglio's heart reflects the compassion of Jesus. Christ's disciples had just come to Him with a question: "Who, then, is the greatest in the kingdom of heaven?" (Matthew 18:1). Calling a small child to Him, He told His disciples, "Unless you change and become like little children, you will never enter the kingdom of heaven" (v. 3). Then He gave a stern warning to anyone who would harm a child (v. 6). In fact, children are so special to Him that Jesus told us, "Their angels in heaven always see the face of my Father in heaven" (v. 10).

How comforting, then, that Jesus's love for children is connected to His love for us all! That's why He invites us, through childlike faith, to become His sons and daughters. Tim Gustafson

Two Kingdoms

Matthew 22:15–22

Render therefore to Caesar the things that are Caesar's, and to God the things that are God's. —Matthew 22:21 NKJV

In a report in *USA Today*, Rick Hampson wrote: "The young generally don't have the old-time political religion. They look at voting and see a quaint, irrational act." One graduate was quoted as saying, "I don't care enough to care about why I don't care." I wonder if this is how we as Jesus-followers sometimes view our civic responsibility!

The insights of Jesus in Matthew 22 helped His followers think clearly about their civic duty in the world. The Jews were required to pay taxes to the Roman government. They hated this taxation because the money went directly into Caesar's treasury, where some of it supported the pagan temples and decadent lifestyle of the Roman aristocracy. They may have questioned whether they even had a civic responsibility to Caesar. Jesus reminded them, however, that they had dual citizenship. They lived in a world with two kingdoms—Caesar's kingdom (human authority) and God's kingdom (spiritual authority). They had responsibilities to both, but their greater responsibility was to God and His kingdom (Acts 5:28–29).

As followers of Christ, we are commanded to cooperate with our leaders, but we are called to give God our ultimate obedience and commitment. **Marvin Williams**

Love's Long Reach

Psalm 139:1–10

Oh, the depths of the riches of the wisdom and knowledge of God! —Romans 11:33

Mary Lee is a sixteen-foot, 3,500-pound great white shark tagged by oceanographers off the east coast of the US in 2012. The transmitter attached to her dorsal fin would be tracked by satellite when she surfaced. For the next five years Mary Lee's movements were observed online by everyone from researchers to surfers, up and down the coast. She was tracked for nearly forty-thousand miles until one day her signal stopped—probably because the battery on her transmitter expired.

Human knowledge and technology reach only so far. Those "following" Mary Lee lost track of her, but you and I can never evade God's awareness throughout every moment of our lives. David prayed, "Where can I go from your Spirit? Where can I flee from your presence? If I go up to the heavens, you are there; if I make my bed in the depths, you are there" (Psalm 139:7–8). "Such knowledge is too wonderful for me," he exclaims gratefully (v. 6).

God chooses to know us because He loves us. He cares enough not only to observe our lives but also to enter into them and make them new. He drew near through Christ's life, death, and resurrection, so we could know Him in return and love Him for eternity. We can never go beyond the reach of God's love. James Banks

Liberated by Jesus

Mark 5:1–20

[He] began to tell . . . how much Jesus had done for him. —Mark 5:20

"I lived with my mother so long that *she* moved out!" Those were the words of KC, whose life before sobriety and surrender to Jesus was not pretty. He candidly admits supporting his drug habit by stealing—even from loved ones. That life is behind him now, and he rehearses this by noting the years, months, and days he's been clean. When KC and I regularly sit down to study God's Word together, I'm looking at a changed man.

Mark 5:15 speaks of a former demon-possessed individual who had also been changed. Prior to his healing, *helpless*, *hopeless*, *homeless*, and *desperate* were words that fit the man (vv. 3–5). But all of that changed after Jesus liberated him (v. 13). But, as with KC, his life before Jesus was far from normal. His internal turmoil that he expressed externally is not unlike what people experience today. Some hurting people dwell in abandoned buildings, vehicles, or other places; some live in their own homes but are emotionally alone. Invisible chains shackle hearts and minds to the point that they distance themselves from others.

In Jesus, we have the one who can be trusted with our pain and the shame of the past and present. And, as with the demon-possessed man and KC, He waits with open arms of mercy for all who run to Him today (v. 19).

Arthur Jackson

Divided in Love

Ephesians 4:2–6

Be completely humble and gentle; be patient, bearing with one another in love. —Ephesians 4:2

When public debate erupted over a controversial Singapore law, it divided Christians who had differing views on the subject. Some called others "narrow-minded" or accused them of compromising their faith.

Controversies can cause sharp divisions among God's family, bringing much hurt and discouragement. I've been made to feel small over personal convictions on how I apply the Bible's teachings to my life. And I'm sure I've been equally guilty of criticizing others I disagree with.

I wonder if the problem lies not in what or even in how we express our views but in the attitudes of our hearts when we do so. Are we just disagreeing with views, or are we seeking to tear down the people behind them?

Sure, there are times when we do need to address false teaching or explain our stand. But Ephesians 4:2–6 reminds us to do so with humility, gentleness, patience, and love. And, above all else, we are to make every effort "to keep the unity of the Spirit" (v. 3).

Some controversies will remain unresolved. God's Word, however, reminds us that our goal should always be to build up people's faith, not tear them down (v. 29). Are we putting others down to win an argument? Or are we allowing God to help us understand His truths in His time and His way, remembering that fellow believers in Jesus share one faith in one Lord (vv. 4–6)? **Leslie Koh**

Is Fear Healthy?

2 Chronicles 17:3–10

Wisdom's instruction is to fear the LORD. —Proverbs 15:33

During a severe thunderstorm, a mother tucked her child into bed and turned off the light. Frightened by the tempest, he asked, "Mommy, will you sleep with me?" Hugging him, she replied, "I can't, dear. I have to sleep with Daddy." Stepping out of the room, she heard, "That big sissy!"

Fear is real. But it's not always negative. In 2 Chronicles 17:3–10, we read about a healthy, positive fear that prevented neighboring countries from going to war against Judah. What had caused this fear? We are told that "the fear of the LORD fell on all the kingdoms of the lands surrounding Judah, so that they did not go to war against Jehoshaphat" (v. 10).

A respectful fear of the Lord was also what King Jehoshaphat desired for his own people. So, he made it a priority that they be taught God's Word. He knew that if the people were in awe of the Almighty, they would humble themselves and obey Him. Doing what was right would bring prosperity to Judah and respect from neighboring countries.

Proverbs 15:33 declares, "Wisdom's instruction is to fear the LORD." Those who fear Him act with wisdom; they walk faithfully before Him as they obey His commands. **Albert Lee**

Run Toward Challenge

2 Kings 6:8–17

He looked and saw the hills full of horses and chariots of fire all around Elisha. —2 Kings 6:17

Tom chased the young men who were stealing his friend's bike. He didn't have a plan. He only knew he needed to get it back. To his surprise, the three thieves looked his way, dropped the bike and backed away. Tom was both relieved and impressed with himself as he picked up the bike and turned around. That's when he saw Jeff, his muscular friend who had been trailing close behind.

Elisha's servant panicked when he saw his town surrounded by an enemy army. He ran to Elisha, "Oh no, my lord! What shall we do?" Elisha told him to relax. "Those who are with us are more than those who are with them." Then God opened the servant's eyes, and he "saw the hills full of horses and chariots of fire all around Elisha" (vv. 15–17).

If you strive to follow Jesus, you may find yourself in some dicey situations. You may risk your reputation, and perhaps even your security, because you're determined to do what's right. You may lose sleep wondering how it will all turn out.

Remember, you're not alone. You don't have to be stronger or smarter than the challenge before you. Jesus is with you, and His power is greater than all rivals. Ask yourself Paul's question, "If God is for us, who can be against us?" (Romans 8:31). Really, who? No one. Run toward your challenge, with God right with you. **Mike Wittmer**

Who "Completes" You?

Colossians 2:6–15

So you also are complete through your union with Christ. —Colossians 2:10 NLT

In a popular movie from the '90s, an actor plays a success-driven sports agent whose marriage begins to crumble. Attempting to win back his wife, Dorothy, he looks into her eyes and says, "You complete me." It's a heart warming message that echoes a tale in Greek philosophy. According to that myth, each of us is a "half" that must find our "other half" to become whole.

The belief that a romantic partner "completes" us is now part of popular culture. But is it true? I talk to many married couples who still feel incomplete because they haven't been able to have children and others who've had kids but feel something else is missing. Ultimately, no human can fully complete us.

The apostle Paul gives another solution. "For in Christ lives all the fullness of God in a human body. So you also are complete through your union with Christ" (Colossians 2:9–10 NLT). Jesus doesn't just forgive us and liberate us, He also completes us by bringing the life of God into our lives (vv. 13–15).

Marriage is great, but it can't make us whole. Only Jesus can do that. Instead of expecting a person, career, or anything else to complete us, let's accept God's invitation to let His fullness fill our lives more and more. **Sheridan Voysey**

Sticks, Bricks, and God

Job 1:18–22

The LORD gave and the LORD has taken away; may the name of the LORD be praised. —Job 1:21

After praying about what God was calling them to do in the next phase of their lives, Mark and Nina determined that moving to the urban core of the city was the step they needed to take. They purchased a vacant house and renovation was well underway—then came the storm. Mark wrote in a text message to me: "We had a surprise this morning. The tornado that came through Jefferson City took out our renovation—down to sticks and bricks. God is up to something."

Uncontrollable storms are not the only things that surprise us and create confusion in our lives. Keeping our minds on God in the middle of misfortune, however, is one of the keys of survival.

The weather catastrophe in Job's life, which resulted in his loss of property and the death of his children (Job 1:19), was but one of the shocking surprises he faced. Prior to that, three messengers had come bearing bad news (vv. 13–17).

On any given day, we can go from feasting to mourning, from celebrating life to processing death, or some other life challenge. Our lives can swiftly be reduced to "sticks and bricks"—financially, relationally, physically, emotionally, spiritually. But God is mightier than any storm. Surviving life's trials requires faith that's focused on Him—faith that enables us to say with Job and others, "May the name of the LORD be praised" (v. 21). **Arthur Jackson**

Just-in-Case Idols

Jeremiah 11:9–13

They have followed other gods to serve them. —Jeremiah 11:10

Sam checks his retirement account twice each day. He saved for thirty years, and with the boost of a rising stock market, finally had enough to retire. As long as stocks don't plunge. This fear keeps Sam worrying about his balance.

Jeremiah warned about this: "You, Judah, have as many gods as you have towns; and the altars you have set up to burn incense to that shameful god Baal are as many as the streets of Jerusalem" (11:13).

The idolatry of the people of Judah was remarkable. They knew that the Lord is God. How could they worship anyone else? They were hedging their bets. They needed the Lord for the afterlife, because only the true God could raise them from the dead. But what about the present? Pagan gods promised health, wealth, and fertility, so why not pray to them too—just in case?

Can you see how Judah's idolatry is also our temptation? It's good to have talent, education, and money. But if we're not careful, we might shift our confidence to them. We know we'll need God when we die, and we'll ask Him to bless us now. But we'll also lean on these lesser gods, just in case.

Where is your trust? Back up idols are still idols. Thank God for His many gifts, and tell Him you're not relying on any of them. Your faith is riding entirely on Him.
Mike Wittmer

Show Them the Moon

Psalm 19:1–4

The heavens declare the glory of God;
the skies proclaim the work of his hands. —Psalm 19:1

"Don't ever miss the chance to show your babies the moon!" she said. Before our midweek prayer service began, a group of us talked about the previous night's harvest moon. The full moon was striking, as it seemed to sit on the horizon. Mrs. Webb was the elder voice in our conversation, a gray-haired lover of God's grand creation. She knew that my wife and I had two children in our home at the time, and she wanted to help me train them in a way worth going. Don't ever miss the chance to show your babies the moon!

Mrs. Webb would've made a good psalmist. Her brand of attentiveness is reflected in David's description of the heavenly bodies that "have no speech. . . . Yet their voice goes out into all the earth, their words to the ends of the world" (Psalm 19:3–4). Neither the psalmist nor Mrs. Webb had any intention of worshipping the moon or the stars, but rather the creative hands behind them. The heavens and skies reveal nothing less than the glory of God (v. 1).

We too can encourage those around us—from babies and teenagers to spouses and neighbors—to stop, look, and listen. Declarations and proclamations of God's glory are all around us. Drawing attention to the work of His hands in turn leads to worshipping the awesome God behind the whole show. Don't ever miss the chance.

John Blase

Growing Up

Ephesians 4:1–16

From him the whole body . . . grows and builds itself up in love. —Ephesians 4:16

Watching young boys and girls play T-ball is entertaining. In this version of baseball, young players often run to the wrong base or don't know what to do with the ball if they happen to catch it. If we were watching a professional baseball game, these mistakes would not be so funny.

It's all a matter of maturity.

It's okay for young athletes to struggle—not knowing what to do or not getting everything exactly right. They are trying and learning. So we coach them and patiently guide them toward maturity. Then we celebrate their success as later they play with skill as a team.

Something similar happens in the life of those who follow Jesus. Paul pointed out that the church needs people who will "be patient, bearing with one another in love" (Ephesians 4:2). And we need a variety of "coaches" (pastors, teachers, spiritual mentors) to help us all move toward "unity in the faith" as we strive to "become mature" (v. 13).

The goal as we listen to preaching and teaching and enjoy life together in the church is to grow up to maturity in Christ (v. 15). Each of us is on this journey, and we can encourage each other on the road to growth in Jesus.

Dave Branon

Mercy's Lament

Lamentations 2:10–13, 18–19

My heart is poured out on the ground . . . because children and infants faint in the streets of the city. —Lamentations 2:11

As artillery rounds fell around him with an earth shaking *whoomp*, the young soldier prayed fervently, "Lord, if you get me through this, I'll go to that Bible school Mom wanted me to attend." God honored his focused prayer. My dad survived World War II, went to Moody Bible Institute, and invested his life in ministry.

Another warrior from another era endured a different kind of crisis that drove him to God, but his problems arose when he avoided combat. As King David's troops fought the Ammonites, David was back at his palace casting more than just a glance at another man's wife (see 2 Samuel 11). In Psalm 39, David chronicles the painful process of restoration from the terrible sin that resulted. "The turmoil within me grew worse," he wrote. "The more I thought about it, the hotter I got" (vv. 2–3 NLT).

David's broken spirit caused him to reflect: "Show me, LORD, my life's end and the number of my days; let me know how fleeting my life is" (v. 4). Amid his renewed focus, David didn't despair. He had nowhere else to turn. "But now, LORD, what do I look for? My hope is in you" (v. 7). David would survive this personal battle and go on to serve God.

What motivates our prayer life doesn't matter as much as the focus of our prayer. God is our source of hope. He wants us to share our heart with Him. Tim Gustafson

A Fragile Stone

Matthew 16:13–20

Simon Peter answered, "You are the Messiah, the Son of the living God." —Matthew 16:16

When writing on the life of Simon Peter, songwriter and author Michael Card described the apostle as "a fragile stone." It is a term filled with contrast, yet one that aptly describes Peter.

Throughout Peter's life, we see this contrast lived out as he displayed moments of courage followed by spiritual failure. After his declaration of Christ as the Son of God, Jesus said to him, "And I tell you that you are Peter, and on this rock I will build my church, and the gates of Hades will not overcome it" (Matthew 16:18). A rock. A stone. Peter, whose name means "a small stone," proved to be fragile when he tried to dissuade Jesus from going to the cross, and when he denied Him three times after His arrest.

Peter, the "fragile stone," reminds us that no amount of personal strength or talent can make us adequate for this life and its challenges. Only as we rest in the strength of Christ will we find His provision. When we acknowledge our frailty and dependence on Him, Christ's strength can empower us for the troubles life throws our way.

Like Peter, we are all "fragile stones." How grateful we can be for His strength that is made perfect in our weakness (2 Corinthians 12:9–10). **Bill Crowder**

Set Free

Romans 8:1–2, 15–17

Therefore, there is now no condemnation for those who are in Christ Jesus. —Romans 8:1

When I was a boy in the village, something about chickens fascinated me. Whenever I caught one, I held it down for a few moments and then gently released it. Thinking I was still holding it, the chicken remained down; even though it was free to dash away, it felt trapped.

When we put our faith in Jesus, He graciously delivers us from sin and the hold Satan had on us. However, because it may take time to change our sinful habits and behavior, Satan can make us still feel trapped. But God's Spirit has set us free; He doesn't enslave us. Paul told the Romans, "Therefore, there is now no condemnation for those who are in Christ Jesus, because through Christ Jesus the law of the Spirit who gives life has set you free from the law of sin and death" (Romans 8:1–2).

Through our Bible reading, prayer, and the power of the Holy Spirit, God works in us to cleanse us and to help us live for Him. The Bible encourages us to be confident in our walk with Jesus without feeling trapped by Satan. Jesus said, "If the Son sets you free, you will be free indeed" (John 8:36). The freedom we have in Christ is a great comfort, and it can spur us on to love Him and serve Him. Lawrence Darmani

MAY 29

The Heart of Christ

Luke 19:37–44

Oh, that . . . my eyes [were] a fountain of tears! I would weep day and night for the slain of my people! —Jeremiah 9:1

I was filling out an online survey when I came to this question: "What is something that is true about you that most people would not guess?" The answer is that I am very sentimental. I get choked up at the movies when the violins start to swell, eyes fill with tears, and the boy finds his long-lost dog—or something comparable. I'm just a softie when it comes to those things.

It's easy and safe to get emotional over fictional characters and events. But it's a different matter to feel deep sadness and grief over real people and their needs. Heartache for the wayward, the suffering, the lost, and the broken tends to mirror the heart and compassion of Jesus, who wept over wayward Jerusalem (Luke 19:41).

When Jeremiah's people were drifting far from God and His love, the prophet also felt the need to weep. He sensed the burden of God's heart and the brokenness of His people. Weeping seemed the only appropriate response (Jeremiah 9:1).

As we see the condition of the fallen world and the spiritual lostness of the people who surround us, let's ask God to give us a heart that mirrors the heart of Christ—a heart that weeps with Him for a lost world and then reaches out to them in love. Bill Crowder

The Question of Revenge

1 Samuel 24:1–4, 11–18

[Saul said], "The Lord delivered me into your hands, but you did not kill me." —1 Samuel 24:18

The farmer climbed into his truck and began his morning inspection of the crops. On reaching the farthest edge of the property, his blood began to boil. Someone had used the farm's seclusion to illegally dump their trash—again.

As he filled the truck with the bags of food scraps, the farmer found an envelope. On it was printed the offender's address. Here was an opportunity too good to ignore. That night he drove to the offender's house and filled his garden with not just the dumped trash but his own!

Revenge is sweet, some say, but is it right? In 1 Samuel 24, David and his men were hiding in a cave to escape a murderous King Saul. When Saul wandered into the same cave to relieve himself, David's men saw a too-good-to-ignore opportunity for David to get revenge (vv. 3–4). But David went against this desire to get even. "The Lord forbid that I should do such a thing to my master," he said (v. 6). When Saul discovered that David chose to spare his life, he was incredulous. "You are more righteous than I," he exclaimed (vv. 17–18).

As we or our loved ones face injustice, opportunities to take revenge on offenders may well come. Will we give in to these desires, as the farmer did, or go against them, like David? Will we choose righteousness over revenge? **Sheridan Voysey**

MAY 31

Verify the Truth

Acts 17:10–13

[The Bereans] examined the Scriptures every day to see if what Paul said was true. —Acts 17:11

"A deadly jungle spider has migrated to the US and is killing people." This was the story sent to me and to others on my friend's email list. The story sounded plausible—lots of scientific names and real-life situations. But when I checked it out on reliable websites, I found it was not true—it was an Internet hoax. Its lack of authenticity could be verified only by consulting a trusted source.

A group of first-century believers living in Macedonia understood the importance of confirming what they were hearing. The folks in Berea "received the message with great eagerness and examined the Scriptures every day to see if what Paul said was true" (Acts 17:11). They wanted to make sure that what Paul was preaching to them lined up with the teachings of the Old Testament. Perhaps he was telling them that there was evidence in the Old Testament that the Messiah would suffer and die for sin. They needed to verify that with the source.

When we hear spiritual ideas that disturb us, we need to be cautious. Let's search the Scriptures for ourselves, listen to trustworthy sources, and seek wisdom from Jesus, our Lord. **Dave Branon**

JUNE 1

Redemption's Hope

Acts 9:1–4, 10–18

Everyone who calls on the name of the LORD will be saved. —Acts 2:21

The man seemed beyond redemption. His crimes included eight shootings (killing six) and starting nearly 1,500 fires that terrorized New York City in the 1970s. He left letters at his crime scenes taunting the police, and he was eventually apprehended and given consecutive sentences of twenty-five years to life for each murder.

Yet God reached down to this man. Today he is a believer in Christ who spends time daily in the Scriptures, has expressed deep regret to his victims' families, and continues to pray for them. Although imprisoned for more than four decades, this man, who seemed beyond redemption, finds hope in God and claims, "My freedom is found in one word: Jesus."

Scripture tells of another unlikely conversion. Before he met the risen Christ on the road to Damascus, Saul (also called Paul) was "breathing out murderous threats against the Lord's disciples" (Acts 9:1). Yet Paul's heart and life were transformed by Jesus (vv. 17–18), and he became one of the most powerful witnesses for Him in history. The man who once plotted the death of Christians devoted his life to spreading the hope of the gospel.

Redemption is always a miraculous work of God. Some stories are more dramatic, but the underlying truth remains the same: None of us deserves His forgiveness, yet Jesus is a powerful Savior! He "[saves] completely those who come to God through him" (Hebrews 7:25). **James Banks**

JUNE 2

Thumb Time

1 Corinthians 12:20–27

Now you are the body of Christ, and each one of you is a part of it. —1 Corinthians 12:27

Attend any rodeo with riding and roping competition and you'll see them—competitors with four fingers on one hand and a nub where their thumb should be. It's a common injury in the sport—a thumb gets caught between a rope on one end and a decent-sized steer pulling on the other, and the thumb is usually the loser. It's not a career-ending injury, but the absence of a thumb changes things. Without using your thumb, try to brush your teeth or button a shirt or comb your hair or tie your shoes or even eat. That little overlooked member of your body plays a significant role.

The apostle Paul indicates a similar scenario in the church. The often less visible and frequently less vocal members can sometimes experience an "I don't need you" response from the others (1 Corinthians 12:21). Usually this is unspoken, but there are times when it's said aloud.

God calls us to have equal concern and respect for one other (v. 25). Each one of us is a part of Christ's body (v. 27), regardless of the gifting we've received, and we need each other. Some of us are eyes and ears, so to speak, and some of us are thumbs. But each of us plays a vital role in the church, the body of Christ—sometimes more than meets the eye. **John Blase**

Stronger than Hate

Luke 23:32–34, 44–46

Father, forgive them, for they do not know what they are doing. —Luke 23:34

Within twenty-four hours of his mother Sharonda's tragic death, Chris found himself uttering these powerful, grace-filled words: "Love is stronger than hate." His mother, along with eight others, had been killed at a Wednesday night Bible study in Charleston, South Carolina. What was it that had so shaped this teenager's life that these words could flow from his lips and his heart? Chris is a believer in Jesus whose mother had "loved everybody with all her heart."

In Luke 23:26–49, we get a front row seat to an execution scene that included two criminals and the innocent Jesus (v. 32). All three were crucified (v. 33). Amid the gasps and sighs and the likely groans from those hanging on the crosses, the following words of Jesus could be heard: "Father, forgive them, for they do not know what they are doing" (v. 34). The hate-filled initiative of the religious leaders had resulted in the crucifixion of the very One who championed love. Though in agony, Jesus's love continued to triumph.

How have you or someone you love been the target of hate, ill will, bitterness, or ugliness? Perhaps your pain can prompt your prayers. Then let the example of Jesus and people like Chris encourage you by the power of the Spirit to choose love over hate. **Arthur Jackson**

JUNE 4

Is God There?

Isaiah 8:16–18

I will wait for the LORD. . . . I will put my trust in him. —Isaiah 8:17

Lela was dying of cancer, and her husband, Timothy, couldn't understand why a loving God would let his wife suffer. She had served Him faithfully as a Bible teacher and mentor to many. "Why did you let this happen?" he cried. Yet despite his pain and doubts, Timothy continued to be faithful in his walk with God.

"So why do you still believe in God?" I asked him frankly. "What keeps you from turning away from Him?"

"Because of what has happened before," Timothy replied. While he couldn't "see" God now, he recalled the times when God had helped and protected him. These were signs that God was still there caring for his family. "I know the God I believe in will come through in His own way," he said.

Timothy's words echo Isaiah's expression of trust in Isaiah 8:17. Even when he couldn't feel God's presence as his people braced for trouble from their enemies, he would "wait for the LORD." He trusted in God because of the signs He had given of His continuing presence (v. 18).

There are times when we might feel as if God isn't with us in our troubles. That's when we depend on what we can see of His works in our lives—in the past and present. They're the visible reminders of an invisible God—a God who is always with us and will answer in His own time and way. **Leslie Koh**

Facing Our Fears

Judges 6

When the angel of the LORD appeared to Gideon, he said, "The LORD is with you, mighty warrior." —Judges 6:12

A mother asked her five-year-old son to go to the pantry to get her a can of tomato soup. But he refused and protested, "It's dark in there." Mom assured Johnny, "It's okay. Don't be afraid. Jesus is in there." So, Johnny opened the door slowly and seeing that it was dark, shouted, "Jesus, can you hand me a can of tomato soup?"

This humorous story of Johnny's fear reminds me of Gideon. The Lord appeared to Gideon, calling him a "mighty warrior" (Judges 6:12) and then telling him to deliver Israel out of Midian's hand (v. 14). But Gideon's fearful reply was, "My clan is the weakest in Manasseh, and I am the least in my family" (v. 15). Even after the Lord told Gideon that with His help he would defeat the Midianites (v. 16), he was still afraid. Then Gideon asked the Lord for signs to confirm God's will and empowerment (vv. 17, 36–40). So, why did the Lord address fearful Gideon as a "mighty warrior"? Because of who Gideon would one day become with the Lord's help.

We too may doubt our own abilities and potential. But let us never doubt what God can do with us when we trust and obey Him. Gideon's God is the same God who will help us accomplish everything He asks us to do. Albert Lee

Beware the Rupert

2 Corinthians 11:3–4, 12–15

Satan himself masquerades as
an angel of light. —2 Corinthians 11:14

In the June 6, 1944, D-Day invasion of Europe, an armada of Allied ships assaulted the beaches of Normandy, France. Simultaneously, thousands of airplanes dropped paratroopers into the action. Along with the paratroopers, the Allies also dropped hundreds of rubber dummies behind the enemy lines. Called "Ruperts," these dummies with parachutes were intended to simulate an attack to confuse the enemy. As the Ruperts landed, some German outposts were tricked into fighting the "paradummies," creating a vital crack in the walls of Fortress Europe.

We accept that kind of deception as part of a legitimate military operation designed to thwart oppressive forces. What we should not accept is the deception Satan throws our way. Paul explained that the devil "masquerades as an angel of light" (2 Corinthians 11:14), and his servants appear to be people who are promoting righteousness (v. 15).

We must be alert! Our spiritual enemy would love to have followers of Christ distracted by false teaching and faulty doctrine. But as we keep our eyes on Jesus and the clear teachings of Scripture, our Lord can keep us aimed in the right direction.

Don't be tricked by Satan's Ruperts. **Bill Crowder**

Listen to His Promptings

Acts 16:6–19

When they came to the border of Mysia, they tried to enter Bithynia, but the Spirit of Jesus would not allow them to. —Acts 16:7

On Friday, my day of rest as a pastor, the Holy Spirit prompted me to call a young single mother in our faith community to see if her car had been repaired. I had some reservations about making the call, but I obeyed.

Little did I know that my obedience would help save her life. She said later: "Friday at work I was planning on taking my life, but in a time of need, I believe God was there for me. He had Pastor Williams call me, and just by listening to his voice, let me know that God loved me."

The apostle Paul must have had reservations when the Holy Spirit prompted him and his team not to go into the provinces of Asia (where Mysia was located) and Bithynia. Instead, they felt the Spirit's call to go into Macedonia to preach the good news. In each situation, they obeyed the Spirit's promptings. As a result, Paul and his team were instrumental in giving birth to a new faith community in Philippi (Acts 16:11–15).

As believers in Christ who are indwelt by the Holy Spirit (Ephesians 2:22), our desire should be to please Him. Let's not grieve the Holy Spirit (Ephesians 4:30) by ignoring His gentle promptings. When we obey Him, we might be used by God to lead someone to Christ, to disciple new believers—or even to help save somebody's life.

Marvin Williams

JUNE 8

The Good News

Acts 13:32–39

We tell you the good news: What God promised our ancestors he has fulfilled for us. —Acts 13:32–33

In 1941, as Hitler's reign was expanding across Europe, novelist John Steinbeck was asked to help with the war effort. He wasn't asked to fight or visit troops on the front line but to instead write a story. The result was *The Moon Is Down*, a novel about a peaceful land that gets invaded by an evil regime. Printed on underground presses and secretly distributed throughout occupied countries, the novel sent a message: The Allies were coming! And by imitating the novel's characters, readers could help secure their freedom. Through *The Moon Is Down*, Steinbeck brought good news to people under Nazi rule—their liberation was near.

Like the characters in Steinbeck's story, Jews in the first century were an occupied people under brutal Roman rule. But centuries before, God had promised to send an Ally to liberate them and bring peace to the world (Isaiah 11). Joy erupted when that Ally arrived! "We tell you the good news," Paul said. "What God promised our ancestors he has fulfilled for us . . . by raising up Jesus" (Acts 13:32–33). Through Jesus's resurrection and offer of forgiveness, the world's restoration had begun (vv. 38–39; Romans 8:21).

Since then, this story has spread throughout the globe, bringing peace and freedom wherever it's embraced. Jesus has been raised from the dead. Our liberation from sin and evil has begun. In Him we're free! **Sheridan Voysey**

Shackled but Not Silent

Acts 16:25–34

About midnight Paul and Silas were praying and singing hymns to God, and the other prisoners were listening to them. —Acts 16:25

In the summer of 1963, after an all-night bus ride, US civil rights activist Fannie Lou Hamer and six other black passengers stopped to eat at a diner in Winona, Mississippi. After law enforcement officers forced them to leave, they were arrested and jailed. But the humiliation wouldn't end with unlawful arrest. All received severe beatings, but Fannie's was the worst. After a brutal attack that left her near death, she burst out in song: "Paul and Silas was bound in jail, let my people go." And she didn't sing alone. Other prisoners, restrained in body but not in soul, joined her in worship.

According to Acts 16, Paul and Silas found themselves in a difficult place when they were imprisoned for telling others about Jesus. But discomfort didn't dampen their faith. "About midnight Paul and Silas were praying and singing hymns to God" (v. 25). Their bold worship created the opportunity to continue to talk about Jesus. "Then they spoke the word of the Lord to [the jailer] and to all the others in his house" (v. 32).

Most of us will not likely face the extreme circumstances encountered by Paul, Silas, or Fannie, but each of us will face uncomfortable situations. When that happens, our strength comes from our faithful God. May there be a song in our hearts that will honor Him and give us boldness to speak for Him—even in the midst of trouble. **Arthur Jackson**

JUNE 10

Water and Life

John 4:1–15

Jesus answered, "Everyone who drinks this water will be thirsty again, but whoever drinks the water I give them will never thirst." –John 4:13–14

As Dave Mueller reached down and turned the handle, water rushed from the spigot into a blue bucket. Around him people applauded. They celebrated as they saw fresh, clean water flowing in their community for the first time. Having a clean source of water was about to change the lives of this group of people in Kenya.

Dave and his wife, Joy, work hard to meet people's needs by bringing them water. But they don't stop with H_2O. As they help bring people clean water, they also tell them about Jesus Christ.

Two thousand years ago, a man named Jesus stood at a Samaritan well and talked with a woman who was there to get clean drinking water for her physical health. But Jesus told her that what she needed even more than that was living water for her spiritual health.

As history has marched on and humanity has become more sophisticated, life still filters down to two truths: Without clean water, we will die. More importantly, without Jesus Christ, the source of living water, we are already dead in our sins.

Water is essential to our existence—both physically with H_2O and spiritually with Jesus. Have you tasted of the water of life that Jesus, the Savior, provides? **Dave Branon**

Storm Chasers

Psalm 107:23–32

He stilled the storm to a whisper; the waves of the sea were hushed. —Psalm 107:29

"Chasing tornadoes," says Warren Faidley, "is often like a giant game of 3D-chess played out over thousands of square miles." The photojournalist and storm chaser adds: "Being in the right place at the right time is a symphony of forecasting and navigation while dodging everything from softball-sized hailstones to dust storms and slow-moving farm equipment."

Faidley's words make my palms sweat and my heart beat faster. While admiring the raw courage and scientific hunger storm chasers display, I balk at throwing myself into the middle of potentially fatal weather events.

In my experience, however, I don't have to chase storms in life—they seem to be chasing me. That experience is mirrored by Psalm 107 as it describes sailors trapped in a storm. They were being chased by the consequences of their wrong choices, but the psalmist says, "They cried out to the Lord in their trouble, and he brought them out of their distress. He stilled the storm to a whisper; the waves of the sea were hushed. They were glad when it grew calm" (Psalm 107:28–30).

Whether the storms of life are of our own making or the result of living in a broken world, our Father is greater. When we are being chased by storms, He alone is able to calm them—or to calm the storm within us. Bill Crowder

JUNE 12

A Glimmer on the Sea

Ephesians 2:1–5, 11–13

At that time you were separate from Christ. . . . without hope and without God in the world. —Ephesians 2:12

"I lay on my bed full of stale liquor and despair," wrote journalist Malcolm Muggeridge of a particularly dismal evening during his work as a World War II spy. "Alone in the universe, in eternity, with no glimmer of light."

In such a condition, he did the only thing he thought sensible; he tried to drown himself. Driving to the nearby Madagascar coast, he began the long swim into the ocean until he grew exhausted. Looking back, he glimpsed the distant coastal lights. For no reason clear to him at the time, he started swimming back toward the lights. Despite his fatigue, he recalls "an overwhelming joy."

Muggeridge didn't know exactly how, but he knew God had reached him in that dark moment, infusing him with a hope that could only be supernatural. The apostle Paul wrote often about such hope. In Ephesians he noted that, before knowing Christ, each of us is "dead in [our] transgressions and sins. . . . without hope and without God in the world" (2:1, 12). But "God, who is rich in mercy, made us alive with Christ even when we were dead" (vv. 4–5).

This world tries to drag us into the depths, but there's no reason to succumb to despair. As Muggeridge said about his swim in the sea, "It became clear to me that there was no darkness, only the possibility of losing sight of a light which shone eternally." **Tim Gustafson**

Lovable!

Jeremiah 31:1–6

I have loved you with an everlasting love; I have drawn you with unfailing kindness. —Jeremiah 31:3

"Lovable!"

That exclamation came from my daughter as she got ready one morning. I didn't know what she meant. Then she tapped her shirt, a hand-me-down from a cousin. Across the front was that word: Lovable. I gave her a big hug, and she smiled with pure joy. "You are lovable!" I echoed. Her smile grew even bigger, if that was possible, as she skipped away, repeating the word over and over again.

I'm hardly a perfect father. But that moment was perfect. In that spontaneous, beautiful interaction, I glimpsed in my girl's radiant face what receiving unconditional love looked like: It was a portrait of delight. She knew the word on her shirt corresponded completely with how her daddy felt about her.

How many of us know in our hearts that we are loved by a Father whose affection for us is limitless? Sometimes we struggle with this truth.

The Israelites did. They wondered if their trials meant God no longer loved them. But in Jeremiah 31:3, the prophet reminds them of what God said in the past: "I have loved you with an everlasting love." We too long for such unconditional love. Yet the wounds, disappointments, and mistakes we experience can make us feel anything but lovable.

But God opens His heart—the heart of a perfect Father—and invites us to experience and rest in His love.

Adam Holz

JUNE 14

Don't Let It Grow

Hebrews 12:14–25

See to it that no one falls short of the grace of God and that no bitter root grows up to cause trouble and defile many. —Hebrews 12:15

In June 1966, celebrated boxer Rubin "Hurricane" Carter, along with an acquaintance, were convicted of murder in a highly publicized and racially charged trial. The boxer maintained his innocence and became his own jailhouse lawyer. After serving nineteen years, Carter was released when the verdict was overturned. As a free man, he reflected: "Wouldn't anyone under those circumstances have a right to be bitter? . . . I've learned that bitterness only consumes the vessel that contains it. And for me to permit bitterness to control or infect my life in any way whatsoever would be to allow those who imprisoned me to take even more than . . . they've already taken."

I believe bitterness is what the writer of Hebrews had in mind when he penned his warnings. In today's text, some of the Christians may have been considering returning to Judaism because of persecution and injustice. Like a small root that grows into a great tree, bitterness could spring up in their hearts and overshadow their deepest Christian relationships (12:15).

When we hold on to disappointment, a poisonous root of bitterness begins to grow. Let's allow the Spirit to fill us so He can heal the hurt that causes bitterness.
Marvin Williams

The Long Way

Exodus 13:17–18

God did not lead them on the road through the Philistine country, though that was shorter. —Exodus 13:17

As his peers were promoted one by one, Benjamin couldn't help but feel a little envious. "How come you're not a manager yet? You deserve it," friends told him. But Ben decided to leave his career to God. "If this is God's plan for me, I'll just do my job well," he replied.

Several years later, Ben was finally promoted. By then, his added experience enabled him to do his job confidently, which won him the respect of subordinates. Some of his peers, meanwhile, were still struggling with their supervisory responsibilities, as they had been promoted before they were ready. Ben realized God had taken him "the long way around" so he would be better prepared for his role.

When God led the Israelites out of Egypt (Exodus 13:17–18), He chose a longer way because the shorter route to Canaan was fraught with risk. The longer journey, note Bible commentators, also gave them more time to strengthen themselves physically, mentally, and spiritually for subsequent battles.

The shortest way isn't always the best. Sometimes God lets us take the longer route in life, whether it's in our career or other endeavors, so we can be better prepared for the journey ahead. Even when things don't seem to happen quickly enough, we can trust in God—the one who leads and guides us. Leslie Koh

JUNE 16

Buy without Money

Isaiah 55:1–5

Give ear and come to me; listen, that you may live. —Isaiah 55:3

A story was told of a wealthy man who felt his son needed to learn gratefulness. So, he sent him to stay with a poor farmer's family. After one month, the son returned. The father asked, "Now don't you appreciate what we have?" The boy thought for a moment and said, "The family I stayed with is better off. With what they've planted, they enjoy meals together. And they always seem to have time for one another."

This story reminds us that money can't buy everything. Even though our bodies can live on what money can buy, money can't keep our souls from withering away. In Isaiah 55, we read: "Come, all you who are thirsty, come to the waters; and you who have no money, come, buy and eat!" (v. 1).

Is it possible to buy what truly satisfies without money? Yes, the prophet Isaiah is pointing to the grace of God. This gift is so invaluable that no price tag is adequate. And the one who offers it—Jesus Christ—has paid the full price with His death. When we acknowledge our thirst for God, ask forgiveness for our sins, and accept the finished work of Christ on the cross, we will find spiritual food that satisfies—and our soul will live forever!

He's calling, "Give ear and come to me" (Isaiah 55:3).

Albert Lee

Dying for Others

1 John 3:16–17

I am the good shepherd. The good shepherd lays down his life for the sheep. —John 10:11

I love birds, which is why I bought six caged birds and carried them home to our daughter Alice, who began to care for them daily. Then one of the birds fell ill and died. We wondered if the birds would be more likely to thrive if they were not caged. So, we freed the surviving five and observed them fly away in jubilation.

Alice then pointed out, "Do you realize, Daddy, that it was the death of one bird that caused us to free the rest?"

Isn't that what the Lord Jesus did for us? Just as one man's sin (Adam's) brought condemnation to the world, so one man's righteousness (Jesus's) brought salvation to those who believe (Romans 5:12–19). Jesus said, "I am the good shepherd. The good shepherd lays down his life for the sheep" (John 10:11).

John makes it more practical when he says, "Jesus Christ laid down his life for us. And we ought to lay down our lives for our brothers and sisters" (1 John 3:16). This won't likely mean literal death, but as we align our lives with Jesus's example of sacrificial love, we find that we "lay down our lives" (v. 17). For instance, we might choose to deprive ourselves of material goods in order to share them with others or perhaps we will give up our free time to be with someone who needs comfort and companionship.

Who do you need to sacrifice for today? Lawrence Darmani

Abba Father

Romans 8:12–17

A father to the fatherless, a defender of widows,
is God in his holy dwelling. —Psalm 68:5

The scene belonged on a funny Father's Day card. As a dad muscled a lawn mower ahead of him with one hand, he expertly towed a child's wagon behind him with the other. In the wagon sat his three-year-old daughter, delighted at the noisy tour of their yard. This might not be the safest choice, but who says men can't multitask?

If you had a good dad, a scene like that can invoke fantastic memories. But for many, "Dad" is an incomplete concept. Where are we to turn if our fathers are gone, or if they fail us, or even if they wound us?

King David certainly had his shortcomings as a father, but he understood the paternal nature of God. "A father to the fatherless," he wrote, "a defender of widows, is God in his holy dwelling. God sets the lonely in families" (Psalm 68:5–6). The apostle Paul expanded on that idea: "The Spirit you received brought about your adoption to sonship." Then, using the Aramaic word for *father*—a term young children would use for their dad—Paul added, "By him we cry, 'Abba, Father'" (Romans 8:15). This is the same word Jesus used when He prayed in anguish to His Father the night He was betrayed (Mark 14:36).

What a privilege to come to God using the same intimate term for "father" that Jesus used! Our Abba Father welcomes into His family anyone who will turn to Him through faith in Jesus Christ. **Tim Gustafson**

Grace Outside the Box

2 Samuel 9:1–7

Mephibosheth ate at David's table like one of the king's sons. —2 Samuel 9:11

Tom worked for a law firm that advised Bob's company. They became friends—until Tom embezzled thousands of dollars from the company. Bob was hurt and angry when he found out, but he received wise counsel from his vice president, a believer in Christ. The VP noticed Tom was deeply ashamed and repentant, and he advised Bob to drop the charges and hire Tom. "Pay him a modest salary so he can make restitution. You'll never have a more grateful, loyal employee." Bob did, and Tom was.

Mephibosheth, grandson of King Saul, hadn't done anything wrong, but he was in a tough spot when David became king. Most kings killed the royal bloodline. But David loved King Saul's son Jonathan, and he treated his surviving son as his own (see 2 Samuel 9). His grace won a friend for life. Mephibosheth marveled that he "deserved nothing but death from my lord the king, but you gave your servant a place" (19:28). He remained loyal to David, even when David's son Absalom chased David from Jerusalem (2 Samuel 16:1–4; 19:24–30).

Do you want a loyal friend for life? Someone so extraordinary may require you to do something extraordinary. When common sense says punish, choose grace. Hold the person accountable, but give the undeserving a chance to make things right. You may never find a more grateful, devoted friend. Think outside the box, with grace. Mike Wittmer

JUNE 20

I Am His Hands

1 Corinthians 12:12–21

The eye cannot say to the hand,
"I don't need you!" —1 Corinthians 12:21

Jia Haixia lost his sight in the year 2000. His friend Jia Wenqi lost his arms as a child. But they've found a way around their disabilities. "I am his hands, and he is my eyes," Haixia says. Together, they're transforming their village in China.

Since 2002 the friends have been on a mission to regenerate a wasteland near their home. Each day Haixia climbs on Wenqi's back to cross a river to the site. Wenqi then "hands" Haixia a shovel with his foot, before Haixia places a pail on a pole between Wenqi's cheek and shoulder. And as one digs and the other waters, the two plant trees—more than ten thousand so far. "Working together, we don't feel disabled at all," Haixia says. "We're a team."

The apostle Paul likens the church to a body, each part needing the other to function. If the church were all eyes, there'd be no hearing; if all ears, there'd be no sense of smell (1 Corinthians 12:14–17). "The eye cannot say to the hand, 'I don't need you!'" Paul says (v. 21). Each of us plays a role in the church based on our spiritual gifts (vv. 7–11, 18). Like Jia Haixia and Jia Wenqi, when we combine our strengths, we can bring change to the world.

Two men combining their abilities to regenerate a wasteland. What a picture of the church in action! **Sheridan Voysey**

With Respect

Ezra 5:6–17

If it pleases the king, let a search be made in the royal archives of Babylon to see if King Cyrus . . . did in fact issue a decree. —Ezra 5:17

The citizens of Israel were having some trouble with the government. It was the late 500s BC, and the Jewish people were eager to complete their temple that had been destroyed in 586 BC by Babylon. However, the governor of their region was not sure they should be doing that, so he sent a note to King Darius (Ezra 5:6–17).

In the letter, the governor says he found the Jews working on the temple and asks the king if they had permission to do so. The letter also records the Jews' respectful response that they had indeed been given permission by an earlier king (Cyrus) to rebuild.

When the king checked out their story, he found it to be true: King Cyrus had said they could build the temple. Darius had not only given them permission to rebuild but he also paid for it! (See 6:1–12). After the Jews finished building the temple, they celebrated "with joy" because they knew God had "[changed] the attitude of the king" (6:22).

When we see a situation that needs to be addressed, we honor God when we plead our case in a respectful way, trust that He is in control of every situation, and express gratitude for the outcome. **Dave Branon**

JUNE 22

Looks Can Be Deceiving

Matthew 15:1–11

These people honor me with their lips,
but their hearts are far from me. —Matthew 15:8

On June 22, 2002, a thirty-three-year-old pitching star for the St. Louis Cardinals was found dead in his Chicago hotel room. He was young, physically active, and appeared to be in good health. However, the autopsy revealed that he had a 90 percent blockage in two of three coronary arteries, an enlarged heart, and a blood clot in one of the arteries. His appearance misled many to think that he was physically healthy.

Jesus said that appearances can deceive people into thinking they are spiritually healthy. After the Pharisees accused Him and His followers of breaking religious traditions by not washing their hands before they ate, Jesus said that the Pharisees had laid aside commands of God for man-made, religious traditions. He reminded them that kingdom righteousness was not an outside-in job but an inside-out, transforming work of God. Jesus said that they looked impressive spiritually, but their hearts were diseased and distant: "[They] honor me with their lips, but their hearts are far from me" (Matthew 15:8). Their talk never matched their walk, thus producing the illegitimate child of hypocrisy.

Spiritual health is not determined by how we look but by how we live. Let's ask God to search us, know our hearts, test us, and lead us in His way (Psalm 139:23–24).

Marvin Williams

Where Are You Headed?

2 Samuel 12:1–14

Then Nathan said to David, "You are the man!" —2 Samuel 12:7

In northern Thailand, the Wild Boars youth soccer team decided to explore a cave together. After an hour they turned to go back and found that the entrance to the cave was flooded. Rising water pushed them deeper into the cave, day after day, until they were finally trapped more than two miles (four kilometers) inside. When they were heroically rescued two weeks later, many wondered how they had become so hopelessly trapped. Answer: one step at a time.

In Israel, Nathan confronted David for killing his loyal soldier, Uriah. How did the man "after [God's] own heart" (1 Samuel 13:14) become guilty of murder? One step at a time. David didn't go from zero to murder in one afternoon. He warmed up to it, over time, as one bad decision bled into others. It started with a second glance that turned into a lustful stare. He abused his kingly power by sending for Bathsheba, then tried to cover up her pregnancy by calling her husband home from the front. When Uriah refused to visit his wife while his comrades were at war, David decided he would have to die.

We may not be guilty of murder or trapped in a cave of our own making, but we're either moving toward Jesus or toward trouble. Big problems don't develop overnight. They break upon us gradually, one step at a time. Mike Wittmer

JUNE 24

The Leaning Tower

Matthew 7:24–27

Everyone who hears these words of mine and puts them into practice is like a wise man who built his house on the rock. —Matthew 7:24

You've probably heard of the famous Leaning Tower of Pisa in Italy, but have you heard of the leaning tower of San Francisco? It's called the Millennium Tower. Built in 2008, this fifty-eight-story skyscraper stands proudly—but slightly crookedly—in downtown San Francisco.

The problem? Its engineers didn't dig a deep enough foundation. So now they're being forced to retrofit the foundation with repairs that may cost more than the entire tower did when it was originally built—a fix that some believe is necessary to keep it from collapsing during an earthquake.

The painful lesson here? Foundations matter. When your foundation isn't solid, catastrophe could ensue. Jesus taught something similar. In Matthew 7:24–27, He contrasts two builders, one who built on a rock, another on sand. When a storm inevitably came, only the house with a solid foundation was left standing.

What does this mean for us? Jesus clearly states that our lives must be built upon Him, through obedience and trust (v. 24). When we rest in Him, our lives can find solid ground through God's power and unending grace.

Christ doesn't promise us that we'll never face storms. But He does say that because He's our rock, those storms and torrents will never wash away our faith-fortified foundation in Him. **Adam Holz**

Lion, Lamb, Savior

Revelation 5:1–7

The Lion of the tribe of Judah, the Root of David, has triumphed. —Revelation 5:5

Two stately stone lions watch over the entrance to the New York Public Library. Hewn from marble, they've stood there proudly since the library's dedication in 1911. They were first nicknamed Leo Lenox and Leo Astor to honor the library's founders. But during the Great Depression, New York's Mayor Fiorello LaGuardia renamed them Fortitude and Patience, virtues he thought New Yorkers should demonstrate in those challenging years. The lions are still called Fortitude and Patience today.

The Bible describes a living, powerful Lion who also gives encouragement in trouble and is known by other names. In his vision of heaven, the apostle John wept when he saw that no one was able to open the sealed scroll containing God's plan of judgment and redemption. Then John was told, "Do not weep! See, the Lion of the tribe of Judah . . . has triumphed. He is able to open the scroll and its seven seals" (Revelation 5:5).

Yet in the very next verse, John describes something else entirely: "Then I saw a Lamb, looking as if it had been slain, standing at the center of the throne" (v. 6). The Lion and the Lamb are the same person: Jesus. He's the conquering King and "the Lamb of God, who takes away the sin of the world!" (John 1:29). Through His strength and His cross, we receive mercy and forgiveness so we can live in joy and stand in wonder of our eternal God! James Banks

Now Go!

Exodus 4:10–17

Now go; I will help you speak and will teach you what to say. —Exodus 4:12

More than ten thousand evangelists and Christian leaders sat in a giant auditorium in Amsterdam in 1986 listening to world-renowned evangelist Billy Graham. I sat among them, listening as he narrated some of his experiences. Then, to my surprise, he said, "Let me tell you: every time I stand before the congregation of God's people to preach, I tremble and my knees wobble!"

What! I wondered. *How can such a great preacher who has enthralled millions with his powerful sermons exhibit trembling and wobbling knees?* Then he went on to describe not fear and stage fright but intense humility and meekness as he felt inadequate for the daunting task to which God had called him. He relied on God for strength, not on his own eloquence.

Moses felt inadequate when God sent him to deliver the enslaved Israelites from their four-hundred-year captivity in Egypt. Moses pleaded with the Lord to send someone else, with the excuse that he had never been a good speaker (see Exodus 4:10, 13).

We may have similar fears when God calls us to do something for Him. But His encouragement to Moses can also spur us on: "Now go; I will help you speak and will teach you what to say."

As Billy Graham said that day, "When God calls you, do not be afraid of trembling and wobbling knees, for He will be with you!" Lawrence Darmani

Difficult People

Proverbs 15:1–7, 18

A gentle answer turns away wrath, but a harsh word stirs up anger. —Proverbs 15:1

Lucy Worsley is a British historian and TV presenter. Like most people in the public eye, she sometimes receives nasty mail—in her case, it's sometimes about a mild speech impediment that makes her *r*'s sound like *w*'s. One person wrote this: "Lucy, I'll be blunt: Please try harder to correct your lazy speech or remove *r*'s from your scripts—I couldn't sit through your TV series because it made me so annoyed. Regards, Darren."

For some people, an insensitive comment like this might trigger an equally rude reply. But here's how Lucy responded: "Oh Darren, I think you've used the anonymity of the Internet to say something you probably wouldn't say to my face. Please reconsider your unkind words! Lucy."

Lucy's measured response worked. Darren apologized and vowed not to send anyone such an email again.

"A gentle answer turns away wrath," Proverbs says, "but a harsh word stirs up anger" (15:1). While the hot-tempered person stirs things up, the patient person calms them down (v. 18). When we get a critical comment from a colleague, a snide remark from a family member, or a nasty reply from a stranger, we have a choice: to choose angry words that fuel the flames or gentle words that douse them.

May God help us to speak words that turn away wrath—and perhaps even help difficult people to change.

Sheridan Voysey

JUNE 28

The Ultimate Wave

Colossians 1:1–8

The gospel is bearing fruit
and growing. —Colossians 1:6

People love doing "the wave." At sporting events and concerts around the world, it begins when a few people stand and raise their hands. A moment later, those seated beside them do the same. The goal is to have one sequential flowing movement work its way around an entire stadium. Once it reaches the end, those who started it smile and cheer—and keep the movement going.

The first recorded incident of the wave occurred at a Major League Baseball game between the Oakland Athletics and the New York Yankees in 1981.

I love joining in the wave because it's fun. But it's also occurred to me that the happiness and togetherness we experience while doing it is reminiscent of the gospel—the good news of salvation in Jesus that unites believers everywhere in praise and hope. This "ultimate wave" started over twenty centuries ago in Jerusalem. Writing to the members of the church in Colossae, Paul described it this way: "The gospel is bearing fruit and growing throughout the whole world—just as it has been doing among you since the day you heard it and truly understood God's grace" (Colossians 1:6). The natural result of this good news is "faith and love that spring from the hope stored up for [us] in heaven" (v. 5).

As believers in Jesus, we're part of the greatest wave in history. Keep it going! Once it's done, we'll see the smile of the One who started it all. **James Banks**

What's Wrong with the World?

1 Timothy 1:12–17

Christ Jesus came into the world to save sinners—
of whom I am the worst. —1 Timothy 1:15

There is an oft heard story that *The London Times* posed a question to readers at the turn of the twentieth century: "What's wrong with the world?"

That's quite the question, isn't it? Someone might quickly respond, "Well, how much time do you have for me to tell you?" And that would be fair, as there seems to be so much that's wrong with our world. As the story goes, *The Times* received a number of responses, but one in particular has endured in its brief brilliance. The English writer, poet, and philosopher G. K. Chesterton (1874–1936) penned this four-word response, a refreshing surprise to the usual passing-of-the-buck: "Dear Sirs, I am."

Whether the story is factual or not is up for debate. But that response? It's nothing but true. Long before Chesterton came along, there was an apostle named Paul. Far from being a lifelong model citizen, Paul confessed his past shortcomings: "I was once a blasphemer and a persecutor and a violent man" (1 Timothy 1:13). After naming who Jesus came to save ("sinners"), he goes on to make a very Chesterton-like qualification: "of whom I am the worst" (v. 15). Paul knew exactly what was and is wrong with the world. And he further knew the only hope of making things right—"the grace of our Lord" (v. 14). What an amazing reality! This enduring truth lifts our eyes to the light of Christ's saving love. **John Blase**

Look-alikes

2 Corinthians 3:17–42

We all . . . are being transformed into his image with ever-increasing glory, which comes from the Lord, who is the Spirit. —2 Corinthians 3:18

They say we all have one: *Doppelgangers* some call them. Look-alikes. People unrelated to us who look very much like us.

Mine happens to be a star in the music field. When I attended one of his concerts, I got a lot of double takes from fellow fans during intermission. But alas, I am no James Taylor when it comes to singing and strumming a guitar. We just happen to look alike.

Who do you look like? As you ponder that question, reflect on 2 Corinthians 3:18, where Paul tells us that we "are being transformed into [the Lord's] image." As we seek to honor Jesus with our lives, one of our goals is to take on His image. Of course, this doesn't mean we have to grow a beard and wear sandals—it means that the Holy Spirit helps us demonstrate Christlike characteristics in how we live. For example, in attitude (humility), in character (loving), and in compassion (coming alongside the down and out), we are to look like Jesus and imitate Him.

As we "contemplate the Lord's glory," (v. 18) by fixing our eyes on Jesus, we can grow more and more like Him. What an amazing thing it would be if people could observe us and say, "I see Jesus in you!" **Dave Branon**

JULY 1

Free Indeed

John 8:31–36

If the Son sets you free, you will be free indeed. —John 8:36

The movie *Amistad* tells the story of West African slaves in 1839 taking over the boat that was transporting them and then killing the captain and some of the crew. Eventually they were recaptured, imprisoned, and taken to trial. An unforgettable courtroom scene features Cinqué, leader of the slaves, passionately pleading for freedom. Three simple words—repeated with increasing force by a shackled man with broken English—eventually silenced the courtroom, "Give us free!" Justice was served and the men were freed.

Most people today aren't in danger of being physically bound, yet true liberation from the spiritual bondage of sin remains elusive. The words of Jesus in John 8:36 offer sweet relief: "So if the Son sets you free, you will be free indeed." Jesus pointed to himself as the source of true emancipation because He offers forgiveness to anyone who believes in Him. Though some in Christ's audience claimed freedom (v. 33), their words, attitudes, and actions regarding Jesus betrayed their claim.

Jesus longs to hear those who would echo Cinqué's plea and say, "Give me freedom!" With compassion He awaits the cries of those who are shackled by unbelief or fear or failure. Freedom is a matter of the heart. True liberty is given to those who believe that Jesus is God's Son, who was sent into the world to break the power of sin's hold on us through His death and resurrection. **Arthur Jackson**

Unashamed Loyalty

Psalm 34:1–4

Glorify the LORD with me; let us exalt his name together. —Psalm 34:3

Sports fans love to sing their teams' praises. By wearing logos, posting notes on Facebook about their beloved teams, or talking about them with friends, fans leave no doubt where their loyalty stands. My own Detroit Tigers caps, shirts, and conversations indicate that I am right there with those who do this.

Our sports loyalties should pale when compared with our truest and greatest loyalty: Our loyalty to our Lord. I think of such unashamed loyalty when I read Psalm 34, where David draws our attention to someone vastly more vital than anything else on earth.

David says, "I will extol the LORD at all times" (v. 1), and we are left to wonder about the gaps in our lives when we live as if God is not our source of truth, light, and salvation. He says, "His praise will always be on my lips" (v. 1), and we think about how many times we praise things of this world more than we praise Him. David says, "My soul shall make its boast in the LORD" (v. 2 NKJV), and we realize that we boast about our own small successes more than what Jesus has done for us.

It's not wrong to enjoy our teams, our interests, and our accomplishments. But our highest praise goes to our Lord. "Glorify the LORD with me; let us exalt his name together" (v. 3). **Dave Branon**

Longing for God

Nehemiah 1:5–11

Even if your exiled people are at the farthest horizon, I will gather them from there and bring them to the place I have chosen. —Nehemiah 1:9

When Conner and Sarah Smith moved five miles up the road, their cat S'mores expressed his displeasure by running away. One day Sarah saw a current photo of their old farmhouse on social media. There was S'mores in the picture!

Happily, the Smiths went to retrieve him. S'mores ran away again. Guess where he went? The Smiths couldn't stop the inevitable; S'mores would always return "home."

Nehemiah served in a prestigious position in the king's court in Susa, but his heart was elsewhere. He had just heard news of the sad condition of "the city where my ancestors are buried" (Nehemiah 2:3). And so he prayed, "Remember the instruction you gave your servant Moses, . . . 'If you return to me and obey my commands, then even if your exiled people are at the farthest horizon, I will gather them from there and bring them to the place I have chosen as a dwelling for my Name'" (1:8–9).

Home is where the heart is, they say. In Nehemiah's case, longing for home was more than being tied to the land. It was communion with God that he most desired. Jerusalem was "the place I have chosen as a dwelling for my Name," God said.

The dissatisfaction we sense deep down is actually a longing for God. We're yearning to be home with Him.

Tim Gustafson

JULY 4

Truth, Lies, and Vigilantes

Exodus 23:1–9

Do not spread false reports. —Exodus 23:1

During the 2018 baseball season, a Chicago Cubs coach wanted to give a baseball to a young boy sitting by the dugout. But when the coach tossed the ball toward him, a man scooped it up instead. Video of the event went viral. News outlets and social media skewered this "brute" of a man. Those viewers, however, didn't know the whole story. They didn't know that earlier, that man had helped the young boy snag a foul ball. So, they agreed to share any additional balls that came their way. Unfortunately, it took twenty-four hours before the true story emerged. The mob had already done its damage, demonizing an innocent man.

Too often, we think we have all the facts when we only have fragments. In our modern gotcha culture, with snippets of dramatic video and inflamed tweets, it's easy to condemn people without hearing the full story. However, Scripture warns us not to "spread false reports" (Exodus 23:1). We must do everything possible to confirm the truth before leveling accusations, making sure not to participate in lies. We should be cautious whenever a vigilante spirit takes hold, whenever passions ignite and waves of judgment swell. We want to safeguard ourselves from "follow[ing] the crowd in doing wrong" (v. 2).

As believers in Jesus, may God help us not to spread falsehoods. May He provide what we need to exhibit wisdom and to make certain our words are actually true. **Winn Collier**

Long-Awaited Reunion

1 Thessalonians 4:13–18

We who are still alive and are left will be caught up together with them in the clouds to meet the LORD in the air. And so we will be with the LORD forever. —1 Thessalonians 4:17

As a boy, I had a collie named Prince Boy, a great dog that I really loved. One day, he disappeared. I didn't know if he had been stolen or if he had simply run away—but I was devastated. I searched everywhere. In fact, one of my earliest childhood memories is of climbing a tall tree from which I could scan our neighborhood in hopes of spotting him. I desperately wanted my beloved dog back. For weeks, I was always watching and hoping to see Prince Boy again. But we were never reunited.

There's a much greater sense of loss when we think we'll never again see a loved one who dies. But for those who know and love the Lord, death's parting is only temporary. One day we will be reunited forever!

Paul assured the Thessalonians, "The dead in Christ will rise first. After that, we who are still alive and are left will be caught up together with them in the clouds to meet the Lord in the air. And so we will be with the Lord forever" (1 Thessalonians 4:16–17). The words that provide comfort to the grieving heart are *together* and *we*. These words of reunion indicate that followers of Christ don't ever have to experience permanent separation. For us, death is not a goodbye; it's a "see you later." **Bill Crowder**

JULY 6

In His Presence

Psalm 116:1–7

Return to your rest, my soul, for the LORD has been good to you. —Psalm 116:7

"Daddy, will you read to me?" my daughter asked. It's not an unusual question for a child to make of a parent. But my daughter was eleven at the time. It seemed that such requests came less frequently than they did when she was younger. "Yes," I said happily, and she curled up next to me on the couch.

As I read to her from J. R. R Tolkien's *The Fellowship of the Ring*, she practically melted into me. It was one of those glorious moments as a parent, when we feel perhaps just an inkling of the perfect love our Father has for us and His deep desire for us to enjoy His presence and love for us.

I realized in that moment that I'm a lot like my eleven-year-old. Much of the time, I'm focused on being independent. It's so easy to lose touch with God's love for us, a tender and protective love that Psalm 116 describes as "gracious and righteous . . . full of compassion" (v. 5). It's a love where, like my daughter, I can rest in my Father—at home in His delight for me.

Psalm 116:7 suggests that we might need to regularly remind ourselves of God's good love, and then accept his companionship: "Return to your rest, my soul, for the LORD has been good to you." And indeed, He has. **Adam Holz**

Able to Help

Hebrews 2:14–18

Because he himself suffered when he was tempted, he is able to help those who are being tempted. —Hebrews 2:18

Joe's eight-week "break" from his job as a crisis care worker at a New York City church was not a vacation. In his words, it was "to live again among the homeless, to become one of them, to remember what hungry, tired, and forgotten feel like." Joe's first stint on the streets had come nine years earlier when he arrived from Pittsburgh without a job or a place to stay. For thirteen days he lived on the streets with little food or sleep. That's how God had prepared him for decades of ministry to needy people.

When Jesus came to earth, He also chose to share the experiences of those He came to save. "Since the children have flesh and blood, he too shared in their humanity so that by his death he might break the power of him who holds the power of death—that is, the devil" (Hebrews 2:14). From birth to death, nothing was missing from Christ's human experience—except sin (4:15). Because He conquered sin, He can help us when we're tempted to sin.

And Jesus doesn't need to reacquaint himself with our earthly cares. The one who saves us remains connected to us and is deeply interested in us. Whatever life brings, we can be assured that the one who rescued us from our greatest foe, the devil (2:14), stands ready to help us in our times of greatest need. **Arthur Jackson**

When God Says No

Isaiah 25:1–5

In perfect faithfulness you have done wonderful things,
things planned long ago. —Isaiah 25:1

When I was conscripted into the military at age eighteen, as all young Singaporean men are, I prayed desperately for an easy posting. A clerk or driver, perhaps. Not being particularly strong, I hoped to be spared the rigors of combat training. But one evening as I read my Bible, one verse leaped off the page: "My grace is sufficient for you" (2 Corinthians 12:9).

My heart dropped—but it shouldn't have. God had answered my prayers. Even if I received a difficult assignment, He would provide for me.

I ended up as an armored infantryman, doing things I didn't always enjoy. Looking back now, though, I'm grateful God didn't give me what I wanted. The training and experience toughened me physically and mentally and gave me confidence to enter adulthood.

In Isaiah 25:1–5, after prophesying Israel's punishment and subsequent deliverance from her enemies, the prophet praises God for His plans. All these "wonderful things," Isaiah notes, had been "planned long ago" (v. 1), yet they included some arduous times.

It can be hard to hear God saying no—and that can be even harder to understand when we're praying for something good. But that's when we need to hold on to the truth of God's good plans. We may not understand why, but we can keep trusting in His love, goodness, and faithfulness. **Leslie Koh**

Godly Sorrow

2 Corinthians 7:5–10

I am happy, not because you were made sorry, but because your sorrow led you to repentance. For you became sorrowful as God intended. —2 Corinthians 7:9

Thieves stole nearly $5,000 in sound and office equipment from a church in West Virginia, only to break in the following night to return the items they had taken. Apparently, the guilt of stealing from a church weighed so heavily on their conscience that they felt the need to correct their criminal behavior of breaking the commandment: "You shall not steal" (Exodus 20:15). Their actions make me think about the differences between worldly sorrow and godly sorrow.

Paul praised the Corinthians for understanding this difference. His first letter to them was biting, as he addressed issues of sin. His words caused sorrow among them, and because of this Paul rejoiced. Why? Their sorrow did not stop at just feeling sad about getting caught or suffering the unpleasant consequences of their sins. Their sorrow was godly sorrow, a genuine remorse for their sins. This led them to repentance—a change in their thinking that led to a renouncing of their sin and turning to God. Their repentance ultimately led to deliverance from their sinful habits.

Repenting is not something we can do unless we have the prompting of the Holy Spirit; it's a gift from God. Pray for repentance today (2 Timothy 2:24–26).

Marvin Williams

JULY 10

What's Your Song?

Deuteronomy 31:15–22

So Moses wrote down this song that day and taught it to the Israelites. —Deuteronomy 31:22

Most Americans knew little about Alexander Hamilton—until 2015, when Lin-Manuel Miranda wrote his hit musical *Hamilton*. Now schoolchildren know Hamilton's story by heart. They sing it to each other on the bus and at recess. He's their favorite founding father.

God knows the power of music, and He told Moses to "write down this song and teach it to the Israelites and have them sing it" (Deuteronomy 31:19). God knew that long after Moses was gone, when He had delivered Israel into the promised land, they would rebel and worship other gods. So, He told Moses, "This song will testify against them, because it will not be forgotten by their descendants" (v. 21).

Songs are nearly impossible to forget, so it's wise to be selective about what we sing. Some songs are just for fun, and that's fine; but we benefit most from songs that boast in Jesus and encourage our faith. One of the ways we "[make] the most of every opportunity" is when we speak "to one another with psalms, hymns, and songs from the Spirit." So "sing and make music from your heart to the Lord" (see Ephesians 5:15–19).

Songs can be an indicator of the direction of our heart. Do the words make much of Jesus? Do we sing them wholeheartedly? What we sing will influence what we believe, so choose wisely and sing loudly. **Mike Wittmer**

Your Money's No Good Here

Ephesians 2:1–9

For it is by grace you have been saved, through faith—and this is not from yourselves, it is the gift of God. —Ephesians 2:8

London's Café Rendezvous has nice lighting, comfortable couches, and the smell of coffee in the air. What it doesn't have are prices. Originally started as a business by a local church, the café was transformed a year after it started. The managers felt that God was calling them to do something radical—make everything on the menu free. Today you can order a coffee, cake, or sandwich without cost. There isn't even a donation jar. It's all a gift.

I asked the manager why they were so generous. "We're just trying to treat people the way God treats us," he said. "God gives to us whether we thank him or not. He's generous to us beyond our imaginations."

Jesus died to rescue us from our sins and reconcile us with God. He rose from the grave and is alive now. Because of this, every wrong thing we've done can be forgiven, and we can have new life today (Ephesians 2:1–5). And one of the most amazing things about this is that it's all free. We can't buy the new life Jesus offers. We can't even donate toward the cost (vv. 8–9). It's all a gift.

As the folks at Café Rendezvous serve their cakes and coffees, they give people a glimpse of God's generosity. You and I are offered eternal life for free because Jesus has paid the bill. All we have to do is trust in His free offer of salvation. Sheridan Voysey

Sharing a Burger

James 2:14–17

Do not forget to do good and to share, for with such sacrifices God is well pleased. —Hebrews 13:16 NKJV

Several years ago, Lee Geysbeek of Compassion International told about a woman who had the opportunity to travel to a distant land to visit the child she sponsored. She decided to take the child, who was living in abject poverty, to a restaurant.

The boy ordered a hamburger, and the sponsor ordered a salad. When the food came to the table, the boy, who assuredly had never had such a meal in his life, surveyed the scene. He looked at his huge hamburger and over at his sponsor's small salad. Then he took his knife and cut the burger in half, offered it to his sponsor, rubbed his tummy, and asked, "Hungry?"

A child who had next to nothing his whole life was willing to share half of what he had with someone he thought might need more. This child can be a good reminder the next time we meet someone in physical, emotional, or spiritual need. As followers of Jesus, our faith in Him should be mirrored through our actions (James 2:17).

We encounter people in need every day. Some around the globe, some simply around the corner. Some in need of a warm meal, others a kind word. Because we have experienced the selfless love of Christ, what a difference we could make by doing good and sharing with others (Hebrews 13:16). **Dave Branon**

Front Porch Relief

Philippians 4:14–20

I have learned the secret of being content in any and every situation. —Philippians 4:12

On a particularly hot day, eight-year-old Carmine McDaniel wanted to make sure his neighborhood mail carrier stayed cool and hydrated. So, he left a cooler filled with a sports drink and water bottles on their front step. The family security camera recorded the mail carrier's reaction: "Oh man, water and Gatorade. Thank God; thank you!"

Carmine's mom says, "Carmine feels that it's his 'duty' to supply the mailman with a cool beverage even if we're not home."

This story warms our hearts, but it can serve to remind us that there is One who will "meet all your needs," as the apostle Paul phrased it. Though Paul was languishing in jail and uncertain about his future, he expressed joy for the Christians in Philippi because God had met his needs through their financial gift to him. The Philippian church was not wealthy, but they were generous, giving to Paul and others out of their poverty (see 2 Corinthians 8:1–4). As the Philippians had met Paul's needs, so God would meet theirs, "according to the riches of his glory in Christ Jesus" (Philippians 4:19).

God often sends vertical help through horizontal means. Put another way, He sends us what we need through the help of other people. When we trust Him for what we need, we learn, as Paul did, the secret of true contentment (vv. 12–13). **Marvin Williams**

Outside the Camp

Hebrews 13:11–16

Jesus also suffered outside the city gate to make the people holy through his own blood. —Hebrews 13:12

Friday was market day in the rural town in Ghana where I grew up. After all these years, I still recall one particular vendor. Her fingers and toes eroded by Hansen's disease (leprosy), she would crouch on her mat and scoop her produce with a hollowed-out gourd. Some avoided her. My mother made it a point to buy from her regularly. I saw her only on market days. Then she would disappear outside the town.

In the time of the ancient Israelites, diseases like leprosy meant living "outside the camp." It was a forlorn existence. Israelite law said of such people, "They must live alone" (Leviticus 13:46). Outside the camp was also where the carcasses of the sacrificial bulls were burned (4:12). Outside the camp was not where you wanted to be.

This harsh reality breathes life into the statement about Jesus in Hebrews 13: "Let us, then, go to him outside the camp, bearing the disgrace he bore" (v. 13). Jesus was crucified outside the gates of Jerusalem, a significant point when we study the Hebrew sacrificial system.

We want to be popular, to be honored, to live comfortable lives. But God calls us to go "outside the camp"—where the disgrace is. That's where we'll find the vendor with Hansen's disease. That's where we'll find people the world has rejected. That's where we'll find Jesus. Tim Gustafson

Living with the Lights On

Psalm 119:9–16, 97–105

Your word is a lamp for my feet, a light on my path. —Psalm 119:105

A work assignment had taken my coworker and me on a two-hundred-fifty-mile journey, and it was late when we began our trip home. An aging body with aging eyes makes me a bit uneasy about nighttime driving; nevertheless, I opted to drive first. My hands gripped the steering wheel, and my eyes gazed intently at dimly lit roads. While driving I found I could see better when lights from vehicles behind me beamed on the highway ahead. I was much relieved when my friend eventually took the wheel of his vehicle. That's when he discovered I had been driving with my fog lights on—and not the headlights!

Psalm 119 is the masterful composition of one who understood that God's Word provides us with light for everyday living (v. 105). Yet, how often do we find ourselves in situations similar to my uncomfortable night on the highway? We needlessly strain to see, and we sometimes stray from the best paths because we forget to use the light of God's Word. Psalm 119 encourages us to be intentional about "hitting the light switch."

What happens when we do? We find wisdom for purity (vv. 9–11); we discover fresh motivation and encouragement for avoiding detours (vv. 101–102). And when we live with the lights on, the psalmist's praise is likely to become our praise: "Oh, how I love your law! I meditate on it all day long" (v. 97). **Arthur Jackson**

JULY 16

Restored Failures

Psalm 145:1–16

The LORD upholds all who fall and lifts up all who are bowed down. —Psalm 145:14

A guest band was leading praise and worship at our church, and their passion for the Lord was moving. We could see—and feel—their enthusiasm.

Then the musicians revealed that they were all ex-prisoners. Suddenly their songs took on special meaning, and I saw why their words of praise meant so much to them. Their worship was a testimony of lives broken and restored.

The world may embrace success. But stories of past failure offer people hope too. They assure us that God loves us no matter how many times we have failed. Pastor Gary Inrig says that what we call the Hall of Faith in Hebrews 11 could well be entitled God's Hall of Reclaimed Failures. "There is scarcely an individual in that chapter without a serious blemish in his or her life," he observes. "But God is in the business of restoring failures. . . . That is a great principle of God's grace."

I love the comfort of Psalm 145, which speaks of God's "wonderful works" (vv. 5–6) and glorious kingdom (v. 11). It describes His compassion (vv. 8–9) and faithfulness (v. 13)—then immediately tells us that He lifts up those who have fallen (v. 14). All His attributes are expressed when He picks us up. He is indeed the one who restores.

Have you failed before? We all have. Have you been restored? Everyone who has been redeemed by Jesus is a story of God's grace. **Leslie Koh**

Slum Songs

Isaiah 35

They will enter Zion with singing; everlasting joy will crown their heads. —Isaiah 35:10

Cateura is a small slum in Paraguay, South America. Desperately poor, its villagers survive by recycling items from its rubbish dump. But from these unpromising conditions something beautiful has emerged—an orchestra.

With a violin costing more than a house in Cateura, the orchestra had to get creative, crafting its own instruments from their garbage supply. Violins are made from oil cans with bent forks as tailpieces. Saxophones have come from drainpipes with bottle tops for keys. Cellos are made from tin drums with food rollers for tuning pegs. Hearing Mozart played on these contraptions is a beautiful thing. The orchestra has gone on tour in many countries, lifting the sights of its young members.

Violins from landfills. Music from slums. That's symbolic of what God does. When the prophet Isaiah envisioned God's new creation, a similar picture of beauty-from-poverty emerged, with barren lands bursting into blooming flowers (Isaiah 35:1–2), deserts flowing with streams (vv. 6–7), castaway war tools crafted into garden instruments (2:4), and impoverished people becoming whole to the sounds of joyful songs (35:5–6, 10).

"The world sends us garbage," Cateura's orchestra director says. "We send back music." And as they do, they give the world a glimpse of the future, when God will wipe away the tears of every eye and poverty will be no more. **Sheridan Voysey**

No More Running

Jonah 2:1–10

In my distress I called to the Lord, and he answered me.
From deep in the realm of the dead I called for help,
and you listened to my cry. —Jonah 2:2

On July 18, 1983, a US Air Force captain disappeared from Albuquerque, New Mexico, without a trace. Thirty-five years later, authorities found him in California. *The New York Times* reported that, "depressed about his job," he had simply run away.

Thirty-five years on the run! Half a lifetime spent looking over his shoulder! I can only imagine that anxiety and paranoia were this man's constant companions.

But I have to admit that I also know a bit about being "on the run." No, I've never abruptly fled something in my life . . . physically. But at times I know there's something God wants me to do, something I need to face or confess. And I don't want to. So, in my own way, I run too.

The prophet Jonah is infamous for literally running from God's assignment to preach to the city of Nineveh (see Jonah 1:1–3). But, of course, he couldn't outrun God. You've probably heard what happened (vv. 4, 17): A storm. A fish. A swallowing. And in the belly of the beast, a reckoning, in which Jonah faced what he'd done and cried to God for help (2:2)

Jonah wasn't a perfect prophet. But I take comfort in his remarkable story, because, even despite Jonah's stubbornness, God never let go of him. The Lord still answered the man's desperate prayer, graciously restoring His reluctant servant (v. 2)—just as He does with us. **Adam Holz**

A Timely Word

Ephesians 4:17–32

A person finds joy in giving an apt reply—and how good is a timely word! —Proverbs 15:23

In Liverpool, England, on the eve of the 2006 British Open Championship, professional golfer Graeme McDowell was in trouble. The next day he was starting the tournament clueless about what was causing his struggles on the course.

While he was out for the evening, McDowell got a surprise. A stranger, an avid golf fan, recognized him and commented that he had noticed a flaw in his swing. The next day, Graeme tested that advice on the driving range, and to his great shock he discovered that the fan had been correct. Satisfied with the value of the change, Graeme implemented the suggestion and finished the first day of the British Open in first place! All because a stranger took time to speak a word of help.

Words are like that. They are powerful instruments for good or for ill. We can use words in destructive ways, or we can use words to build and encourage. This must be what Solomon had in mind when he said, "A person finds joy in giving an apt reply—and how good is a timely word!" (Proverbs 15:23).

In a world where words are often wielded as weapons, let's use our words as tools to build up the hearts of others.

Bill Crowder

Relaxing with Purpose

Proverbs 30:24–31

Four things on earth are small, yet they are extremely wise. —Proverbs 30:24

Ramesh loves to tell others about Jesus. He boldly speaks with coworkers, and one weekend each month he returns to his village to evangelize from house to house. His enthusiasm is contagious—especially since he's learned the value of taking time to rest and relax.

Ramesh used to spend every weekend and most evenings proclaiming the gospel. His wife and children missed him when he was out, and they found him exhausting when he was around. He needed to make every minute and conversation count. He couldn't enjoy games or small talk. Ramesh was wound too tight.

He was awakened to his imbalance by the honest words of his wife, the counsel of friends, and somewhat obscure passages of Scripture. Proverbs 30 mentions trivial things, such as ants, roosters, and locusts. It marvels how "a lizard can be caught with the hand, yet it is found in kings' palaces" (v. 28). Ramesh wondered how something so mundane made it into the Bible. Observing lizards required significant downtime. Someone saw a lizard darting around the palace, thought, *That's interesting*, and paused to watch some more.

Perhaps God included it in His Word to remind us to balance work with rest. We need hours to daydream about lizards, catch one with our kids, and simply relax with family and friends. May God give us wisdom to know when to work, when to serve, and when to relax! **Mike Wittmer**

A Hundred Years from Now

Job 19:21–27

I know that my redeemer lives, and that in the end he will stand on the earth. —Job 19:25

"I just want people to remember me a hundred years from now," said screenwriter Rod Serling in 1975. Creator of the TV series *The Twilight Zone*, Serling wanted people to say of him, "He was a writer." Most of us can identify with Serling's desire to leave a legacy—something to give our lives a sense of meaning and permanence.

The story of Job shows us a man struggling with meaning amid life's fleeting days. In a moment, not just his possessions but those most precious to him, his children, were taken. Then his friends accused him of deserving this fate. Job cried out: "Oh, that my words were recorded, that they were written on a scroll, that they were inscribed with an iron tool on lead, or engraved in rock forever!" (Job 19:23–24).

Job's words have been "engraved in rock forever." We have them in the Bible. Yet Job needed even more meaning in his life than the legacy he'd leave behind. He discovered it in the character of God. "I know that my redeemer lives," Job declared, "and that in the end he will stand on the earth" (19:25). This knowledge gave him the right longing. "I myself will see him," Job said. "How my heart yearns within me!" (v. 27).

In the end, Job didn't find what he expected. He found much more—permanence and the Source of all meaning (42:1–6). Tim Gustafson

JULY 22

Room 5020

Genesis 50:15–20

You intended to harm me, but God intended it for good to accomplish what is now being done. —Genesis 50:20

Jay Bufton turned his hospital room into a lighthouse.

The fifty-two-year-old husband, father, high school teacher, and coach was dying of cancer, but his room—Room 5020—became a beacon of hope for friends, family, and hospital workers. Because of his joyful attitude and strong faith, nurses wanted to be assigned to Jay. Some even came to see him during off-hours.

Even as his once-athletic body was wasting away, he greeted anyone and everyone with a smile and encouragement. One friend said, "Every time I visited Jay he was upbeat, positive, and filled with hope. He was, even while looking cancer and death in the face, living out his faith."

At Jay's funeral, one speaker noted that Room 5020 had a special meaning. He pointed to Genesis 50:20, in which Joseph says that although his brothers sold him into slavery, God turned the tables and accomplished something good: "the saving of many lives." Cancer invaded Jay's life, but by recognizing God's hand at work, Jay could say that "God intended it for good." That's why Jay could use even the ravages of cancer as an open door to tell others about Jesus.

What a legacy of unwavering trust in our Savior even as death was knocking at the door! What a testimony of confidence in our good and trustworthy God! Dave Branon

God-ography

Hebrews 11:1–6

Without faith it is impossible to please God, because anyone who comes to him must believe that he exists and that he rewards those who earnestly seek Him. —Hebrews 11:6

A National Geographic survey reported that many young Americans are geographically illiterate. According to the survey, 63 percent of Americans aged eighteen to twenty-four failed to correctly locate Iraq on a map of the Middle East. The results for US geography are even more dismal. Half could not find New York State on the map, a third could not find Louisiana, and 48 percent could not locate Mississippi.

Understanding geography is helpful in daily life, but "God-ography" (finding God) is infinitely more crucial—for now and for eternity.

In Hebrews 11:6 we are told that to find God and please Him, we first must believe that He exists. How can we prove that God exists? Finding God is a matter of faith—confidence in Him and commitment to Him. This confidence and commitment should remain strong even though the objects of our faith are unseen. The writer of Hebrews and the apostle John agree that ultimately the way to find the Lord and please Him is by believing in His Son Jesus (Hebrews 11:6; John 14:6).

Finding God is solely a work of God. Those who seek Him will find Him because God will give them a heart to recognize Him as Lord (Jeremiah 29:13–14). Marvin Williams

When All Seems Lost

Psalm 22:1–5

My God, my God, why have you forsaken me? —Psalm 22:1

Within the short span of six months, Gerald's life fell apart.

An economic crisis destroyed his business and took away his wealth. What's worse, a tragic accident took his son's life. Overcome by shock, his mother had a heart attack and died, his wife went into depression, and his two young daughters remained inconsolable. All he could do was echo the words of the psalmist, "My God, my God, why have you forsaken me?" (Psalm 22:1).

The only thing that kept Gerald going was the hope that God, who raised Jesus to life, would one day deliver him and his family from their pain to an eternal life of joy. It was a hope that God would answer his desperate cries for help. In his despair, like the psalmist David, he determined to trust God in the midst of his suffering. He held on to the hope that God would deliver and save him (vv. 4–5).

That hope sustained Gerald. Over the years, whenever he was asked how he was, he could only say, "Well, I'm trusting God."

God honored that trust, giving Gerald the comfort, strength, and courage to keep going through the years. His family slowly recovered from the crisis, and soon Gerald welcomed the birth of his first grandchild. Even though the pain of loss is still real, His cry is now a testimony of God's faithfulness. "I'm no longer asking, 'Why have you forsaken me?' God has blessed me."

When it seems there's nothing left, with God there is still hope. **Leslie Koh**

The "Chewing" Years

1 Peter 2:1–11

Blessed are those who hunger and thirst for righteousness, for they will be filled. —Matthew 5:6

A few years ago, my wife gave me a Labrador retriever puppy we named Max. One day when Max was spending time with me in my study, I was concentrating at my desk when I heard the sound of paper ripping behind me. I turned to find a guilty-looking puppy with a book wide open and a page dangling from his mouth.

Our veterinarian told us that Max was going through his "chewing years." As puppies lose their milk teeth and permanent ones grow, they soothe their gums by chewing almost anything. We had to watch Max carefully to ensure he wasn't gnawing on something that could harm him, and we pointed him to safer alternatives.

Max's urge to chew—and my responsibility to watch him—caused me to think about what we "chew on" in our minds and hearts. Do we carefully consider what we are feeding our eternal souls when we read or surf the web or watch TV? The Bible encourages us, "Like newborn babies, crave pure spiritual milk, so that by it you may grow up in your salvation, now that you have tasted that the Lord is good" (1 Peter 2:2–3). We need to fill ourselves daily with God's Word and His truth if we are to thrive as followers of Christ. Only then can we grow to maturity in Him. **James Banks**

Even a Taco

Matthew 10:37–42

If anyone gives even a cup of cold water . . . that person will certainly not lose their reward. —Matthew 10:42

Ashton and Austin Samuelson graduated from a Christian college with a strong desire to serve Jesus. However, neither felt called to a traditional ministry in the church. But what about ministry in the world? Absolutely. They blended their burden to end childhood hunger with their God-given entrepreneurial skills, and in 2014 launched a restaurant that serves tacos.

But this isn't just any restaurant. The Samuelsons operate from a buy-one-give-one philosophy. For every meal bought, they donate money to provide a meal specifically designed to meet the nutritional needs of malnourished children. So far, they've made contributions in more than sixty countries. Their goal is to be a part of ending childhood hunger—one taco at a time.

Jesus's words in Matthew 10 are not cryptic. They are astoundingly clear: devotion is evidenced by actions, not words (vv. 37–42). One of those actions is giving to the "little ones." For the Samuelsons, that focus is giving to children. But take note, the "little ones" isn't a phrase limited to chronological age. Christ is calling us to give to any who are of "little account" in the eyes of this world: the poor, the sick, the prisoner, the refugee, those disadvantaged in any way. And give what? Well, Jesus says "even a cup of cold water" (v. 42). If something as small and simple as a cup of cold water classifies, then a taco surely fits right in line too. John Blase

An Anchor When You're Afraid

Isaiah 51:12–16

I, even I, am he who comforts you. —Isaiah 51:12

Are you a worrier? I am. I wrestle with anxiety almost daily. I worry about big things. I worry about small things. Sometimes, it seems like I worry about everything. Once in my teens, I called the police when my parents were four hours late getting home.

Scripture repeatedly tells us not to be afraid. Because of God's goodness and power, and because He sent Jesus to die for us and gave us His Holy Spirit to guide us, our fears don't have to rule our lives. We may well face hard things, but God has promised to be with us through it all.

One passage that has helped me profoundly in fearful moments is Isaiah 51:12–16. Here, God reminded His people, who had endured tremendous suffering, that He was still with them, and that His comforting presence is the ultimate reality. No matter how bad things may seem: "I, even I, am he who comforts you," He told them through the prophet Isaiah (v. 12).

I love that promise. Those eight words have been an emotion-steadying anchor for my soul. I've clung to this promise repeatedly when life has felt overwhelming, when my own "constant terror" (v. 13) has felt oppressive. Through this passage, God reminds me to lift my eyes from my fears and in faith and dependence look to the one who "stretches out the heavens" (v. 13)—the one who promises to comfort us. Adam Holz

Who Needs Me?

1 Kings 19:9–12, 15–18

When you get there, anoint Hazael king over Aram. –1 Kings 19:15

While on a red-eye flight to Washington, DC, opinion writer Arthur Brooks overheard an elderly woman whisper to her husband, "It's not true that no one needs you anymore." The man murmured something about wishing he were dead, and his wife replied, "Oh, stop saying that." When the flight ended, Brooks turned around and immediately recognized the man. He was a world-famous hero. Other passengers shook his hand, and the pilot thanked him for the courage he displayed decades ago. How had this giant sunk into despair?

The prophet Elijah defeated 450 prophets of Baal bravely and single-handedly—or so he thought (1 Kings 18). Yet he hadn't really done it alone; God was there all along! But later, feeling all alone, he asked God to take his life.

God lifted Elijah's spirits by taking him into His presence and giving him new people to serve. He was told he must go and "anoint Hazael king over Aram," Jehu "king over Israel," and Elisha "to succeed you as prophet" (19:15–16). Invigorated with renewed purpose, Elijah found and mentored his successor Elisha.

Your great victories may lie in the rearview mirror. You may feel your life has peaked, or that it never did. No matter. Look around. The battles may seem smaller, the stakes less profound, but there are still others who need you. Serve them well for Jesus's sake, and it will count for His glory. They're your purpose—the reason you're still here. **Mike Wittmer**

Insight from the Spirit

John 16:12–15

When he, the Spirit of truth, comes, he will guide you into all the truth. —John 16:13

As the French soldier dug in the desert sand, reinforcing the defenses of his army's encampment, he had no idea he would make a momentous discovery. Moving another shovelful of sand, he saw a stone. Not just any stone. It was to become known as the Rosetta Stone, containing a listing—written in three scripts—of the good things King Ptolemy V had done for his priests and the people of Egypt. That stone (now housed in the British Museum in London) would be one of the most important archaeological finds of the nineteenth century, helping to unlock the mysteries of the ancient Egyptian writing known as hieroglyphics.

For many of us, much of Scripture is also wrapped in deep mystery. The night before the cross, Jesus promised His followers that He would send the Holy Spirit. He told them, "But when he, the Spirit of truth, comes, he will guide you into all the truth. He will not speak on his own; he will speak only what he hears, and he will tell you what is yet to come" (John 16:13). The Holy Spirit is, in a sense, our divine Rosetta Stone, shedding light on the truth—including truths behind the mysteries of the Bible.

While we're not promised absolute understanding of everything given to us in the Scriptures, we can have confidence that by the Spirit we can comprehend everything necessary for us to follow Jesus. He will guide us into those vital truths. **Bill Crowder**

Who Rules the Waves?

Job 38:1–18

[The LORD] said, "This far you may come and no farther; here is where your proud waves halt." —Job 38:11

English monarch King Canute was one of the most powerful men on earth in the eleventh century. In a now-famous tale, it is said that he ordered his chair to be placed on the shore as the tide was rising. "You are subject to me," he said to the sea. "I command you, therefore, not to rise on to my land, nor to wet the clothing or limbs of your master." But the tide continued to rise, drenching the king's feet.

This story is often told to draw attention to Canute's pride. Actually, it's a story about humility. "Let all the world know that the power of kings is empty," Canute says next, "save Him by whose will heaven, earth, and sea obey." Canute's story makes a point: God is the only all-powerful one.

The Bible character Job discovered the same thing. Compared to the one who laid Earth's foundations (Job 38:4–7), the one who commands morning to appear and night to end (vv. 12–13), the one who stocks the storehouses of the snow and directs the stars (vv. 22, 31–33), we are small. There is only one ruler of the waves, and it is not us (v. 11; Matthew 8:23–27).

Canute's story is good to think about when we begin feeling too clever or proud about ourselves. Think about walking to the beach and telling the tide to halt. Or try commanding the sun to step aside. Those images are great reminders about who is really supreme. Perhaps they will cause us to thank Him for ruling our lives. Sheridan Voysey

United in Separation

Genesis 13:1–9

Let's not have any quarreling between you and me . . . for we are close relatives. —Genesis 13:8

Thrown into a project with his coworker Tim, Alvin faced a major challenge: he and Tim had very different ideas of how to go about it. While they respected each other's opinions, their approaches were so different that conflict seemed imminent. Before conflict could break out, however, the two men agreed to discuss their differences with their boss, who put them on separate teams. It turned out to be a wise move. That day, Alvin learned this lesson: Being united doesn't always mean doing things together.

Abraham must have realized this truth when he suggested that he and his nephew Lot go their separate ways in Bethel (Genesis 13:5–9). Sensing that there wasn't enough room for both of their flocks, Abraham wisely suggested parting company. But first, he stressed that they were "close relatives" (v. 8), reminding Lot of their relationship. Then, with the greatest humility, he let his nephew have the first choice of land (v. 9) even though he, Abraham, was the senior man. It was, as one pastor described it, a "harmonious separation."

Because each of us is uniquely created, we may find that we sometimes work better separately to achieve the same goal. There's a unity in diversity, even among followers of Christ. Let's never forget, however, that we're still brothers and sisters in the family of God. We may do things differently, but we remain united in purpose.
Leslie Koh

AUGUST 1

God Is Listening

Psalm 5

In the morning, LORD, you hear my voice; in the morning
I lay my requests before you and wait expectantly. —Psalm 5:3

The day before Billy Graham was scheduled to be interviewed on *The Today Show*, his director of public relations, Larry Ross, requested a private room for Graham to pray in before the interview. But when Mr. Graham arrived at the studio, his assistant informed Ross that Mr. Graham wouldn't need the room. He said, "Mr. Graham started praying when he got up this morning, he prayed while eating breakfast, he prayed on the way over in the car, and he'll probably be praying all the way through the interview." Ross later said, "That was a great lesson for me to learn as a young man."

Prayerfulness is not an event; it is a way of being in relationship with God. This kind of intimate relationship is developed when God's people view prayerfulness as a way of life. The Psalms encourage us to begin each day by lifting our voice to the Lord (Psalm 5:3); to fill our day with conversations with God (55:17); and in the face of accusations and slander, to give ourselves totally to prayer (109:4). We develop prayer as a way of life because we desire to be with God (42:1–4; 84:1–2; 130:5–6).

Prayer is our way of connecting with God in all life's circumstances. God is always listening. We can talk to Him any time throughout the day. Marvin Williams

Soccer and Shepherds

John 10:11–15

I am the good shepherd; I know my sheep and my sheep know me. —John 10:14

An intriguing element of English soccer is the team anthem sung by the fans at the start of each match. These songs range from the fun ("Glad All Over") to the whimsical ("I'm Forever Blowing Bubbles") to the surprising. "Psalm 23," for instance, is the anthem of the club from West Bromwich Albion. The words of that psalm appear on the façade inside the team's stadium, declaring to everyone who comes to watch the "West Brom Baggies" the care of the good, great, and chief Shepherd.

In Psalm 23, David made his timeless statement, "The Lord is my shepherd" (v. 1). Later, the gospel writer Matthew would tell us, "When [Jesus] saw the crowds, he had compassion on them, because they were harassed and helpless, like sheep without a shepherd" (Matthew 9:36). And in John 10, Jesus declared His love and concern for the human "sheep" of His generation. "I am the good shepherd," He said. "The good shepherd lays down his life for the sheep" (v. 11). Jesus's compassion drove His interactions with the crowds, His responses to their needs, and ultimately, His sacrifice on their (and our) behalf.

"The Lord is my shepherd" is far more than an ancient lyric or a clever slogan. It is the confident statement of what it means to be known and loved by our great God—and what it means to be rescued by His Son. **Bill Crowder**

AUGUST 3

The Triumph of Forgiveness

Psalm 32:4–7

Blessed is the one whose transgressions are forgiven, whose sins are covered. —Psalm 32:1

Mack, having struggled with drug abuse and sexual sin, was desperate. Relationships he valued were in disarray, and his conscience was beating him up. In his misery, he found himself knocking on the door of a church—asking to speak with a pastor. There he found relief in sharing his complicated story and in hearing about God's mercy and forgiveness.

Biblical scholars think Psalm 32 was composed by David after his sexual sin. He compounded his wrongdoing by devising a sinister strategy that resulted in the death of the woman's husband (see 2 Samuel 11–12). While these ugly incidents were behind him when he wrote this psalm, the effects of his actions remained. Psalm 32:3–4 describes the deep struggles he experienced before he acknowledged the ugliness of his deeds; the gnawing effects of unconfessed sin were undeniable. What brought relief? Relief began with confession to God and accepting the forgiveness He offers (v. 5).

What a great place for us to start—at the place of God's mercy—when we say or do things that cause hurt and harm to ourselves and others. The guilt of our sin need not be permanent. There's One whose arms are open wide to receive us when we acknowledge our wrongs and seek His forgiveness. We can join the chorus of those who sing, "Blessed is the one whose transgressions are forgiven, whose sins are covered" (v. 1). **Arthur Jackson**

Windows

Isaiah 55:6–13

You will go out in joy and be led forth in peace. —Isaiah 55:12

Near the foothills of the Himalayas, a visitor noticed a row of houses without windows. His guide explained that some of the villagers feared that demons might sneak into their homes while they slept, so they built impermeable walls. You could tell when a homeowner began to follow Jesus because he put in windows to let in the light.

A similar dynamic may take place in us, though we might not see it quite that way. We live in scary, polarizing times. Satan and his demons instigate angry divisions that split families and friends. I often feel like hiding behind my walls. But Jesus wants me to cut in a window.

Israel sought refuge in higher walls, but God said their security lay with Him. He reigns from heaven, and His word governs all (Isaiah 55:10–11). If Israel would return to Him, God would "have mercy on them" (v. 7) and restore them as His people to bless the world (Genesis 12:1–3). He would lift them up, ultimately leading them in a triumphal parade. Their celebration "will be for the Lord's renown, for an everlasting sign, that will endure forever" (Isaiah 55:13).

Sometimes walls are necessary. Walls with windows are best. They show the world that we trust God for the future. Our fears are real. Our God is greater. Windows open us to Jesus—"the light of the world" (John 8:12)—and to others who need Him. Mike Wittmer

True Success

Exodus 34:1–7

And he passed in front of Moses, proclaiming, "The LORD, the LORD, the compassionate and gracious God, slow to anger, abounding in love and faithfulness." —Exodus 34:6

My interview guest politely answered my questions. I had a feeling, though, that something lurked beneath our interaction. A passing comment brought it out.

"You're inspiring thousands of people," I said.

"Not thousands," he muttered. "Millions."

And as if pitying my ignorance, my guest reminded me of his credentials—the titles he held, the things he'd achieved, the magazine he'd graced. It was an awkward moment.

Ever since that experience, I've been struck by how God revealed himself to Moses on Mount Sinai (Exodus 34:5–7). Here was the Creator of the cosmos and Judge of humanity, but God didn't use His titles. Here was the Maker of a hundred billion galaxies, but such feats weren't mentioned either. Instead, God introduced himself as "the compassionate and gracious God, slow to anger, abounding in love and faithfulness" (v. 6). When He reveals who He is, it isn't His titles or achievements He lists but the kind of character He has.

As people made in God's image and called to follow His example (Genesis 1:27; Ephesians 5:1–2), this is profound. Achievement is good, titles have their place, but what really matters is how compassionate and gracious we're becoming. Our God has modeled what true success is—not what's written on our business cards and résumés, but how we're becoming like Him. Sheridan Voysey

A Risky Detour

2 Timothy 4:1–5

Preach the word; be prepared in season and out of season. —2 Timothy 4:2

What a waste of time, thought Harley. His insurance agent was insisting they meet again. Harley knew it would be yet another boring sales pitch, but he decided to make the most of it by looking for an opportunity to talk to her about his faith.

Noticing that the agent's eyebrows were tattooed, he hesitantly asked why and discovered that the woman did it because she felt it would bring her luck. Harley's question was a risky detour from a routine chat about finances, but it opened the door to a conversation about luck and faith, which gave him an opportunity to talk about why he relied on Jesus. That "wasted" hour turned out to be a divine appointment.

Jesus also took a risky detour. While traveling from Judea to Galilee, He went out of His way to speak to a Samaritan, something unthinkable for a Jew. Worse, she was an adulterous woman who was avoided even by other Samaritans. Yet He ended up having a conversation that led to the salvation of many (John 4:1–26, 39–42).

Are you meeting someone you don't really want to see? Do you keep bumping into a neighbor you normally avoid? The Bible reminds us to be always ready—"in season and out of season"—to share the good news (2 Timothy 4:2). Consider taking a "risky detour." Who knows, God may be giving you a divine opportunity to talk to someone about Him today! Leslie Koh

AUGUST 7

Bees and Snakes

Matthew 7:7–11

If you, then, though you are evil, know how to give good gifts to your children, how much more will your Father in heaven give good gifts to those who ask him! —Matthew 7:11

Some problems have Daddy's name written all over them. For instance, my kids recently discovered that bees had moved into a crack in our concrete front porch. So, armed with bug spray, I went out to do battle.

I got stung. Five times.

I don't like being stung by insects. But better me than my kids or wife. After all, taking care of my family's well-being is at the top of my job description. My children recognized a need, and they asked me to address it. They trusted me to protect them from something they feared.

In Matthew 7, Jesus teaches that we too should bring our needs to God (v. 7) and trust Him with our requests. To illustrate, Jesus gives a case study in character: "Which of you, if your son asks for bread, will give him a stone? Or if he asks for a fish, will give him a snake?" (vv. 9–10). For loving parents, the answer is obvious. But Jesus answers anyway, challenging us not to lose faith in our Father's generous goodness: "If you, then, though you are evil, know how to give good gifts to your children, how much more will your Father in heaven give good gifts to those who ask him!" (v. 11).

I can't imagine loving my kids more than I do. But Jesus assures us that even the best earthly father's love is eclipsed by God's love for us. **Adam Holz**

Who Are You Wearing?

Zechariah 3

I have taken away your sin, and I will put fine garments on you. —Zechariah 3:4

The Argentine women's basketball team came to their tournament game wearing the wrong uniforms. Their navy blue jerseys were too similar to Colombia's dark blue jerseys, and as the visiting team they should have had white uniforms with them. With no time to find replacement uniforms and change, they had to forfeit the game.

In the time of the prophet Zechariah, God showed him a vision in which the high priest Joshua came before God wearing smelly, filthy clothes. Satan sneered and pointed. He's disqualified! Game over! But there was time to change. God rebuked Satan and told His angel to remove Joshua's grubby garments. He turned to Joshua, "See, I have taken away your sin, and I will put fine garments on you" (Zechariah 3:4).

We came into this world wearing the stench of Adam's sin, which we layer over with sin of our own. If we stay in our filthy clothes, we'll lose the game of life. If we become disgusted with our sin and turn to Jesus, He'll dress us from head to toe with himself and His righteousness. It's time to check: Who are we wearing?

The final stanza of the hymn "The Solid Rock" explains how we win. "When He shall come with trumpet sound, / Oh, may I then in Him be found; / Dressed in His righteousness alone, / Faultless to stand before the throne." **Mike Wittmer**

Flight of Ichabod

1 Samuel 4:12–22

The Glory has departed from Israel, for the ark of God has been captured. —1 Samuel 4:22

In "The Legend of Sleepy Hollow," Washington Irving tells of Ichabod Crane, a schoolteacher who seeks to marry a beautiful young woman named Katrina. Key to the story is a headless horseman who haunts the colonial countryside. One night, Ichabod encounters a ghostly apparition on horseback and flees the region in terror. It's clear to the reader that this "horseman" is actually a rival suitor for Katrina, who then marries her.

Ichabod is a name first seen in the Bible, and it too has a gloomy backstory. While at war with the Philistines, Israel carried the sacred ark of the covenant into battle. Bad move. Israel's army was routed and the ark captured. Hophni and Phinehas, the sons of the high priest Eli, were killed (1 Samuel 4:17). Eli too would die (v. 18). When the pregnant wife of Phinehas heard the news, "she went into labor and gave birth, but was overcome by her labor pains" (v. 19). With her last words she named her son Ichabod (literally, "no glory"). "The Glory has departed from Israel," she gasped (v. 22).

Thankfully, God was unfolding a much larger story. His glory would ultimately be revealed in Jesus, who said of His disciples, "I have given them the glory that you [the Father] gave me" (John 17:22).

No one knows where the ark is today, but no matter. Ichabod has fled. Through Jesus, God has given us His very glory! Tim Gustafson

Three Friends

Daniel 1:11–21

A friend loves at all times, and a brother is born for a time of adversity. —Proverbs 17:17

The Old Testament characters Job and Daniel had much in common. Both went through serious trials and challenges. Both had great success because of the blessing of God's presence in their lives. Both are viewed as giants of the faith, one for his patience in suffering and the other for his purity in an impure culture.

Job and Daniel had something else in common—each had three significant friends. Here, however, the similarities end. Job's friends became a thorn in his side, offering him condemnation when he needed compassion and companionship. As Job struggled with loss and grief, Eliphaz, Bildad, and Zophar seemed bent on intensifying his pain rather than helping him in his adversity

Daniel's three friends were very different. Taken captive together, Daniel and his companions, Shadrach, Meshach, and Abednego, supported and strengthened one another in difficult times. They stood together in honoring God (Daniel 1) and in prayer (2:17–18), and in refusing to bow before the king's image (3:16–18). That's the kind of friend we need.

So, what kind of friend am I? Proverbs 17:17 says, "A friend loves at all times." Who needs you to be a friend today? **Bill Crowder**

AUGUST 11

A Warm Welcome for All

Hebrews 13:1–3

Let us do good to all people, especially to those who belong to the family of believers. —Galatians 6:10

On a vacation, my wife and I visited a famous athletic complex. The gates were wide open, and it appeared that we were welcome to visit. We enjoyed touring the grounds and admiring the well-manicured sports fields. As we were about to leave, someone stopped us and coldly told us we were not supposed to be there. Suddenly, we were reminded that we were outsiders—and it felt uncomfortable.

On that vacation we also visited a church. Again, the doors were open, so we walked in. What a difference! Many people greeted us warmly and made us feel right at home. We walked out of that church service knowing we were welcomed and accepted.

Sadly, it isn't uncommon for outsiders to receive the unspoken message "you're not supposed to be here" when they visit a church. But Scripture calls us to be hospitable to all. Jesus said we are to love our neighbors as ourselves, which surely means welcoming them into our lives and our churches (Matthew 22:39). In Hebrews, we're reminded to "show hospitality to strangers" (13:2). Both Luke and Paul instruct us to show active love to people with social and physical needs (Luke 14:13–14; Romans 12:13). And among the body of believers, we have a special responsibility to show love (Galatians 6:10).

When we welcome all people openly and with Christlike love, we reflect our Savior's love and compassion. **Dave Branon**

Trust the Light

John 12:25–33, 35–36

Believe in the light . . . so that you may become children of light. —John 12:36

The weather forecast said "bomb cyclone." That's what happens when a winter storm rapidly intensifies as the atmospheric pressure drops.

By the time night fell, the blizzard conditions made the highway to the Denver airport almost impossible to see. Almost. But when it's your daughter who's flying home to visit, you do what you have to do. You pack extra clothes and water (just in case you get stranded on the highway), drive very slowly, pray without ceasing, and last but not least, trust your headlights. And sometimes you can achieve the almost impossible.

Jesus foretold of a storm on the horizon, one that would involve His death (John 12:31–33), and one that would challenge His followers to stay faithful and serve (v. 26). It was going to get dark and be almost impossible to see. Almost. So, what did Jesus tell them to do? Believe, or trust, the Light (v. 36). That was the only way they could keep going forward and stay faithful.

Jesus would be with them only a little while longer. But He sent the Holy Spirit—and as believers we have Him as our constant guide to light the way. We too will face dark times when it's almost impossible to see the way ahead. Almost. But by believing, or trusting in the Light, we can press on. **John Blase**

Unchanging Love

Psalm 103:13–22

The world and its desires pass away, but whoever does the will of God lives forever. —1 John 2:17

When I was in high school, I played on the varsity tennis team. I spent many hours of my teenage years trying to improve my skills on four concrete courts located just two blocks from my home.

The last time I visited that city, one of the first things I did was drive to the tennis courts, hoping to watch others play and reminisce for a moment. But the old courts, so familiar to my memory, were nowhere to be seen. In their place was a vacant field, inhabited only by an occasional weed waving silently in the breeze.

That afternoon remains in my mind as a stark reminder of the brevity of life. One of the places where I expended some of my best youthful strength no longer existed! Reflecting on that experience later brought me to this truth, expressed by an aging King David: "The life of mortals is like grass, they flourish like a flower of the field; the wind blows over it and it is gone, and its place remembers it no more. But from everlasting to everlasting the Lord's love is with those who fear him" (Psalm 103:15–17).

We grow older and the world around us may change, but God's love doesn't. He can always be trusted to take care of those who turn to Him. James Banks

Christ Living in Us

Galatians 2:15–21

I have finished the race, I have kept the faith. Now there is in store for me the crown of righteousness. —2 Timothy 4:7–8

The Ironman Triathlon consists of a 2.4-mile swim, a 112-mile bike ride, and a 26.2-mile run. It is not an easy feat for anyone to accomplish. But Dick Hoyt participated in the race and completed it with his physically disabled son, Rick. When Dick swam, he pulled Rick in a small boat. When Dick cycled, Rick was in a seat-pod on the bike. When Dick ran, he pushed Rick along in a wheelchair. Rick was dependent on his dad in order to finish the race. He couldn't do it without him.

We see a parallel between their story and our own Christian life. Just as Rick was dependent on his dad, we are dependent on Christ to complete our Christian race.

As we strive to live a God-pleasing life, we realize that in spite of our best intentions and determination, we often stumble and fall short. By our strength alone, it is impossible. Oh, how we need the Lord's help! And it has been provided. Paul declares it with these insightful words, "I no longer live, but Christ lives in me. The life I now live in the body, I live by faith in the Son of God" (Galatians 2:20).

We cannot finish the Christian race on our own. We must do so by depending on Jesus living in us. **Albert Lee**

Building Bridges

John 4:7–14, 39–42

There is neither Jew nor Gentile, neither slave nor free, nor is there male and female, for you are all one in Christ Jesus. —Galatians 3:28

In our neighborhood, high concrete walls surround our homes. Many of these walls are enhanced with electric barbed wires lining the top. The purpose? To ward off robbers.

Frequent power outages are also a problem in our community. These outages render the front gate bell useless. Because of the wall, a visitor may be kept out in the scorching sun or torrential rain during these outages. Yet even when the gate bell works, to admit the visitor might depend on who they are. Our fence walls serve a good purpose, but they can become walls of discrimination—even when the visitor is obviously not an intruder.

The Samaritan woman whom Jesus met at the well had a similar difficulty with discrimination. The Jews had nothing to do with Samaritans. When Jesus asked her for a drink, she said, "You are a Jew and I am a Samaritan woman. How can you ask me for a drink?" (John 4:9). As she began to open up to Jesus, she had a life-changing experience that positively affected her and her neighbors (vv. 39–42). Jesus became the bridge that broke the wall of hostility and favoritism.

The lure to discriminate is real, and we need to identify it in our lives. As Jesus showed us, we can reach out to all people regardless of nationality, social status, or reputation. He came to build bridges. **Lawrence Darmani**

New Humanity

Acts 2:1–12

When they heard this sound, a crowd came together in bewilderment, because each one heard their own language being spoken. —Acts 2:6

While I was visiting London's Tate Modern art gallery, one work caught my attention. Created by Brazilian artist Cildo Meireles, it was a giant tower made of hundreds of old radios. Each radio was turned on and tuned to a different station, creating a cacophony of confusing, indecipherable speech. Meireles aptly called the sculpture *Babel.*

The title is appropriate. At the original tower of Babel, God thwarted humanity's attempt to seize heaven by confusing mankind's languages (Genesis 11:1–9). No longer able to communicate with one another, humanity fractured into tribes of various dialects (vv. 10–26). Divided by language, we've struggled to understand each other ever since.

There's a second part to the story. When the Holy Spirit came upon the first Christians at Pentecost, He enabled them to praise God in the various languages of those visiting Jerusalem that day (Acts 2:1–12). Through this miracle, everyone heard the same message, no matter their nationality or language. The confusion of Babel was reversed.

In a world of ethnic and cultural division, this is good news. Through Jesus, God is forming a new humanity from every nation, tribe, and tongue (Revelation 7:9). As I stood at Tate Modern, I imagined all those radios suddenly tuning to a new signal and playing the same song to all in the room: "Amazing grace, how sweet the sound."

Sheridan Voysey

AUGUST 17

Change

Matthew 3:2–12

Repent, for the kingdom of heaven has come near. . . .
Produce fruit in keeping with repentance. —Matthew 3:2, 8

Medical studies have shown that even though people who have had heart-bypass surgery are told that they must change their lifestyle or die, about 90 percent do not change. Typically, two years after surgery the patients haven't altered their lifestyle. It seems that most would rather die than change.

Just as doctors preach a physical message of change to prevent death, John the Baptist came preaching a spiritual message of change. "Repent, for the kingdom of heaven has come near!" (Matthew 3:2). He was preparing the way for the ultimate manifestation of God's reign—the Messiah, Jesus.

Repentance means to change one's mind and attitude about God, which ultimately changes a person's actions and decisions. Those who repent and accept Christ's provision of forgiveness from their sins through His death on the cross will escape spiritual death (John 3:16). Repentance involves confessing sin with godly sorrow and then forsaking sin. John the Baptist was calling people to turn from one way of living to ways that honor God.

Today, the Lord is still calling us to repent and then to respond with "fruit in keeping with repentance" (Matthew 3:8). Marvin Williams

How Did I Get Here?

Job 2:1–10

Shall we accept good from God, and not trouble? —Job 2:10

Tiffani awoke in the pitch-black darkness of an Air Canada jet. Still wearing her seat belt, she'd slept while the other passengers exited and the plane was parked. Why didn't anyone wake her? How did she get here? She shook the cobwebs from her brain and tried to remember.

Have you found yourself in a place you never expected? You're too young to have this disease, and there's no cure. Your last review was excellent; why is your position being eliminated? You were enjoying the best years of your marriage. Now you're starting over as a single parent with a part-time job.

How did I get here? Job may have wondered as "he sat among the ashes" (Job 2:8). He'd lost his children, his wealth, and his health in no time flat. He couldn't have guessed how he got here; he just knew he had to remember.

Job remembered his Creator and how good He'd been. He told his wife, "Shall we accept good from God, and not trouble?" (v. 10). Job remembered he could count on this good God to be faithful. So he lamented. He screamed at the heavens. He mourned in hope, "I know that my redeemer lives." And he confessed that "in my flesh I will see God" (19:25–26). Job clung to hope as he remembered how the story began and how it ends. We may wonder how we got here, but we know who will get us through.

Mike Wittmer

AUGUST 19

Practicing What We Preach

1 John 2:7–11

Anyone who claims to be in the light but hates a brother or sister is still in the darkness. —1 John 2:9

Pastor and writer Eugene Peterson had the opportunity to hear a lecture by Swiss physician and highly respected pastoral counselor Paul Tournier. Peterson had read the doctor's works, and he admired Tournier's approach to healing. The lecture left a deep impression on Peterson. As he listened, he had the feeling that Tournier lived what he spoke and spoke what he lived. Peterson chose this word to describe his experience: "Congruence. It is the best word I can come up with."

Congruence—it's what some refer to as "practicing what you preach" or "walking your talk." The apostle John stresses that if any of us "claims to be in the light but hates a brother or sister," then we're "still in the darkness" (1 John 2:9). In essence, our lives simply don't match up with our words. John goes further to say such people "do not know where they are going" (v. 11). The word he chose to describe how incongruence leaves us? *Blind.*

Living closely aligned to God by allowing the light of His Word to illuminate our paths keeps us from living blind. The result is a godly vision that gives clarity and focus to our days—our words and actions match up. When others observe this, the impression is not necessarily that of someone who knows everywhere he's going but of someone who clearly knows who he's following.

John Blase

Taming the Untamable

James 3:1–12

No human being can tame the tongue. —James 3:8

From Vietnamese pot-bellied pigs to Siberian foxes, humans have learned to tame wild animals. People enjoy teaching monkeys to "act" in commercials or training deer to eat out of their hands. As the apostle James put it, "Every kind of beast and bird, of reptile and creature of the sea, is tamed and has been tamed by mankind" (3:7 NKJV).

But there is something we cannot tame. All of us have trouble getting a little thing called the tongue under control. "No man can tame the tongue," James tells us (v. 8 NKJV).

Why? Because while our words may be on the tip of our tongue, they originate from deep within us. "From the mouth speaks what the heart is full of" (Matthew 12:34). And thus the tongue can be used for both good and evil (James 3:9). Or, as scholar Peter Davids put it, "On the one hand, [the tongue] is very religious, but, on the other, it can be most profane."

If we cannot tame this unruly tongue of ours, is it destined to be a daily problem for us, always prone to speak evil? (v. 10). By God's grace, no. We are not left to our own devices. We can ask the Lord to "set a guard" over our mouth; He will "keep watch over the door of [our] lips" (Psalm 141:3). He can tame the untamable. **Dave Branon**

Generation

2 Kings 20:1–6, 16–19

Hezekiah turned his face to the wall and prayed to the Lord. —2 Kings 20:2

"Never trust anyone over thirty," said young environmentalist Jack Weinberg in 1964. His comment stereotyped an entire generation—something Weinberg later regretted. Looking back, he said, "Something I said off the top of my head . . . became completely distorted and misunderstood."

Have you heard disparaging comments aimed at millennials? Or vice versa? Ill thoughts directed from one generation toward another can cut both ways.

Although he was an excellent king, Hezekiah showed a lack of concern for another generation. When as a young man Hezekiah was struck with a terminal illness (2 Kings 20:1), he cried out to God for his life (vv. 2–3). God gave him fifteen more years (v. 6).

But when Hezekiah received the terrible news that his children would one day be taken captive, the royal tears were conspicuously absent (vv. 16–18). He thought, "Will there not be peace and security in my lifetime?" (v. 19). It may have been that Hezekiah didn't apply the passion he had for his own well-being to the next generation.

God calls us to a love that dares to cross the lines dividing us. The older generation needs the fresh idealism and creativity of the younger, who in turn can benefit from the wisdom and experience of their predecessors. This is no time for snarky memes and cutting slogans; it's the time for thoughtful exchange of ideas. We're in this together.

Tim Gustafson

Prayerful Wrestling

Genesis 32:24–32

Jacob was left alone, and a man wrestled with him till daybreak. —Genesis 32:24

Dennis's life was transformed after someone gave him a New Testament. Reading it captivated him, and it became his constant companion. Within six months, two life-changing events occurred in his life. He placed his faith in Jesus for the forgiveness of his sins, and he was diagnosed with a brain tumor after experiencing severe headaches. Because of the unbearable pain, he became bedridden and unable to work. One painful, sleepless night he found himself crying out to God. Sleep finally came at 4:30 a.m.

Bodily pain can cause us to cry out to God, but other excruciating life circumstances also compel us to run to Him. Centuries before Dennis's night of wrestling, a desperate Jacob faced off with God (Genesis 32:24–32). For Jacob, the problem was unfinished family business. He had wronged his brother Esau (chapter 27), and he feared that payback was coming. In seeking God's help in this difficult situation, Jacob encountered God face-to-face (32:30) and emerged from it a changed man.

And so did Dennis. After pleading with God in prayer, Dennis was able to stand up after being bedridden, and the doctor's examination showed no signs of the tumor. Although God doesn't always choose to miraculously heal us, we can be confident that He hears our prayers and will give us what we need for our situation. In our desperation we offer sincere prayers to God and leave the results to Him! **Arthur Jackson**

AUGUST 23

Walking God's Way

Isaiah 30:15–21

Whether you turn to the right or to the left,
your ears will hear a voice behind you, saying,
"This is the way; walk in it." —Isaiah 30:21

"We're going *this* way," I said as I touched my son's shoulder and redirected him through the crowd to follow his mom and sisters in front of us. I'd done this more often as the day wore on at the amusement park our family was visiting. He was getting tired and more easily distracted. *Why can't he just follow them?* I wondered.

Then it hit me: *How often do I do exactly the same thing? How often do I veer from obediently walking with God, enchanted by the temptations to pursue what I want instead of seeking His ways?*

Think of Isaiah's words from God for Israel: "Whether you turn to the right or to the left, your ears will hear a voice behind you, saying, 'This is the way; walk in it'" (Isaiah 30:21). Earlier in that chapter, God had rebuked His people for their rebelliousness. But if they would trust His strength instead of their own ways (v. 15), He promised to show His graciousness and compassion (v. 18).

One expression of God's graciousness is His promise to guide us by His Spirit. That happens as we talk to Him about our desires and ask in prayer what He has for us. I'm thankful God patiently directs us, day by day, step-by-step, as we trust Him and listen for His voice. **Adam Holz**

Wearing Our Courage

2 Kings 1:9–15

If I am a man of God, may fire come down from heaven. —2 Kings 1:10

Andrew lives in a country that's closed to the gospel. When I asked how he keeps his faith a secret, he said he doesn't. He wears a button that advertises his church, and whenever he's arrested, he tells the police that "they need Jesus too." Andrew has courage because he knows who's on his side.

Elijah refused to be intimidated, even when the king of Israel sent fifty soldiers to arrest him (2 Kings 1:9). The prophet knew God was with him, and he called down fire that consumed the platoon. The king sent more soldiers, and Elijah did it again (v. 12). The king sent more, but the third platoon had heard about the others. The captain begged Elijah to spare his soldiers' lives. They were more afraid of him than he'd ever been of them, so the angel of the Lord told Elijah it was safe to go with them (vv. 13–15).

Jesus doesn't want us to call down fire on our enemies. When the disciples asked if they could call down fire on a Samaritan village, Jesus rebuked them (Luke 9:51–55). We're living in a different time. But Jesus does want us to have Elijah's boldness—to be ready to tell everyone about the Savior who died for them. It may seem like one person taking on fifty, but it's actually One on fifty. Jesus provides what we need to courageously love and reach out to others. Mike Wittmer

AUGUST 25

Alternatives to Revenge

Deuteronomy 19:16–21; Matthew 5:38–45

Do not seek revenge . . . , but love your neighbor as yourself. —Leviticus 19:18

One Sunday while preaching, a pastor was accosted and punched by a man. He continued preaching, and the man was arrested. The pastor prayed for him and even visited him in jail a few days later. What an example of the way to respond to insult and injury!

While there is a place for self-defense, personal revenge was forbidden in the Old Testament: "Do not seek revenge or bear a grudge against anyone among your people, but love your neighbor as yourself" (Leviticus 19:18; see also Deuteronomy 32:35). Revenge was also forbidden by Jesus and the apostles (Matthew 5:38–45; Romans 12:17; 1 Peter 3:9).

The Old Testament law exacted like for like (Exodus 21:23–25; Deuteronomy 19:21), which ensured that judicial punishment was not unjust or malicious. But there was a larger principle looming when it came to personal revenge: Justice must be done, but it must be left in the hands of God or the authorities ordained by God.

Instead of returning injury and insult, may we live by Christ-honoring and Spirit-empowered alternatives: Live at peace with everyone (Romans 12:18), submit to a spiritual mediator (1 Corinthians 6:1–6), and leave it in the hands of authorities and, most of all, in God's hands.

Marvin Williams

Unseen Danger

James 1:13–25

Each one is tempted when he is drawn away by his own desires and enticed. —James 1:14 NKJV

When I was a young child, our family escaped a serious tragedy. Most of the main appliances in the house, as well as the furnace, were fueled by natural gas, but a small leak that developed in one of the gas lines put our lives at risk. As the gas poured into our little house that day, our family was overcome by the lethal fumes and we lost consciousness. Had we not been discovered by a neighbor who happened to stop by for a visit, we all could have been killed by this dangerous, unseen enemy.

As followers of Christ, we can also find ourselves surrounded by unseen dangers. The toxic realities of temptation and the weaknesses of our own human frailty can endanger our lives and relationships. Unlike the natural gas in my childhood home, however, these unseen dangers do not come from outside of us—they reside within us. James wrote, "Each one is tempted when he is drawn away by his own desires and enticed" (James 1:14 NKJV).

Our natural tendency to sin, compounded by blind spots that prevent us from seeing our own weaknesses, can lead to toxic choices that ruin us. It is only by submitting to God as He shows us our hearts in His Word (vv. 23–25) that we can live a life that pleases our heavenly Father. Bill Crowder

AUGUST 27

Touched by Grace

Luke 6:27–36

Love your enemies, do good to those who hate you. —Luke 6:27

In Leif Enger's novel *Peace Like a River*, Jeremiah Land is a single father of three working as a janitor at a local school. He's also a man of deep, sometimes miraculous, faith. As the story goes on, his faith is often tested.

Jeremiah's school is run by Chester Holden, a mean-spirited superintendent with a skin condition. Despite Jeremiah's excellent work ethic—mopping up a sewage spill without complaint, picking up broken bottles the superintendent smashed—Holden wants him gone. One day, in front of all the students, he accuses Jeremiah of drunkenness and fires him. It's a humiliating scene.

How does Jeremiah respond? He could threaten legal action for unfair dismissal or make accusations of his own. He could slink away, accepting the injustice. Think for a moment what you might do.

"Love your enemies," Jesus says, "do good to those who hate you, bless those who curse you, pray for those who mistreat you" (Luke 6:27–28). These challenging words aren't meant to excuse evil or stop justice from being pursued. Instead, they call us to imitate God (v. 36) by asking a profound question: How can I help my enemy become all God wants him or her to be?

Jeremiah looks at Holden for a moment, then reaches up and touches his face. Holden steps back defensively, then feels his chin and cheeks in wonder. His scarred skin has been healed. An enemy touched by grace. **Sheridan Voysey**

Feeling Insignificant?

Psalm 139:7–16

I praise you because I am fearfully and wonderfully made. —Psalm 139:14

We are among approximately eight billion people who coexist on a tiny planet that resides in a small section of a rather insignificant solar system. Our earth is just one miniscule blue dot among millions of celestial bodies that God created. On the gigantic canvas that is our universe, our beautiful, majestic Earth appears as a tiny speck of dust.

That could make us feel extremely unimportant and inconsequential. However, God's Word suggests that just the opposite is true. Our great God, who "measured the waters in the hollow of his hand" (Isaiah 40:12), has singled out each person on this planet as supremely important, for we are each made in His image.

For instance, He has created everything for us to enjoy (1 Timothy 6:17). Also, for all who have trusted Jesus as Savior, God has given purpose (Ephesians 2:10). And then there's this: Despite the vastness of this world, God cares specifically about each of us. Psalm 139 says He knows what we are going to say and what we are thinking. We can't escape His presence, and He planned our earthly existence before we were born.

We don't need to feel unimportant; the God of the universe is extremely interested in every last one of us!

Dave Branon

Words That Endure

Jeremiah 36:27–32

This word came to Jeremiah from the LORD. —Jeremiah 36:1

In the early nineteenth century, Thomas Carlyle gave a manuscript to philosopher John Stuart Mill to review. Somehow, whether accidentally or intentionally, the manuscript got tossed into a fire. It was Carlyle's only copy. Undaunted, he set to work rewriting the lost chapters. Mere flames couldn't stop the story, which remained intact in his mind. Out of great loss, Carlyle produced his monumental work *The French Revolution*.

In the waning days of ancient Judah's decadent kingdom, God told the prophet Jeremiah, "Take a scroll and write on it all the words I have spoken to you" (Jeremiah 36:2). The message revealed God's tender heart, calling on His people to repent in order to avoid imminent invasion (v. 3).

Jeremiah did as he was told. The scroll soon found its way to Judah's king Jehoiakim, who methodically shredded it and threw it into the fire (vv. 23–25). The king's act of arson only made matters worse. God told Jeremiah to write another scroll with the same message. He said, "[Jehoiakim] will have no one to sit on the throne of David; his body will be thrown out and exposed to the heat by day and the frost by night" (v. 30).

It's possible to burn the words of God by tossing a book into a fire. Possible, but utterly futile. The Word behind the words endures forever. Tim Gustafson

Just Like Dad

John 5:17–20

The Son can do nothing by himself; he can do only what he sees his Father doing, because whatever the Father does the Son also does. —John 5:19

Isn't it fun to see a child mimicking his parents? How often we've seen the young boy in a car seat, gripping his imaginary steering wheel intently while keeping a close eye on the driver to see what Daddy does next.

I remember doing the same thing when I was young. Nothing gave me greater pleasure than doing exactly what my dad did—and I'm sure he got an even bigger kick out of watching me copy his actions.

I would like to think God felt the same way when He saw His Son doing exactly what the Father did—reaching out to the lost, helping the needy, and healing the sick. Jesus said, "the Son can do nothing by himself; he can do only what he sees his Father doing, because whatever the Father does the Son also does" (John 5:19).

We too are called to do the same—to "follow God's example, therefore, as dearly loved children and walk in the way of love" (Ephesians 5:1–2). As we continue growing to be more like Jesus, we will seek to love like the Father loves, forgive like He forgives, care like He cares, and live in ways that please Him. It is a delight to copy His actions, in the power of the Spirit, knowing that our reward is the warm smile of a loving Father. Leslie Koh

AUGUST 31

How Deserving Are We?

Deuteronomy 9:1–6

It is not because of your righteousness that the LORD your God is giving you this good land. —Deuteronomy 9:6

I remember the day our secondhand refrigerator finally broke down. As a young newlywed employed by a Christian ministry, I didn't have much money to spend on repairs. Not knowing where to turn for reliable help, I called a friend in the electrical business. He assured me that he would handle the problem. Later that evening, I found a brand-new refrigerator in our kitchen. I asked myself, "What did I do to deserve such help?"

It's easy to think we deserve the help that others graciously give us. When we're successful, we tend to assume that we deserve our possessions. Success goes to our head. It makes us proud and can even turn us away from God.

In Deuteronomy 9, we read of God's reminder to Israel about the reason they would be successful. God wanted His people to remember that He was leading them into the land to fulfill His purpose and promises. They would succeed because of Him, not because of their own righteousness (vv. 4–5). He knew they would be tempted to become ungrateful after they were prospering in the promised land.

Ungratefulness is a temptation for us today as well. If our endeavors are successful, let's make sure we are thankful to God for His goodness, help, and protection.

Albert Lee

SEPTEMBER 1

Finding a Quiet Life

1 Thessalonians 4:9–12

Make it your ambition to lead a quiet life. —1 Thessalonians 4:11

"What do you want to be when you grow up?" We all heard that question as children and sometimes even as adults. The question is born of curiosity, and the answer is often heard as an indication of ambition. My answers morphed over the years, starting with a cowboy, then a truck driver, followed by a soldier, and I entered college set on becoming a doctor. However, I can't recall one time that someone suggested or that I consciously considered pursuing "a quiet life."

Yet that's exactly what Paul told the Thessalonians. First, he urged them to love one another and all of God's family even more (1 Thessalonians 4:10). Then he gave them a general admonition that would cover whatever specific plow they put their hand to. "Make it your ambition to lead a quiet life" (v. 11). Now what did Paul mean by that exactly? He clarified: "You should mind your own business and work with your hands" so outsiders respect you and you're not a burden on anyone (vv. 11–12). We don't want to discourage children from pursuing their giftedness or passions, but maybe we could encourage them that whatever they choose to do, they do with a quiet spirit.

Considering the world we live in, the words *ambitious* and *quiet* couldn't seem further apart. But the Scriptures are always relevant, so perhaps we should consider what it might look like to begin living more quietly. **John Blase**

SEPTEMBER 2

The Empty Bed

Matthew 28:16–20

Go and make disciples of all nations. —Matthew 28:19

I was eager to return to St. James Infirmary in Montego Bay, Jamaica, and reconnect with Rendell, who two years earlier had learned about Jesus's love for him. Evie, a teenager in the high school choir I travel with each spring, had read Scripture with Rendell and explained the gospel, and he personally received Jesus as his Savior.

When I entered the men's section of the home and looked toward Rendell's bed, however, I found it was empty. I went to the nurse's station, and I was told what I didn't want to hear. He had passed away—just five days before we arrived.

Through tears, I texted Evie the sad news. Her response was simple: "Rendell is celebrating with Jesus." Later she said, "It's a good thing we told him about Jesus when we did."

Her words reminded me of the importance of being ready to lovingly share with others the hope we have in Christ. No, it's not always easy to proclaim the gospel message about the One who will be with us always (Matthew 28:20), but when we think about the difference it made for us and for people like Rendell, perhaps we'll be encouraged to be even more ready to "make disciples" wherever we go (v. 19).

I'll never forget the sadness of seeing that empty bed—and also the joy of knowing what a difference one faithful teen made in Rendell's forever life. Dave Branon

The Finish Line

1 Corinthians 9:24–27

Tell Archippus, "See to it that you complete the ministry you have received in the LORD." —Colossians 4:17

When I was in college, I ran on the cross-country team. In the final event of the season, the state's small colleges competed against each other, with about seventy-five runners in the event. We ran the 5K course in the rain and mud on a cold November day.

As I neared the finish line, I spied a runner from one of the other schools just a short distance ahead of me. He became my goal. I ran as hard as I could and passed him just as I crossed the finish line. That last dash meant I finished forty-second in the race, which seemed a lot better than forty-third! It meant our team finished one position higher in the final standings than the team represented by the runner I beat. The point? I didn't give up—I ran all the way through the finish line.

That is a big part of the teaching of Paul as he wrote to Archippus, one of his young ministry protégés: "See to it that you complete the ministry you have received in the Lord" (Colossians 4:17). When we feel discouraged and want to quit, it's good to remember that the Lord, who entrusted us with the privilege of spiritual service, will give us the grace and strength to carry out that service. Let us "run with perseverance" (Hebrews 12:1) so we will receive "a crown that will last forever" (1 Corinthians 9:25). Bill Crowder

SEPTEMBER 4

Truly Humble, Truly Great

Philippians 2:1–11

[Christ Jesus] made himself nothing. —Philippians 2:7

As the American Revolution concluded with England's improbable surrender, many politicians and military leaders sought to make General George Washington a new monarch. The world watched, wondering if Washington would stick to his ideals of freedom and liberty when absolute power was within his grasp.

England's King George III saw another reality, however. He was convinced that if Washington resisted the power pull and returned to his Virginia farm, he would be "the greatest man in the world." The king knew that the greatness evidenced in resisting the allure to power is a sign of true nobility and significance.

Paul knew this same truth and encouraged us to follow Christ's humble way. Even though Jesus was "in very nature God," he "did not consider equality with God something to be used to his own advantage" (Philippians 2:6). Instead, He surrendered His power, became "a servant" and "humbled himself by becoming obedient to death" (vv. 7–8). The one who held all power surrendered every bit of it for the sake of love.

And yet, in the ultimate reversal, God exalted Christ from a criminal's cross "to the highest place" (v. 9). Jesus, who could demand our praise or force us to be obedient, laid down His power in a breathtaking act that won our worship and devotion. Through absolute humility, Jesus demonstrated true greatness, turning the world upside down in the process. **Winn Collier**

Pax Romana

Isaiah 9:1–7

To us a child is born, to us a son is given, and the government will be on his shoulders. —Isaiah 9:6

No one can afford the price of war. In a recent year, one website reported that sixty-four nations were then involved in armed conflicts. When and how will they end? We want peace, but not at the expense of justice.

Jesus was born during a time of "peace," but it came at the cost of heavy-handed oppression. The *Pax Romana* ("Roman Peace") existed only because Rome squashed all dissent.

Seven centuries before that time of relative peace, hostile armies prepared to invade Jerusalem. From the shadow of war, God made a remarkable pronouncement. "On those living in the land of deep darkness a light has dawned," the prophet declared back in Isaiah 9:2. And we have this: "For to us a child is born, to us a son is given. . . . Of the greatness of his government and peace there will be no end" (vv. 6–7). Matthew tells us that Isaiah's prophecy found fulfillment in the Christ-child (Matthew 1:22–23; see also Isaiah 7:14).

We adore the tiny baby in the manger scene. Yet that helpless babe is also the Lord Almighty, "the LORD of Heaven's Armies" (Isaiah 13:13 NLT). He will one day "reign on David's throne and over his kingdom, establishing and upholding it with justice and righteousness" (9:7). Such a regime will not be an oppressive *Pax Romana*. It will be the reign of the true Prince of Peace. Tim Gustafson

SEPTEMBER 6

Marked by Momma

2 Timothy 1:3–7

Continue in what you have learned and have become convinced of, because you know those from whom you learned it. —2 Timothy 3:14

Her name was long, but her years were even longer. Madeline Harriet Orr Jackson Williams lived to be 101 years old, outliving two husbands. Both were preachers. Madeline was my grandmother, and we knew her as Momma. My siblings and I got to know her well; we lived in her home until her second husband whisked her away. Even then she was less than fifty miles away from us. Our grandmother was a hymn-singing, catechism-reciting, piano-playing, God-fearing woman, and my siblings and I have been marked by her faith.

According to 2 Timothy 1:3–7, Timothy's grandmother Lois and his mother, Eunice, had a huge impact on his life. Their living and teaching were rooted in the soil of Scripture (v. 5; 2 Timothy 3:14–16), and eventually their faith blossomed in Timothy's heart. His biblically based upbringing was not only foundational for his relationship with God but it was also vital to his usefulness in the Lord's service (1:6–7).

Today, as well as in Timothy's time, God uses faithful women and men to mark future generations. Our prayers, words, actions, and service can be powerfully used by the Lord while we live and after we're gone. That's why my siblings and I still rehearse things that were passed on to us from Momma. My prayer is that Momma's legacy will not stop with us. **Arthur Jackson**

Loving All

Leviticus 19:33–34

The stranger who dwells among you shall be to you as one born among you, and you shall love him as yourself. —Leviticus 19:34 NKJV

I worship in a church located in a large, open field—a rare commodity on the island of Singapore (we're just twenty-five miles long and fifteen miles wide). Some time back, people from abroad who work in my country started gathering on the church property for a picnic every Sunday.

This evoked a range of responses from fellow churchgoers. Some fretted about the mess the visitors would leave behind. But others saw this as a divine opportunity to extend hospitality to a wonderful group of strangers—without even leaving the church grounds!

The Israelites must have faced similar issues in their time. After they settled in their new land, they had to grapple with how to relate to other peoples. But God expressly commanded them to treat foreigners like their own kind and to love them as themselves (Leviticus 19:34). Many of His laws made special mention of foreigners: they were not to be mistreated or oppressed, and they were to be loved and helped (Exodus 23:9; Deuteronomy 10:19). Centuries later, Jesus would command us to do the same: to love our neighbor as ourselves (Mark 12:31).

We should strive to have God's heart to love others as ourselves, remembering that we too are sojourners on this earth. Yet we have been loved as God's people, treated as His own. **Leslie Koh**

SEPTEMBER 8

Only One Option

Habakkuk 1:1–2:4

Behold the proud, his soul is not upright in him;
but the just shall live by his faith. —Habakkuk 2:4 NKJV

If you were to ask several people to draw a crooked line on a piece of paper, no two lines would be identical. There is a lesson in this: There are many ways to be crooked but only one way to be straight.

The Lord tells us that the righteous person has only one option—to "live by his faith" (Habakkuk 2:4 NKJV). In the chapter prior to this declaration from the Lord, the prophet Habakkuk had complained about the violence and injustice around him. It seemed as if the wicked were swallowing up the righteous (1:13).

God responded to Habakkuk by saying that His people were to be "just" and were to live by faith. They were not to be like the one who is "proud" and "not upright" (2:4 NKJV). A proud and self-sufficient person will rationalize his faults and imperfections. He doesn't want to admit that he needs God. His ways are crooked.

Wickedness seems to prevail in our world. God urges us to live our lives in faith, taking to heart His assurance to Habakkuk that there will be a day of reckoning for the wicked.

The only way to please God now and to be ready for that day of reckoning is to live by faith. Albert Lee

Fight Off Jealousy

1 Corinthians 3:1–10

For since there is jealousy and quarreling among you, are you not worldly? Are you not acting like mere humans? —1 Corinthians 3:3

The story is told of two shopkeepers who were bitter rivals. They spent each day keeping track of each other's business. If one got a customer, he would smile triumphantly at his rival.

One night an angel appeared to one of the shopkeepers in a dream and said, "I will give you anything you ask, but whatever you receive, your competitor will receive twice as much. What is your desire?" The man frowned and then said, "Strike me blind in one eye." Now, that's jealousy of the worst kind!

The self-destructive emotion of jealousy had the potential of tearing apart the Corinthian church. These believers had received the gospel but had not allowed the Holy Spirit to change their hearts. As a result, they became jealous of one another, which led to a divided community. Paul identified their jealousy as a sign of immaturity and worldliness (1 Corinthians 3:3). These believers were not acting like people who had been transformed by the gospel.

One of the clearest indicators that the Holy Spirit is working in our lives is our contentment and our thankfulness for what we have. Then, instead of experiencing jealousy, we can genuinely celebrate the gifts and blessings of others. Marvin Williams

The Death Zone

2 Samuel 11:1–6, 12–15

But David remained
in Jerusalem. —2 Samuel 11:1

In 2019, a climber saw his last sunrise from the peak of Mount Everest. He survived the dangerous ascent, but the high altitude squeezed his heart, and he passed away on the trek down. One medical expert warns climbers not to think of the summit as their journey's end. They must get up and down quickly, remembering that "they're in the death zone."

David survived his dangerous climb to the top. He killed lions and bears, slew Goliath, dodged Saul's spear and pursuing army, and conquered Philistines and Ammonites to become king of the mountain.

But David forgot he was in the death zone. At the peak of his success, as "the LORD gave David victory wherever he went" (2 Samuel 8:6), he committed adultery and murder. His initial mistake? He lingered on the mountaintop. When his army set out for new challenges, he "remained in Jerusalem" (11:1). David had once volunteered to fight Goliath; now he relaxed in the accolades of his triumphs.

It's hard to stay grounded when everyone, including God, says you're special (7:11–16). But we must. If we've achieved some success, we may appropriately celebrate the accomplishment and accept congratulations, but we must keep moving. We're in the death zone. Come down the mountain. Humbly serve others in the valley—asking God to guard your heart and your steps. **Mike Wittmer**

Overcoming Envy

1 Samuel 18:5–9

Saul has slain his thousands, and David his tens of thousands. —1 Samuel 18:7

In the movie *Amadeus*, aging composer Antonio Salieri plays some of his music on the piano for a visiting priest. The embarrassed priest confesses he doesn't recognize the tunes. "What about this one?" Salieri says, playing an instantly familiar melody. "I didn't know you wrote that," the priest says. "I didn't," Salieri replies. "That was Mozart!" As viewers discover, Mozart's success as a composer caused deep envy in Salieri—even leading him to play a part in Mozart's death.

A song lies at the heart of another envy story. After David's victory over Goliath, the Israelites heartily sing, "Saul has slain his thousands, and David his tens of thousands" (1 Samuel 18:7). The comparison doesn't sit well with King Saul. Envious of David's success and afraid of losing his throne (vv. 8–9), Saul begins a prolonged pursuit of David, trying to take his life. Saul had been divinely chosen for his role as king (10:6–7, 24), a status that should've fostered security in him rather than envy.

Like Salieri with music or Saul with power, we're sometimes tempted to envy those with similar but greater gifts than we possess. And whether it's picking fault with their work or belittling their success, we too can seek to damage our "rivals." Since we each have unique callings too (Ephesians 2:10), maybe the best way to overcome envy is to stop comparing ourselves. Let's celebrate each other's successes instead and trust God's direction in our lives.

Sheridan Voysey

Abby's Prayer

Ephesians 6:16–20

I urge . . . that petitions, prayers, intercession and thanksgiving be made for all people. —1 Timothy 2:1

When Abby was a sophomore in high school, she and her mom heard a news story about a young man who'd been critically injured in a plane accident—an accident that took the lives of his father and stepmother. Although they didn't know this person, Abby's mom said, "We need to pray for him and his family." And they did.

Fast forward a few years, and one day Abby walked into a class at her university. A student offered her the seat next to him. That student was Austin Hatch, the plane crash survivor Abby had prayed for. Soon they were dating, and in 2018 they were married.

"It's crazy to think that I was praying for my future husband," Abby said in an interview shortly before they were married. It can be easy to limit our prayers to our own personal needs and for those closest to us, without taking the time to pray for others. However, Paul, writing to the Christians at Ephesus, told them to "pray in the Spirit on all occasions with all kind of prayers and requests. With this in mind, be alert and always keep on praying for all the Lord's people" (Ephesians 6:18). And 1 Timothy 2:1 tells us to pray "for all people," including those in authority.

Let's pray for others—even people we don't know. It's one of the ways we can "carry each other's burdens" (Galatians 6:2). **Dave Branon**

Doing Good

1 Peter 3:8–17

It is better, if it is God's will, to suffer for doing good than for doing evil. —1 Peter 3:17

Joseph (not his real name) was the model of a trusted military officer, rising in his nation's army to the rank of colonel in the special forces. With this came great opportunity, both for good and bad.

When deployed into a region racked with drug trafficking, Joseph was intent on bringing justice to that plagued area. He and his troops began dealing with the criminals to protect the people. Some of his superiors, who were corrupt and took bribes from the drug runners, ordered him to turn his head to let them move their drugs. He repeatedly refused until he was finally arrested and imprisoned for eight years—for doing good.

Sadly, we live in a world where at times doing good brings suffering. This was true for Joseph; his payment for serving his people was unjust imprisonment.

The apostle Peter, having also been jailed for doing good, understood that kind of heartache. He gave us this perspective: "It is better, if it is God's will, to suffer for doing good than for doing evil" (1 Peter 3:17).

As Joseph shared the stories of what God taught him in prison, I learned that the justice of God is not hampered by the evil of men. Doing good is still pleasing in His sight—even when we're mistreated by the world for it. **Bill Crowder**

Our Chief Task

Matthew 7:12–23

I am the way and the truth and the life. No one comes to the Father except through me. —John 14:6

When a British scholar called on the world's religions to work together for worldwide unity, people everywhere applauded. Pointing out that the major religions share a belief in the Golden Rule, she suggested, "The chief task of our time is to build a global society where people of all persuasions can live together in peace and harmony."

Jesus cited the Golden Rule in His Sermon on the Mount: "Do to others what you would have them do to you" (Matthew 7:12). In the same sermon, He said, "Love your enemies and pray for those who persecute you" (5:44). Putting those radical commands into practice would indeed go a long way toward peace and harmony. But immediately following the Golden Rule, Jesus called for discernment. "Watch out for false prophets," He warned. "They come to you in sheep's clothing, but inwardly they are ferocious wolves" (7:15).

Respect for others and discernment of the truth go hand in hand. If we have the truth, we have a message worth telling. But God extends to everyone the freedom to choose Him or reject Him. Our responsibility is to lovingly present the truth and respect the personal choice of others just as God does.

Our respect for others is vital to winning their respect for us. It's an important step in gaining an opportunity to convey the message of Jesus, who said, "I am the way and the truth and the life" (John 14:6). **Tim Gustafson**

Objects in Mirror

Philippians 3:7–14

Forgetting what is behind and straining toward what is ahead, I press on toward the goal to win the prize for which God has called me heavenward in Christ Jesus. —Philippians 3:13–14

"Must. Go. Faster." That's what Dr. Ian Malcolm, played by Jeff Goldblum, says in an iconic scene from the 1993 movie *Jurassic Park* as he and two other characters flee in a Jeep from a rampaging tyrannosaurus. When the driver looks in the rearview mirror, he sees the raging reptile's jaw—right above the words: "OBJECTS IN MIRROR MAY BE CLOSER THAN THEY APPEAR."

The scene is a masterful combination of intensity and grim humor. But sometimes it feels as if the "monsters" from our past never stop pursuing us. We look in the "mirror" of our lives and see mistakes looming right there, threatening to consume us with guilt or shame.

The apostle Paul understood the past's potentially paralyzing power. He had spent years trying to live perfectly apart from Christ, and he had even persecuted Christians (Philippians 3:1–9). Regret over his past could easily have crippled him. But Paul found such beauty and power in his relationship with Christ that he was compelled to let go of his old life (vv. 8–9). That freed him to look forward in faith instead of backward in fear or regret: "One thing I do: Forgetting what is behind and straining toward what is ahead, I press on toward the goal" (vv. 13–14).

Our redemption in Christ has freed us to live for Him. We don't have to let those "objects in [our] mirror" dictate our direction as we continue forward. **Adam Holz**

SEPTEMBER 16

Wait

1 Samuel 13:7–14

"You have done a foolish thing," Samuel said [to Saul]. "You have not kept the commandment the LORD your God gave you." —1 Samuel 13:13

In an act of impatience, a man in San Francisco, California, tried to beat traffic by swerving around a lane of cars that had come to a stop. However, the lane he pulled into had just been laid with fresh cement, and his Porsche 911 got stuck. This driver paid a high price for his impatience.

The Scriptures tell of a king who also paid a high price for his impatience. Eager for God to bless the Israelites in their battle against the Philistines, Saul acted impatiently. When Samuel did not arrive at the appointed time to offer a sacrifice for God's favor, Saul became impatient and disobeyed God's command (1 Samuel 13:8–9, 13). Impatience led Saul to think he was above the law and to take on an unauthorized position of priest. He thought he could disobey God without serious consequences. He was wrong.

When Samuel arrived, he rebuked Saul for his disobedience and prophesied that Saul would lose the kingdom (vv. 13–14). Saul's refusal to wait for the development of God's plan caused him to act in haste, and in his haste he lost his way (see Proverbs 19:2). His impatience was the ultimate display of a lack of faith.

The Lord will provide His guiding presence as we wait patiently for Him to bring about His will. Marvin Williams

Love Your "Samaritan"

Acts 1:1–8

You will be my witnesses in Jerusalem, and in all Judea and Samaria. —Acts 1:8

I ducked into a room before she saw me. I was ashamed of hiding, but I didn't want to deal with her right then—or ever. I longed to tell her off, to put her in her place. Though I'd been annoyed by her past behavior, it's likely I had irritated her even more!

The Jews and Samaritans also shared a mutually irritating relationship. In the eyes of the Jews, the Samaritans had spoiled the Jewish bloodline and faith, erecting a rival religion on Mount Gerizim (John 4:20). In fact, the Jews so despised Samaritans they walked the long way around rather than take the direct route through their country.

Jesus revealed a better way. He brought salvation for all people, including Samaritans. So, He ventured into the heart of Samaria to bring living water to a sinful woman and her town (vv. 4–42). In His last words to His disciples, He told them to follow His example. They were to share His good news with everyone, beginning in Jerusalem and dispersing through Samaria until they reached "the ends of the earth" (Acts 1:8). Samaria was more than the next geographical sequence. It was the most painful part of the mission. The disciples had to overcome lifetimes of prejudice to love people they didn't like.

Does Jesus matter more to us than our grievances? There's only one way to be sure. Love your "Samaritan."

Mike Wittmer

SEPTEMBER 18

Finding Hope

Ephesians 4:32–5:10

Follow God's example, therefore, as dearly loved children and walk in the way of love. —Ephesians 5:1–2

I once spoke at a secular conference for childless couples. Heartbroken over their infertility, many attendees despaired at their future. Having walked the childless path too, I tried to encourage them. "You can have a meaningful identity without becoming parents," I said. "I believe you are fearfully and wonderfully made, and there's new purpose for you to find."

A woman later approached me in tears. "Thank you," she said. "I've felt worthless being childless and needed to hear that I'm fearfully and wonderfully made." I asked the woman if she was a believer in Jesus. "I walked away from God years ago," she said. "But I need a relationship with Him again."

Times like this remind me how profound the gospel is. Some identities, like "mother" and "father," are hard for some to attain. Others, like those based on a career, can be lost through unemployment. But through Jesus we become God's "dearly loved children"—an identity that can never be stolen (Ephesians 5:1). And then we can "walk in the way of love"—a life purpose that transcends any role or employment status (v. 2)

All human beings are "fearfully and wonderfully made" (Psalm 139:14), and those who follow Jesus become children of God (John 1:12–13). Once in despair, that woman left in hope—about to find an identity and purpose bigger than this world can give. **Sheridan Voysey**

The Way to Success

Joshua 1:1–9

Keep this Book of the Law always on your lips; meditate on it. . . . Then you will be prosperous and successful. —Joshua 1:8

During the Chinese New Year it is customary for *hongbaos* (small red envelopes containing money) to be given away. When parents give *hongbaos* to their children, it is also to wish them prosperity and success. Knowing that this sincere wish is insufficient, however, they also remind their children to study hard. Chinese people generally believe that a good education is the key to one's success in life.

In Joshua 1, God told Joshua that his ways could prosper as he assumed Moses's leadership role. But he and the people needed to display courage in the face of stiff opposition as they entered the promised land (v. 6). God promised to give them success if they heeded His "Book of the Law" (v. 8).

Believers today also need to live according to God's Word if we are to enjoy success in our spiritual walk. The Bible contains not only the dos and don'ts for living but also records the life experiences of those who pleased or displeased God.

We, like Joshua, have God's promise that He will be with us always (v. 9; Matthew 28:20). That should give us strength to face the challenges and difficulties that inevitably arise as we seek to please Him. **Albert Lee**

SEPTEMBER 20

Great News

Psalm 51:1–7

Have mercy on me, O God, according to your unfailing love. —Psalm 51:1

The article in the local newspaper was short but heartwarming. After attending a faith-based program on building stronger family ties, a group of prison inmates was given a rare treat of an open visit with their families. Some hadn't seen their children in years. Instead of talking through a glass panel, they could touch and hold their loved ones. The tears flowed freely as families grew closer and wounds began to heal.

For most readers, it was just a story. But for these families, holding one another was a life-changing event—and for some, the process of forgiveness and reconciliation was begun.

God's forgiveness of our sin and offer of reconciliation, made possible through His Son, is more than a mere fact of the Christian faith. The article's news of reconciliation reminds us that Jesus's sacrifice is great news not just for the world but also for you and me.

In times when we're overwhelmed by guilt for something we've done, the idea of reconciliation is great news that we cling to. That's when the fact of God's unending mercy becomes personal to us. Because of Jesus's death on our behalf, we can come to the Father washed clean, "whiter than snow" (Psalm 51:7). In those times when we know we don't deserve God's mercy, we can grasp the one thing that helps the most: God's unfailing love and compassion (v. 1). **Leslie Koh**

Unlimited

Isaiah 40:21–28

The LORD is the everlasting God, the Creator of the ends of the earth. He will not grow tired or weary. —Isaiah 40:28

There I am, sitting in the shopping mall food court, my body tense and my stomach knotted over looming work deadlines. As I unwrap my burger and take a bite, people rush around me, fretting over their own tasks. *How limited we all are,* I think to myself, *limited in time, energy, and capacity.*

I consider writing a new to-do list and prioritizing the urgent tasks, but as I pull out a pen another thought enters my mind: a thought of One who is infinite and unlimited, who effortlessly accomplishes all that He desires.

This God, Isaiah says, can measure the oceans in the hollow of His hand and collect the dust of the earth in a basket (Isaiah 40:12). He names the stars of the heavens and directs their path (v. 26), knows the rulers of the world and oversees their careers (v. 23), considers islands mere specks of dust and the nations like drops in the sea (v. 15). "To whom will you compare me?" He asks (v. 25). "The LORD is the everlasting God," Isaiah replies. "He will not grow tired or weary" (v. 28).

Stress and strain are never good for us, but on this day they deliver to me a powerful lesson. The unlimited God is not like me! He accomplishes everything He wishes—in the world and in me. I finish my burger and pause once more. And silently worship. **Sheridan Voysey**

SEPTEMBER 22

Powerful and Loving

Deuteronomy 4:5–8, 11–14

You came near and stood at the foot of the mountain while it blazed with fire to the very heavens, with black clouds and deep darkness. —Deuteronomy 4:11

In 2020, the Ecuadorian volcano Sangay erupted. The BBC described "a dark ash plume which reached a height of more than 12,000m." The discharge covered four provinces (about 198,000 acres) in gray ash and grimy soot. The sky turned dingy and grim, and the air was thick—making it difficult to breathe. Farmer Feliciano Inga described the unnerving scene to *El Comercio* newspaper: "We didn't know where all this dust was coming from. . . . We saw the sky go dark and grew afraid."

The Israelites experienced a similar fear at the base of Mount Sinai, as they "stood at the foot of the mountain while it blazed with fire . . . with black clouds and deep darkness" (Deuteronomy 4:11). God's voice thundered, and the people trembled. It's an awesome, knee-buckling experience to encounter the living God. "Then the Lord spoke," and they "heard the sound of words but saw no form" (v. 12). The voice that rattled their bones provided life and hope. God gave Israel the Ten Commandments and renewed His covenant with them. The voice from the dark cloud caused them to quake, but it also wooed and loved them with tenacity (Exodus 34:6–7).

God is powerful, beyond our reach, even startling. And yet He's also full of love, always reaching out to us. A God both powerful and loving—this is who we desperately need. **Winn Collier**

Loved, Handsome, Gifted

Romans 8:15–17

The Spirit you received brought about your adoption to sonship. —Romans 8:15

Malcolm appeared confident as a teenager. But this confidence was a mask. In truth, a turbulent home left him fearful, desperate for approval, and feeling falsely responsible for his family's problems. "For as far back as I remember," he says, "every morning I would go into the bathroom, look in the mirror, and say out loud to myself, 'You are stupid, you are ugly, and it's your fault.'"

Malcolm's self-loathing continued until he was twenty-one, when he had a divine revelation of his identity in Jesus. "I realized that God loved me unconditionally, and nothing would ever change that," he recalls. "I could never embarrass God, and He would never reject me." In time, Malcolm looked in the mirror and spoke to himself differently. "You are loved, you are handsome, you are gifted," he said, "and it's not your fault."

Malcolm's experience illustrates what God's Spirit does for the believer in Jesus—He frees us from fear by revealing how profoundly loved we are (Romans 8:15, 38–39), and He confirms that we are children of God with all the benefits that brings (8:16–17; 12:6–8). As a result, we can see ourselves correctly by having our thinking renewed (12:2–3).

Years later, Malcolm still whispers those words each day—reinforcing who God says he is. In the Father's eyes he is loved, he is handsome, and he is gifted. And so are we. Sheridan Voysey

SEPTEMBER 24

The Search for Peace

Philippians 4:4–12

The peace of God, which transcends all understanding, will guard your hearts and your minds. —Philippians 4:7

At the height of their popularity, creativity, and wealth, the Beatles produced a controversial project called *The White Album*. It signaled the breakup of the band by featuring pieces that were primarily individual in nature instead of collaborative.

It also revealed a growing disenchantment with everything their fame had produced. In his song "I'm So Tired," John Lennon expressed the emptiness of his "successful" and wealthy life with this profound idea: He would give it all up—all his accomplishments—for some peace of mind. All that he had, all that he had done, and all that he had become could not meet this simple, yet deep, personal need.

The world we live in cannot offer peace. It offers only poor options. Pleasure, power, and possessions are no substitute for peace of heart and mind.

The apostle Paul reminded the believers at Philippi, "The peace of God, which transcends all understanding, will guard your hearts and your minds in Christ Jesus" (Philippians 4:7). This is the peace God brings to those who have been reconciled to God by faith in His Son Jesus (Ephesians 2:14–16). It is a peace we are supposed to share with a world that is desperate for it.

Peace—real peace—is found only in a relationship with Jesus. Have you received the peace He offers? **Bill Crowder**

Bad Faith, Good Faith

Romans 4:18–25

[Abraham] did not waver through unbelief regarding the promise of God, but was strengthened in his faith and gave glory to God. —Romans 4:20

"You gotta have faith," people say. But what does that mean? Is any faith good faith?

"Believe in yourself and all that you are," wrote one positive thinker a century ago. "Know that there is something inside you that is greater than any obstacle." As nice as that may sound, it falls to pieces when it crashes into reality. We need a faith in something bigger than ourselves.

God promised Abram he would have a multitude of descendants (Genesis 15:4–5), so he faced a huge obstacle—he was old and childless. When he and Sarah got tired of waiting for God to make good on His promise, they tried to overcome that obstacle on their own. As a result, they fractured their family and created a lot of unnecessary dissension (see Genesis 16 and 21:8–21).

Nothing Abraham did in his own strength worked. But ultimately, he became known as a man of tremendous faith. Paul wrote of him, "Against all hope, Abraham in hope believed and so became the father of many nations, just as it had been said to him, 'So shall your offspring be'" (Romans 4:18). This faith, said Paul, "was credited to him as righteousness" (v. 22).

Abraham's faith was in something far bigger than himself—the one and only God. It's the object of our faith that makes all the difference. Tim Gustafson

SEPTEMBER 26

Who Are You?

Ezekiel 32:2–10

You are like a lion among the nations;
you are like a monster in the seas. —Ezekiel 32:2

The leader of our video conference said, "Good morning!" I said "Hello" back, but I wasn't looking at him. I was distracted by my own image on the screen. Do I look like this? I looked at the smiling faces of the others on the call. That looks like them. So yes, this must be me. I should lose some weight. And get a haircut.

In his own mind, Pharaoh was pretty great. He was "a lion among the nations . . . a monster in the seas" (Ezekiel 32:2). But then he caught a glimpse of himself from God's perspective. God said he was in trouble and that He would expose his carcass to wild animals, causing "many peoples to be appalled at you, and their kings [to] shudder with horror because of you" (v. 10). Pharaoh was much less impressive than he thought.

We may think we're "spiritually handsome"—until we see our sin as God sees it. Compared to His holy standard, even "our righteous acts are like filthy rags" (Isaiah 64:6). But God also sees something else, something even more true: He sees Jesus, and He sees us in Jesus.

Feeling discouraged about how you are? Remember this is not who you are. If you have put your trust in Jesus, then you're in Jesus, and His holiness drapes over you. You're more handsome than you can imagine.
Mike Wittmer

In the Father's Ways

1 Samuel 8:1–9

[Samuel's sons] turned aside after dishonest gain and accepted bribes and perverted justice. —1 Samuel 8:3

In the 1960s, the bustling community of North Lawndale, on Chicago's West Side, was a pilot community for interracial living. A handful of middle-class African Americans bought homes there on "contract"—which combined the responsibilities of home ownership with the disadvantages of renting. In a contract sale, the buyer accrued no equity, and if he missed a single payment, he would immediately lose his down payment, all his monthly payments, and the property itself. Unscrupulous sellers sold at inflated prices, then the families were evicted when they missed a payment. Another family would buy on contract, and the greed-fueled cycle just kept going.

Samuel appointed his sons to be judges over Israel, but they were driven by greed. His sons "did not follow his ways" (1 Samuel 8:3). In contrast to Samuel's integrity, his sons "turned aside after dishonest gain" and used their position to their own advantage. This unjust behavior displeased the elders of Israel, and it put in motion a cycle of kings that fills the pages of the Old Testament (vv. 4–5).

To refuse to walk in God's ways allows room for the perversion of those values. As a result, injustice flourishes. To walk in His ways means honesty and justice are clearly seen not only in our words but in our deeds as well. Those good deeds are never an end in themselves, but they help others recognize our Father in heaven and honor Him. **John Blase**

SEPTEMBER 28

Be a "Stand-Up" Guy

Jeremiah 26:12–15, 20–24

Ahikam son of Shaphan supported Jeremiah, and so he was not handed over to the people to be put to death. —Jeremiah 26:24

Clifford Williams was sentenced to die for a murder he didn't commit. From death row he vainly filed motions to reconsider the evidence against him. Each petition was denied—for forty-two years. Then attorney Shelley Thibodeau learned of his case. She found that not only was there no evidence to convict Williams but also that another man had confessed to the crime. At the age of seventy-six, Williams was finally exonerated and released.

The prophets Jeremiah and Uriah were also in deep trouble. They had told Judah that God promised to judge His people if they didn't repent (Jeremiah 26:12–13, 20). This message angered the people and officials of Judah, who sought to kill both prophets. They succeeded with Uriah. He fled to Egypt, but he was brought back to face the king, who "had him struck down with a sword" (v. 23). Why didn't they kill Jeremiah? In part because Ahikam "stood up for Jeremiah" (NLT), "and so he was not handed over to the people to be put to death" (v. 24).

We may not know anyone facing death, but we probably know someone who could use our support. Whose rights are trampled. Whose talents are dismissed. Whose voice isn't heard. It may be risky to step out like Thibodeau or Ahikam, but it's so right. Who needs us to stand up for them as God guides us? **Mike Wittmer**

The Problem of Suffering

Job 42:1–9

I am angry with you and your two friends, because you have not spoken the truth about me, as my servant Job has. —Job 42:7

"So what you're saying is, it may not be my fault." The woman's words took me by surprise. I had been a guest speaker at her church, and we were now discussing what I'd shared that morning. "I have a chronic illness," she explained, "and I have prayed, fasted, confessed my sins, and done everything else I was told to do to be healed. But I'm still sick, so I thought I was to blame."

I felt sad at the woman's confession. Having been given a spiritual "formula" to fix her problem, she had blamed herself when the formula hadn't worked. Even worse, this formulaic approach to suffering was disproved generations ago.

Simply put, this old formula says that if you're suffering, you must have sinned. When Job tragically lost his livestock, children, and health, his friends used the formula on him. "Who, being innocent, has ever perished?" Eliphaz said, suspecting Job's guilt (Job 4:7). Bildad even told Job that his children died only because they had sinned (8:4). Ignorant of the real cause of Job's calamities (1:6–2:10), they tormented him with simplistic reasons for his pain, later receiving God's rebuke (42:7).

Suffering is a part of living in a fallen world. As with Job, it can happen for reasons we may never know. But God has a purpose for you that goes beyond the pain you endure. Don't be discouraged by simplistic formulas, but be encouraged in God's love for you. Sheridan Voysey

SEPTEMBER 30

A Goal and a Purpose

Acts 20:17–24

My only aim is to finish the race and complete the task the Lord Jesus has given me. —Acts 20:24

In 2018, endurance athlete Colin O'Brady took a walk that had never been taken before. Pulling a supply sled behind him, O'Brady trekked across Antarctica entirely alone—a total of 932 miles in 54 days. It was a momentous journey of dedication and courage.

Commenting on his time alone with the ice, the cold, and the daunting distance, O'Brady said, "I was locked in a deep flow state [fully immersed in the endeavor] the entire time, equally focused on the end goal, while allowing my mind to recount the profound lessons of this journey."

For those of us who have put our faith in Jesus, that statement might strike a familiar chord. It sounds a lot like our calling as believers: focused on the goal of walking through life in a way that glorifies (honors) God and reveals Him to others. In Acts 20:24, Paul, no stranger to dangerous journeys, said, "I consider my life worth nothing to me; my only aim is to finish the race and complete the task the Lord Jesus has given me—the task of testifying to the good news of God's grace."

As we walk on in our relationship with Jesus, may we recognize what we know about the purpose for our journey and press on to the day we'll see our Savior face-to-face. **Dave Branon**

OCTOBER 1

Defending the Vulnerable

Mark 10:13–16

At just the right time, when we were still powerless, Christ died for the ungodly. —Romans 5:6

When Kathleen's teacher called her to the front of the grammar class to analyze a sentence, she panicked. As a recent transfer student, she hadn't learned that aspect of grammar. The class laughed at her.

Instantly the teacher sprang to her defense. "She can out-write any of you any day of the week!" he explained. Many years later, Kathleen gratefully recalled the moment: "I started that day to try to write as well as he said I could."

Eventually, Kathleen Parker would win a Pulitzer Prize for her writing.

As did Kathleen's teacher, Jesus identified with the defenseless and vulnerable. When His disciples kept children away from Him, He grew angry. "Let the little children come to me," He said, "and do not hinder them" (Mark 10:14). He reached out to a despised ethnic group, making the Good Samaritan the hero of His parable (Luke 10:25–37), and He offered genuine hope to a searching Samaritan woman at Jacob's well (John 4:1–26). He protected and forgave a woman trapped in adultery (John 8:1–11). And though we were utterly helpless, Christ gave His life for all of us (Romans 5:6).

When we defend the vulnerable and the marginalized, we give them a chance to realize their potential. We show them real love, and in a small but significant way we reflect the very heart of Jesus. **Tim Gustafson**

OCTOBER 2

The Measure of Love

John 15:9–17

Greater love has no one than this: to lay down one's life for one's friends. —John 15:13

On October 2, 1954, First Lieutenant James O. Conway was taking off from Boston Logan Airport, flying a plane that carried a load of munitions. When his plane became airborne, he suddenly lost power over Boston's bay. In an instant, Conway faced a brutal choice—eject from the plane and save his own life or crash the plane into the bay causing his own death.

If he ejected, however, the plane would crash into an East Boston neighborhood filled with homes and families. Amazingly, Conway chose to crash the plane into the bay—giving his life for the lives of others.

In John 15:13, Jesus said, "Greater love has no one than this: to lay down one's life for one's friends." The willingness to make the ultimate sacrifice to protect others shows a heart that cares more about the needs of others than the needs of self. Someone once said that "the measure of love is what one is willing to give up for it." God the Father loved so much that He gave up His Son. Christ loved so much that He gave up His life—even taking our sins on himself and dying in our place.

The measure of God's love for you is great. Have you accepted His love personally by trusting Jesus as your Savior? Bill Crowder

Second-Wind Strength

Isaiah 40:27–31

Come to me, all you who are weary and burdened, and I will give you rest. —Matthew 11:28

At the age of fifty-four I entered the Milwaukee marathon with two goals—to finish the race and to do it under five hours. My time would have been amazing if the second 13.1 miles went as well as the first. But the race was grueling, and the second-wind strength I'd hoped for never came. By the time I made it to the finish line, my steady stride had morphed into a painful walk.

Footraces aren't the only things that require second-wind strength; life's race does too. To endure, people who are tired and weary need God's help. Isaiah 40:27–31 beautifully weds poetry and prophecy to comfort and motivate people who need strength to keep going. Timeless words remind fatigued and discouraged people that the Lord isn't detached or uncaring (v. 27), that our plight doesn't escape His notice. These words breathe comfort and assurance, and they remind us of God's limitless power and endless knowledge (v. 28).

The second-wind strength described in verses 29–31 is just right for us—whether we're in the throes of raising and providing for our families, struggling through life under the weight of physical or financial burdens, or discouraged by relational tensions or spiritual challenges. Such is the strength that awaits those who—through meditating on the Scriptures and prayer—wait upon the Lord. Arthur Jackson

Hope Is Our Strategy

Micah 7:1–7

But as for me, I watch in hope for the Lord,
I wait for God my Savior; my God will hear me. —Micah 7:7

My favorite football team has lost eight consecutive games as I write this. With each loss, it's harder to hope this season can be redeemed for them. The coach has made changes weekly, but nothing he's done has resulted in wins. Talking with my coworkers, I've joked that merely wanting a different outcome can't guarantee it. "Hope is not a strategy," I've quipped.

That's true in football. But in our spiritual lives, it's just the opposite. Cultivating hope in God is not just a strategy; clinging to Him in faith and trust is the *only* strategy. This world often disappoints us, but hope can anchor us in God's truth and power during the turbulent times.

Micah understood this reality. He was heartbroken by how Israel had turned away from God. "What misery is mine!" he cried out. "The faithful have been swept from the land; not one upright person remains" (7:1–2). But then he refocused on his true hope: "But as for me, I watch in hope for the Lord, I wait for God my Savior; my God will hear me" (v. 7).

What does it take to maintain hope in harsh times? Micah shows us: Watching. Waiting. Praying. Remembering. God hears our cries even when our circumstances are overwhelming. In these moments, clinging to and acting in response to our hope in God is our strategy, the only strategy that will help us weather life's storms.

Adam Holz

For the Long Run

James 5:7–11

Be patient, then, brothers and sisters, until the LORD's coming. —James 5:7

A recent survey of more than one thousand adults discovered that most people take an average of eighteen minutes to lose their patience while waiting in line. Also, most people lose their patience in only nine minutes while on hold on the phone. Impatience is a common trait.

James wrote to a group of believers who were struggling with being patient for Jesus's return (James 5:7). They were living under exploitation and distressing times, and James encouraged them to "set the timer of their temper" for the long run. Challenging these believers to persevere under suffering, he tried to stimulate them to stand firm and to live sacrificially until the Lord returned to right every wrong. He wrote: "Be patient and stand firm, because the Lord's coming is near" (v. 8).

James called them to be like the farmer who waits patiently for the rain and the harvest (v. 7) and like the prophets and the patriarch Job who demonstrated perseverance in difficulties (vv. 10–11). The finish line was just ahead, and James encouraged the believers not to give up.

When we are being tried in a crucible of distress, God desires to help us continue living by faith and trusting in His compassion and mercy (v. 11). **Marvin Williams**

Stay Together

Ephesians 4:1–6

Keep the unity of the Spirit through the bond of peace. —Ephesians 4:3

Dewberry Baptist Church split in the 1800s over a chicken leg. Various versions of the story exist, but the account told by a current member was that two men fought over the last drumstick at a church potluck. One man said God wanted him to have it. The other replied God didn't care, and he really wanted it. The men became so furious that one moved a couple kilometers down the road and started Dewberry Baptist Church #2. Thankfully, the churches have settled their differences, and everyone concedes the reason for their split was ridiculous.

Jesus agrees. The night before His death Jesus prayed for His followers. May they "be one, Father, just as you are in me and I am in you" (John 7:21). May they "be brought to complete unity. Then the world will know that you sent me" (v. 23).

Paul agrees. He urges us to "make every effort to keep the unity of the Spirit through the bond of peace. There is one body and one Spirit" (Ephesians 4:3–4), and these cannot be divided.

We who weep for Christ's body broken for our sin must not tear apart His body, the church, with our anger, gossip, and cliques. Better to let ourselves be wronged than be guilty of the scandal of church division. Give the other guy the chicken leg—and some pie too! Mike Wittmer

Failing to Do Right

James 4:13–17

If anyone, then, knows the good they ought to do and doesn't do it, it is sin for them. —James 4:17

In his book *Eight Men Out*, Eliot Asinof records the events surrounding the notorious "Black Sox" scandal of 1919. Eight members of the Chicago White Sox baseball club were accused of taking bribes from gamblers in exchange for intentionally losing the World Series. Although they were never convicted in a court of law, all eight were banned from baseball for life.

But one of those players, Buck Weaver, claimed that he had played to win despite knowing about the conspiracy. Though Weaver's performance on the field supported his contention, baseball commissioner Kenesaw Mountain Landis ruled that any player who had knowledge of the scandal, yet chose not to stop it, would still be banned. Weaver was not punished for doing wrong but for failing to do right.

In his letter to the first-century church, James wrote, "If anyone, then, knows the good they ought to do and doesn't do it, it is sin for them" (4:17). In a world filled with evil and darkness, followers of Christ have the opportunity to shine their light. That often means we must resist the urge to do nothing.

When faced with the choice between doing good and failing to do anything at all, we must always choose to do what's right. **Bill Crowder**

Noticing Nature

Matthew 6:25–34

Look at the birds of the air; they do not sow or reap or store away in barns, and yet your heavenly Father feeds them. —Matthew 6:26

A friend and I recently visited a favorite walking spot of mine. Hiking up a windswept hill, we crossed a field of wildflowers that led to a forest of towering pine trees. We descended into a valley where we paused a moment to take it all in—the majesty of clouds high above us, the stream trickling nearby, the songs of numerous birds. Jason and I stood there silently for fifteen minutes, taking it all in.

As it turns out, our actions that day were deeply therapeutic. According to research from the University of Derby, people who stop to contemplate nature experience higher levels of happiness, lower levels of anxiety, and a greater desire to care for the earth. Trekking through the forest isn't enough, though. You have to watch the clouds, listen to the birds. The key isn't being in nature but noticing it.

Could there be a spiritual reason for nature's benefits? Paul said that creation reveals God's power and nature (Romans 1:20). God told Job to look at the sea, sky, and stars for evidence of His presence (Job 38–39). Jesus said that contemplating the "birds of the air" and "flowers of the field" could reveal God's care and reduce anxiety (Matthew 6:25–30).

Scientists wonder why nature affects us so positively. Maybe one reason is that by noticing nature we catch a glimpse of the God who created it and who notices us.

Sheridan Voysey

God's Special Treasure

1 Peter 2:4–10

But you are . . . God's special possession. —1 Peter 2:9

Imagine a vast throne room. Seated on the throne is a great king. He's surrounded by all manner of attendants, each on their best behavior. Now imagine a box that sits at the king's feet. From time to time the king reaches down and runs his hands through the contents. And what's in the box? Jewels, gold, and gemstones particular to the king's tastes. This box holds the king's treasures, a collection that brings him great joy. Can you see that image in your mind's eye?

The Hebrew word for this treasure is *segulah*, and it means "special possession." That word is found in such Old Testament Scriptures as Exodus 19:5, Deuteronomy 7:6, and Psalm 135:4, where it refers to the nation of Israel. But that same word picture shows up in the New Testament by way of the pen of Peter the apostle. He's describing the "people of God," those who "have received mercy" (1 Peter 2:10), a collection that goes beyond the nation of Israel. In other words, he's talking about those who believe in Jesus, both Jew and gentile. And he writes, "But you are . . . God's special possession" (v. 9).

Imagine that! The great and powerful King of heaven considers you among His special treasures. He has rescued you from the grip of sin and death. He claims you as His own. The King's voice says, "This one I love. This one is mine." **John Blase**

OCTOBER 10

Present in the Storm

Psalm 46

The Lord Almighty is with us; the God of Jacob is our fortress. —Psalm 46:7

Fire swept through the home of a family of six from our church. Although the father and son survived, the father was still hospitalized while his wife, mother, and two small children were laid to rest. Unfortunately, heartbreaking events like this continue to happen again and again. When they're replayed, so is the age-old question: Why do bad things happen to good people? And it doesn't surprise us that this old question doesn't have new answers.

Yet the truth that the psalmist puts forth in Psalm 46 has also been replayed and rehearsed and embraced repeatedly. "God is our refuge and strength, an ever-present help in trouble" (v. 1). The conditions described in verses 2–3 are catastrophic—earth and mountains moving and sea waters raging. We shudder when we imagine being in the midst of the stormy conditions poetically pictured here. But sometimes we do find ourselves there—in the swirling throes of a terminal illness, tossed about by a devastating financial crisis, stung and stunned by the deaths of loved ones.

It's tempting to rationalize that the presence of trouble means the absence of God. But the truth of Scripture counters such notions. "The Lord Almighty is with us; the God of Jacob is our fortress" (vv. 7, 11). He is present when our circumstances are unbearable, and we find comfort in His character: He is good, loving, and trustworthy. **Arthur Jackson**

Fleeing to Strength

1 Corinthians 6:12–20

You were bought at a price. Therefore honor God with your bodies. —1 Corinthians 6:20

"Parry four!"

When I began fencing in high school, my coach would shout the correct defensive position ("parry") against the move he was making. When he extended his weapon and lunged, to repel the attack I had to listen and respond immediately.

That example of active listening brings to mind the prompt obedience Scripture calls for in the area of sexual temptation. In 1 Corinthians 6:18 Paul writes to believers tempted to solicit pagan temple prostitutes, telling them to "flee from sexual immorality." Sometimes we are to "stand firm" in challenging circumstances (Galatians 5:1; see Ephesians 6:11), but here the Bible practically shouts our best defense: "Run away!"

Immediate action guards against compromise. Small compromises can lead to devastating defeats. An unrestrained thought, a glance in the wrong place on the Internet, a flirting friendship when you're already married—each are steps that take us where we shouldn't go and put distance between us and God.

When we flee temptation, God also provides a place to run. Through Jesus's death on the cross for our sins, He offers us hope, forgiveness, and a new beginning—no matter where we've been or what we've done. When we run to Jesus in our weakness, He sets us free to live in His strength. **James Banks**

Self-Checking

Lamentations 3:37–42

Let us examine our ways and test them,
and let us return to the LORD. —Lamentations 3:40

Recently I read through a stack of World War II–era letters my dad sent to my mother. He was in North Africa, and she was in West Virginia. Dad, a second lieutenant in the US Army, was tasked with censoring soldiers' letters—keeping sensitive information from enemy eyes. So, it was rather humorous to see—on the outside of his letters to his wife—a stamp that said, "Censored by 2nd Lt. John Branon." Indeed, he had even cut out lines from his own letters!

Self-censoring is really a good idea for all of us. Several times in Scripture, the writers mention the importance of taking a good long look at ourselves to find what's not right—not God-honoring. The psalmist, for example, prayed, "Search me, God, and know my heart. . . . See if there is any offensive way in me" (Psalm 139:23–24). Jeremiah put it like this: "Let us examine our ways and test them, and let us return to the LORD" (Lamentations 3:40). And Paul, speaking of our heart condition at the time of communion, said, "Everyone ought to examine themselves" (1 Corinthians 11:28).

The Holy Spirit can help us turn from any attitudes or actions that don't please God. So, before we head out into the world today, let's stop and seek the Spirit's help in doing some self-checking so we can "return to the LORD" in fellowship with Him. **Dave Branon**

A Longing in Stone

Deuteronomy 34:1–5

I have let you see it with your eyes, but you will not cross over into it. —Deuteronomy 34:4

"Ah, every pier is a longing in stone!" says a line in Fernando Pessoa's Portuguese poem "Ode Marítima." Pessoa's pier represents the emotions we feel as a ship moves slowly away from us. The vessel departs but the pier remains, an enduring monument to hopes and dreams, partings and yearnings. We ache for what's lost, and for what we can't quite reach.

The Portuguese word translated "longing" (*saudade*) refers to a nostalgic yearning we feel—a deep ache that defies definition. The poet is describing the indescribable.

We might say that Mount Nebo was Moses's "longing in stone." From Nebo he gazed into the promised land—a land he would never reach. God's words to Moses—"I have let you see it with your eyes, but you will not cross over into it" (Deuteronomy 34:4)—might seem harsh. But if that's all we see, we miss the heart of what's happening. God is speaking immense comfort to Moses: "This is the land I promised on oath to Abraham, Isaac and Jacob when I said, 'I will give it to your descendants'" (v. 4). Very soon, Moses would leave Nebo for a land far better than Canaan (v. 5).

Life often finds us standing on the pier. Loved ones depart; hopes fade; dreams die. Amid it all we sense echoes of Eden and hints of heaven. Our longings point us to God. He is the fulfillment we yearn for. Tim Gustafson

OCTOBER 14

The Knife Angel

Isaiah 2:1–4

Nation will not take up sword against nation,
nor will they train for war anymore. —Isaiah 2:4

When knife crime rose across the United Kingdom, the British Ironwork Centre came up with an idea. Working with local police forces, the Centre built and placed two hundred deposit boxes around the country and ran an amnesty campaign. One hundred thousand knives were anonymously surrendered, some still with blood on their blades. These were then shipped to artist Alfie Bradley, who blunted them, inscribed some with the names of young knife-crime victims, plus messages of regret from ex-offenders. All 100,000 weapons were then welded together to create the *Knife Angel*—a twenty-seven-foot-high angelic sculpture with shimmering steel wings.

When I stood before the *Knife Angel*, I wondered how many thousands of wounds had been prevented by its existence. I thought too of Isaiah's vision of the new heavens and earth (Isaiah 65:17): a place where children won't die young (v. 20) or grow up in crime-breeding poverty (vv. 22–23) and a place where knife crime is no more because all swords have been reshaped and given more creative purposes (2:4).

That new world isn't yet here, but we are to pray and serve until its arrival (Matthew 6:10). In its own way, the *Knife Angel* gives us a glimpse of God's promised future. Swords become plow shares. Weapons become artworks. In what other ways can we learn to glimpse that future a little more? **Sheridan Voysey**

What's Your Name?

Revelation 2:12–17

I will also give that person a white stone
with a new name written on it. —Revelation 2:17

Someone said we go through life with three names: the name our parents gave us, the name others give us (our reputation), and the name we give ourselves (our character). The name others give us matters, as "a good name is more desirable than great riches; to be esteemed is better than silver or gold" (Proverbs 22:1). But while reputation is important, character matters more.

There's yet another name that's even more important. Jesus told the Christians in Pergamum that though their reputation had suffered some well-deserved hits, He had a new name reserved in heaven for those who fight back and conquer temptation. "To the one who is victorious, I will give . . . a white stone with a new name written on it, known only to the one who receives it" (Revelation 2:17).

We aren't sure why Jesus promised a white stone. Is it an award for winning? A token for admission to the messianic banquet? Perhaps it's similar to what jurors once used to vote for acquittal. We simply don't know. Whatever it is, God promises our new name will wipe away our shame (see Isaiah 62:1–5).

Our reputation may be tattered, and our character may be seemingly beyond repair. But neither name ultimately defines us. It's not what others call you nor even what you call yourself that matters. You are who Jesus says you are. Live into your new name. **Mike Wittmer**

OCTOBER 16

I Invented It

Job 38:4–18

Where were you when I laid the earth's foundations?
Tell me, if you understand. —Job 38:4

Willard S. Boyle, Nobel Prize winner in physics, was the coinventor of the "electronic eye" behind the digital camera and the Hubble telescope. He was in the market for a new digital camera and visited a store in Halifax, Nova Scotia. The salesman tried to explain the complexity of the camera to Boyle, but he stopped because he felt it was too complicated for Boyle to understand. Boyle then bluntly said to the salesman: "No need to explain. I invented it."

After God allowed Satan to test Job by taking away his family, his health, and his possessions (Job 1–2), Job lamented the day of his birth (chapter 3). In the following chapters, Job questioned why God would allow him to endure so much suffering. Then with divine bluntness, God reminded Job that He "invented" life and created the world (chapters 38–41). God invited him to rethink what he had said. In drawing attention to His sovereign power and the depth of His wisdom displayed everywhere on earth (38:4–41), God exposed the immensity of Job's ignorance.

If we're tempted to tell God how life should work, let's remember that He invented it! Let's allow Him to help us humbly acknowledge our ignorance and rely on Him—the Creator of the universe. Marvin Williams

Sowing and Reaping

Galatians 6:7–9

Do not be deceived, God cannot be mocked.
A man reaps what he sows. —Galatians 6:7

It seemed somewhat innocent enough at the time.

I had just come home from high school and told my mom that I was going to a friend's house to play football. She insisted that I stay home and do my homework. Instead, I slipped out the back door and spent the next two hours making tackles and touchdowns in my friend's backyard. But on the last play, I was tackled into a swing set and knocked out my front tooth. It hurt like crazy, but not as badly as telling my parents.

That choice to disobey put me on a ten-year path of dental problems and pain that have continuing implications today. Ballplayer Roy Hobbs said in the movie *The Natural*, "Some mistakes you never stop paying for."

Centuries earlier, Paul captured the same idea in the universal law of sowing and reaping. He said, "A man reaps what he sows" (Galatians 6:7). Our choices often have a reach and impact that we could never imagine. Thus the apostle's words remind us to choose wisely.

The choices we make today produce the consequences we reap tomorrow. It's far better to avoid sin in the first place than to struggle to overcome its consequences.

Lord, we need your wisdom to help us make good choices, and forgiveness when we make bad choices.
Bill Crowder

OCTOBER 18

Whose Prisoner?

Ephesians 3:1–9

This grace was given me: preach to the Gentiles the boundless riches of Christ. —Ephesians 3:8

A story is told of Scottish minister Alexander Whyte (1836–1921), who was able to look at the bleakest situation and yet find something to be thankful for. On a dark Sunday morning when the weather was freezing, wet, and stormy, one of his deacons whispered, "I am sure the preacher won't be able to thank God for anything on a day like this. It's absolutely horrible outside!" The pastor began the service by praying, "We thank Thee, O God, that the weather is not always like this."

The apostle Paul also saw the best in every situation. Consider his circumstances as he wrote to the church in Ephesus while he awaited trial before the Roman emperor Nero. Most people would have concluded that he was a prisoner of Rome. But Paul saw himself as a prisoner of Christ. He thought of his hardship as an opportunity to bring the gospel to the Gentiles.

These words of Paul should challenge us: "Although I am less than the least of all the Lord's people, this grace was given me: to preach to the Gentiles the boundless riches of Christ" (Ephesians 3:8). Paul, a prisoner of Christ, saw himself as being given the privilege to serve God and present the "riches of Christ" to many.

Whose prisoner are we? **Albert Lee**

The Man Who Couldn't Talk

Psalm 96

Great is the LORD and most worthy of praise. —Psalm 96:4

Sitting in his wheelchair at a senior citizens home in Belize, a man joyfully listened as a group of American high school teenagers sang about Jesus. Later, as some of the teens gathered around him and tried to communicate with him, they discovered he couldn't talk. A stroke had robbed him of his ability to speak.

Since they couldn't carry on a conversation with the man, the teens decided to sing to him. As they began to sing, something amazing happened. The man who couldn't talk began to sing. With enthusiasm, he belted out "How Great Thou Art" right along with his new friends.

It was a remarkable moment for everyone. This man's love for God broke through the barriers and poured out in audible worship—heartfelt, joyous worship.

We all have worship barriers from time to time. Maybe it's a relationship conflict or a money problem. Or it could be a heart that's grown a bit cold in its relationship to God.

Our nontalking friend reminds us that the greatness and majesty of our almighty God can overcome any barrier. "O Lord, my God—when I in awesome wonder, consider all the worlds Thy hands have made!"

Struggling in your worship? Reflect on how great our God is by reading a passage such as Psalm 96, and you too may find your obstacles and objections replaced by praise.

Dave Branon

OCTOBER 20

Calming the Storm

Mark 4:35–41

He got up, rebuked the wind and said to the waves, "Quiet! Be still!" Then the wind died down and it was completely calm. —Mark 4:39

While Hurricane Katrina headed toward the coast of Mississippi back in 2005, a retired pastor and his wife left their house and went to a shelter to wait it out. Their daughter pleaded with them to go to Atlanta where she could take care of them, but the couple couldn't get any money because the banks were closed. After the storm, they returned to their home to get a few belongings and were able to salvage only a few soaked family photos. Then, when the man was taking his father's photo out of its frame so it could dry, $366 fell out—precisely the amount needed for two plane tickets to Atlanta.

In the dramatic narrative of Mark 4:35–41, Jesus had instructed His disciples to cross to the other side of the Sea of Galilee, and then He went to sleep in the boat. When a quick and violent storm blew in, the disciples dripped as much with fear and anxiety as water from the waves. They woke Jesus, saying, "Teacher, don't you care if we drown?" (v. 38). Jesus stood up, "rebuked the wind," and with little three words, "Quiet! Be still!" muzzled the waves.

We all experience storms—persecutions, financial troubles, illnesses, disappointments, loneliness—and Jesus does not always prevent them. But He has promised never to leave us or forsake us (Hebrews 13:5). He can keep us calm in the storm because of His very presence—and sometimes He calms the storm. **Marvin Williams**

Navigating Life's Rapids

Psalm 32:8–11

I will instruct you and teach you in the way you should go; I will counsel you with my loving eye on you. —Psalm 32:8

"Everybody on the left, give me three strong forward strokes!" our whitewater raft guide shouted. Those on the left dug in, pulling our raft away from a churning vortex. For several hours, we'd learned the importance of listening to our guide's instructions. His steady voice enabled six people with little rafting experience to work together to plot the safest course down a raging river.

Life has its share of whitewater rapids, doesn't it? One moment, it's smooth sailing. Then, in a flash, we're paddling like mad to avoid suddenly swirling whirlpools. Those tense moments make us keenly aware of our need for a skilled guide, a trusted voice to help us navigate turbulent times.

In Psalm 32, God promises to be that voice: "I will instruct you and teach you in the way you should go" (v. 8). Backing up, we see that confessing our sins (v. 5) and prayerfully seeking Him (v. 6) play a role in hearing Him too. Still, I take comfort in the fact that God promises, "I will counsel you with my loving eye on you" (v. 8), a reminder that His guidance flows from His love. Near the end of the chapter, the psalmist concludes, "The Lord's unfailing love surrounds the one who trusts in him" (v. 10). And as we trust Him, we can rest in His promise to guide us through life's rockiest rapids. Adam Holz

OCTOBER 22

Speak Up!

Colossians 4:2–6

Pray . . . that God may open a door for our message, so that we may proclaim the mystery of Christ. —Colossians 4:3

Brittany exclaimed to her coworker at the restaurant, "There's that man! There's that man!" She was referring to Melvin, who first encountered her under different circumstances. While Melvin was tending to the lawn of his church, the Spirit prompted him to start a conversation with a woman who appeared to be a prostitute. Her reply when he invited her to church was: "Do you know what I do? They wouldn't want me in there." As Melvin told her about the love of Jesus and assured her of His power to change her life, tears streamed down her face. Now, some weeks later, Brittany was working in a new environment, living proof of the power of Jesus to change lives.

In the context of encouraging believers to be devoted to prayer, the apostle Paul made a twofold request: "Pray for us, too, that God may open a door for our message, so that we may proclaim the mystery of Christ, for which I am in chains. Pray that I may proclaim it clearly, as I should" (Colossians 4:3–4).

Have you prayed for opportunities to speak boldly and clearly for Jesus? What a fitting prayer! Such prayers can lead His followers, like Melvin, to speak about Him in unexpected places and to unexpected people. Speaking up for Jesus can seem uncomfortable, but the rewards—changed lives—have a way of compensating for our discomforts. **Arthur Jackson**

A True Disciple of Jesus

John 15:1–8

I am the vine; you are the branches. —John 15:5

When Christian Mustad showed his Van Gogh landscape to art collector Auguste Pellerin, Pellerin took one look and said it wasn't authentic. Mustad hid the painting in his attic, where it remained for fifty years. Mustad died, and the painting was evaluated off and on over the next four decades. Each time it was determined to be a fake—until 2012, when an expert used a computer to count the thread separations in the painting's canvas. He discovered it had been cut from the same canvas as another work of Van Gogh. Mustad had owned a real Van Gogh all along.

Do you feel like a fake? Do you fear that if people examined you, they'd see how little you pray, give, and serve? Are you tempted to hide in the attic, away from prying eyes?

Look deeper, beneath the colors and contours of your life. If you've turned from your own ways and put your faith in Jesus, then you and He belong to the same canvas. To use Jesus's picture, "I am the vine; you are the branches" (John 15:5). Christ and you form a seamless whole.

Resting in Jesus makes you a true disciple of Him. It's also the only way to improve your picture. He said, "If you remain in me and I in you, you will bear much fruit; apart from me you can do nothing" (v. 5). **Mike Wittmer**

OCTOBER 24

Milk Comes First

Hebrews 5:11–6:2

Solid food is for the mature. —Hebrews 5:14

In the seventh century, what is now called the United Kingdom was many kingdoms often at war. When one king, Oswald of Northumbria, became a believer in Jesus, he called for a missionary to bring the gospel to his region. A man named Corman was sent, but things didn't go well. Finding the people "stubborn," "barbarous," and uninterested in his preaching, he returned home frustrated.

"I am of the opinion," a monk named Aidan told Corman, "that you were more severe to your unlearned hearers than you ought to have been." Instead of giving the Northumbrians "the milk of more easy doctrine," Corman had given them teaching they couldn't yet grasp. Aidan went to Northumbria, adapted his preaching to the people's understanding, and thousands became believers in Jesus.

Aidan got this sensitive approach to mission from Scripture. "I gave you milk, not solid food," Paul told the Corinthians, "for you were not yet ready for it" (1 Corinthians 3:2). Before right living can be expected from people, Hebrews says, basic teaching about Jesus, repentance, and baptism must be grasped (Hebrews 5:13–6:2). While maturity should follow (5:14), let's not miss the order. Milk comes before meat. People can't obey teaching they don't understand.

The faith of the Northumbrians ultimately spread to the rest of the country and beyond. Like Aidan, when sharing the gospel with others, let's meet people where they are. **Sheridan Voysey**

Redeeming the Season

Psalm 104:10–23

He made the moon to mark the seasons. —Psalm 104:19

Leisa wanted a way to redeem the season. So many of the autumn decorations she saw seemed to celebrate death, sometimes in gruesome and macabre ways.

Determined to counter the darkness in some small way, Leisa began to write things she was grateful for with a permanent marker on a large pumpkin. "Sunshine" was the first item. Soon visitors were adding to her list. Some entries were whimsical: "doodling," for instance. Others were practical: "a warm house," "a working car." Still others were poignant, like the name of a departed loved one. A chain of gratitude began to wind its way around the pumpkin.

Psalm 104 offers a litany of praise to God for things we easily overlook. "[God] makes springs pour water into the ravines," sang the poet (v. 10). "He makes grass grow for the cattle, and plants for people to cultivate" (v. 14). Even the night is seen as good and fitting. "You bring darkness, it becomes night, and all the beasts of the forest prowl" (v. 20). But then, "The sun rises . . . . People go out to their work, to their labor until evening" (vv. 22–23). For all these things, the psalmist concluded, "I will sing praise to my God as long as I live" (v. 33).

In a world that doesn't know how to deal with death, even the smallest offering of praise to our Creator can become a shining contrast of hope. Tim Gustafson

Preach or Plow?

Ephesians 4:4–16

From [Christ] the whole body, joined and held together by every supporting ligament, grows and builds itself up in love, as each part does its work. —Ephesians 4:16

According to the family legend, two brothers, one named Billy and the other Melvin, were standing on the family's dairy farm one day when they saw an airplane doing some skywriting. The boys watched as the plane sketched out the letters "GP" overhead.

Both brothers decided that what they saw had meaning for them. One thought it meant "Go preach." The other read it as "Go plow." Later, one of the boys, Billy Graham, dedicated himself to preaching the gospel, becoming an icon of evangelism. His brother Melvin went on to faithfully run the family dairy farm for many years.

Skywriting signs aside, if God did call Billy to preach and Melvin to plow, as seems to be the case, they both honored God through their vocations. While Billy had a long preaching career, his success doesn't mean that his brother's obedience to his calling to plow was any less important.

While God does assign some to be in what we call full-time ministry (Ephesians 4:11–12), that doesn't mean those in other jobs and roles aren't doing something just as important. In either case, as Paul said, "each part [should do] its work" (v. 16). That means honoring Jesus by faithfully using the gifts He's given us. When we do, whether we "go preach" or "go plow," we can make a difference for Jesus wherever we serve or work. **Dave Branon**

In Progress or Completed?

Hebrews 10:5–14

For by one sacrifice he has made perfect forever those who are being made holy. —Hebrews 10:14

It's satisfying to finish a job. Each month, for instance, one of my job responsibilities gets moved from one category to another, from "In Progress" to "Completed." I love clicking that "Completed" button. But last month when I clicked it, I thought, *If only I could overcome rough spots in my faith so easily!* It can seem like the Christian life is always in progress, never completed.

Then I remembered Hebrews 10:14. It describes how Christ's sacrifice redeems us totally. So, in one important sense, that "completed button" has been pressed for us. Jesus's death did for us what we couldn't do for ourselves: He made us acceptable in God's eyes when we place our faith in Him. It is finished, as Jesus himself said (John 19:30). Paradoxically, even though His sacrifice is complete and total, we spend the rest of our lives living into that spiritual reality—"being made holy," as the author of Hebrews writes.

The fact that Jesus has finished something that's still being worked out in our lives is hard to understand. When I'm struggling spiritually, it's encouraging to remember that Jesus's sacrifice for me—and for you—is complete . . . even if our living it out in this life is still a work in progress. Nothing can stop His intended end from being achieved eventually: being transformed into His likeness (see 2 Corinthians 3:18). **Adam Holz**

OCTOBER 28

Listening Beyond the Stars

Isaiah 55:6–9

Seek the LORD while he may be found. —Isaiah 55:6

Imagine life without mobile phones, Wi-Fi, GPS, Bluetooth devices, or microwave ovens. That's the way it is in the little town of Green Bank, West Virginia, known as "the quietest town in America." It's also the location of the Green Bank Observatory, the world's largest steerable radio telescope. The telescope needs "quiet" to "listen" to naturally occurring radio waves emitted by the movement of pulsars and galaxies in deep space. It has a surface area larger than a football field and stands in the center of the National Radio Quiet Zone, a 13,000-square-mile area established to prevent electronic interference to the telescope's extreme sensitivity.

This intentional quiet enables scientists to hear "the music of the spheres." It also reminds me of our need to quiet ourselves enough to listen to the One who created the universe. God communicated to a wayward and distracted people through the prophet Isaiah, "Give ear and come to me; listen, that you may live. I will make an everlasting covenant with you" (Isaiah 55:3). God promises His faithful love to all who will seek Him and turn to Him for forgiveness.

We listen intentionally to God by turning from our distractions to meet Him in Scripture and in prayer. God isn't distant. He longs for us to make time for Him so He can be the priority of our daily lives and then for eternity.

James Banks

Burying Our Heads

2 Samuel 12:1–14

If someone is caught in a sin, you who live by the Spirit should restore that person gently. —Galatians 6:1

Contrary to common belief, the ostrich does not bury its head in the sand to ignore danger. An ostrich can run at a speed of forty-five miles per hour, kick powerfully, and peck aggressively with its beak. As the largest and fastest bird in the world, it doesn't need to bury its head.

"Burying your head in the sand" is a saying that describes someone who wants to ignore his shortcomings or those of others. The prophet Nathan did not allow King David to forget his sins of adultery and murder (2 Samuel 12:1–14). It took a brave man to confront a king about his errors. Yet Nathan was obedient to God and wise in his approach.

The apostle Paul urged the early church to confront sin. He said, "If someone is caught in a sin, you who live by the Spirit should restore that person gently. But watch yourselves or you also may be tempted" (Galatians 6:1). We are to confront our brothers and sisters in Christ about their sin with the view of restoring them to fellowship with God. We must also recognize that we are not immune to the same temptations.

We shouldn't go looking for sin in the lives of other believers, of course. But neither should we bury our head in the sand when it needs to be confronted. **Albert Lee**

OCTOBER 30

Behind the Scenes

John 3:22–31

He must become greater; I must become less. —John 3:30

The outreach activities of our church culminated with a city wide service. As the team that had organized and led the events—comprised of our youth music group, counselors, and church leaders—walked onto the stage, we all excitedly applauded and poured out our appreciation for their hard work.

One man, however, was hardly noticeable, yet he was the leader of the team. When I saw him a few days later, I thanked and congratulated him for his work and said, "We hardly noticed you during the program."

"I like to work in the background," he said. He was not concerned with getting recognition for himself. It was time for those who did the work to receive appreciation.

His quiet demeanor was an entire sermon to me. It was a reminder that when serving the Lord, I need not seek to be recognized. I can give honor to God whether or not I'm openly appreciated by others. A Christ-first attitude can subdue any petty jealousies or unhealthy competition.

Jesus, who is "above all" (John 3:31), "must become greater; I must become less" (v. 30). When we have this attitude, we will seek the progress of God's work. It is Christ, not us, who should be the focus of all we do. **Lawrence Darmani**

Tell Me a Story

Mark 4:26–34

He did not say anything to them without using a parable. —Mark 4:34

"Once upon a time . . ."

Those four words just might be among the most powerful in the entire world. Some of my earliest memories as a boy contain a variation on that potent phrase. My mother came home one day with a large, hardcover illustrated edition of biblical stories—*My Good Shepherd Bible Story Book.* Every evening before lights-out, my brother and I would sit expectantly as she read to us of a time long ago filled with interesting people and the God who loved them. Those stories became a lens for how we looked at the great big world.

The undisputed greatest storyteller ever? Jesus of Nazareth. He knows we all carry inside us an innate love for stories, so that was the medium He consistently used to communicate His good news: Once upon a time there was a man who scattered "seed on the ground" (Mark 4:26). Once upon a time there was "a mustard seed" (v. 31), and on and on. Mark's gospel clearly indicates that Jesus used stories in His interactions with everyday people (v. 34) as a way of helping them see the world more clearly and understand more thoroughly the God who loved them.

That's wise to remember as we desire to share with others God's good news of mercy and grace. The use of story is almost impossible to resist. **John Blase**

NOVEMBER 1

Do Whatever

Ecclesiastes 2:17–25

For without him, who can eat or find enjoyment? —Ecclesiastes 2:25

In a recent film, a self-proclaimed "genius" rants to the camera about the world's "horror, corruption, ignorance, and poverty," declaring life to be godless and absurd. While such thinking isn't unusual in many modern films, what's interesting is where it leads. In the end, the lead character implores the audience to do whatever it takes to find happiness—including leaving traditional morality behind.

But will "do whatever" work? Facing his own despair at life's horrors, the Old Testament writer of Ecclesiastes gave it a try long ago, searching for happiness through pleasure (Ecclesiastes 2:1, 10), grand work projects (vv. 4–6), riches (vv. 7–9), and philosophical inquiry (vv. 12–16). And his assessment? "All of it is meaningless, a chasing after the wind" (v. 17). None of these things is immune to death, disaster, or injustice (5:13–17).

Only one thing brings the writer of Ecclesiastes back from despair. Despite life's trials, we find fulfillment when God is part of our living and working: "For without him, who can eat or find enjoyment?" (2:25). "Remember your Creator" he says (12:1). "Fear God and keep his commandments" (v. 13).

Without God as our center, life's pleasures and sorrows lead only to disillusionment. Sheridan Voysey

How They'll Know

Acts 11:19–26

The disciples were called Christians first at Antioch. —Acts 11:26

"The Gathering" in northern Thailand is an interdenominational, international church. On one Sunday, believers in Jesus from Korea, Ghana, Pakistan, China, Bangladesh, the US, the Philippines, and other countries came together in a humble, thread-worn hotel conference room. They sang "In Christ Alone" and "I Am a Child of God," lyrics that were especially poignant in that setting.

No one brings people together like Jesus does. He's been doing it from the start. In the first century, Antioch contained eighteen different ethnic groups, each living in its own part of the city. When believers first came to Antioch, they spread the word about Jesus "only among Jews" (Acts 11:19). That wasn't God's plan for the church, however. Others soon came who "began to speak to Greeks [gentiles] also, telling them the good news about the Lord Jesus," and "a great number of people believed and turned to the Lord" (vv. 20–21). People in the city noticed that Jesus was healing centuries of animosity between Jews and Greeks, and they declared this multiethnic church should be called "Christians," or "little Christs" (v. 26).

It can be challenging for us to reach across ethnic, social, and economic boundaries to embrace those different from us. But this difficulty is our opportunity. If it wasn't hard, we wouldn't need Jesus to do it. And few would notice we're following Him. Mike Wittmer

Strong Conqueror

John 18:10–14, 36–37

My kingdom is from another place. —John 18:36

Most of us hope for good government. We vote, we serve, and we speak out for causes we believe are fair and just. But political solutions remain powerless to change the condition of our hearts.

Many of Jesus's followers anticipated a Messiah who would bring a vigorous political response to Rome and its heavy-handed oppression. Peter was no exception. When Roman soldiers came to arrest Christ, Peter drew his sword and took a swing at the head of the high priest's servant, lopping off his ear in the process.

Jesus halted Peter's one-man war, saying, "Put your sword away! Shall I not drink the cup the Father has given me?" (John 18:11). Hours later, Jesus would tell Pilate, "My kingdom is not of this world. If it were, my servants would fight to prevent my arrest by the Jewish leaders" (v. 36).

The Lord's restraint in that moment, as His life hung in the balance, astonishes us when we ponder the scope of His mission. On a future day, He will lead the armies of heaven into battle. John wrote, "With justice he judges and wages war" (Revelation 19:11).

But as He endured the ordeal of His arrest, trial, and crucifixion, Jesus kept His Father's will in view. By embracing death on the cross, He set in motion a chain of events that truly transforms hearts. And in the process, our Strong Conqueror defeated death itself. **Tim Gustafson**

Money Talks

Luke 12:13–21

For the love of money is a root of all kinds of evil. —1 Timothy 6:10

As I was driving home from the office, I saw a minivan proudly displaying a bumper sticker that read: "Money Talks: Mine Says Goodbye." I think a lot of people can relate to that sentiment.

Much of our living is spent acquiring and using money, which doesn't last. The stock market crashes. Prices go up. Thieves steal others' goods. Things wear out and break down, requiring the acquisition and expenditure of more money to replace what has been lost. The temporary nature of material wealth makes it a poor bargain in the search for security in an insecure world. Money is much better at saying goodbye than it is at sticking around.

Nowhere does the Bible say it's wrong to have money or the things that money can buy. Where we lose our way is when money becomes the driving purpose of our lives. Like the rich man and his barns (Luke 12:13–21), we end up pursuing the accumulation of things that eventually will be forfeited—if not in life, then certainly at death.

How tragic to live our entire lives, only to end them with nothing of eternal worth to show for our labors. To paraphrase Jesus's words, it is much better to be rich toward God than to work for treasure that can't last (v. 21). **Bill Crowder**

NOVEMBER 5

Blocked Prayers

Mark 11:20–25

When you stand praying, if you hold anything against anyone, forgive them, so that your Father in heaven may forgive you your sins. —Mark 11:25

For fourteen years, the Mars rover *Opportunity* communicated with the people at NASA's Jet Propulsion Laboratory. After it landed in 2004, it traversed twenty-eight miles, took thousands of images, and analyzed many materials. But in 2018, communication between *Opportunity* and scientists ended when a major dust storm coated its solar panels, causing the rover to lose power.

Is it possible that we can allow "dust" to block our communication with Someone outside of our world? When it comes to prayer—communicating with God—there are certain things that can get in the way. Scripture says that sin can block our relationship with God. "If I had cherished sin in my heart, the Lord would not have listened" (Psalm 66:18). Jesus instructs, "When you stand praying, if you hold anything against anyone, forgive them, so that your Father in heaven may forgive you your sins" (Mark 11:25). Our communication with God can also be hindered by doubt and relationship problems (James 1:5–7; 1 Peter 3:7).

Opportunity's blockage of communication seems to be permanent. But our prayers don't have to be blocked. By the work of the Holy Spirit, God lovingly draws us to restored communication with Him. As we confess our sins and turn to Him, by God's grace we experience the greatest communication the universe has ever known: one-to-one prayer between us and our holy God. **Dave Branon**

Together We Win

Exodus 17:8–13

Two are better than one . . . : If either of them falls down, one can help the other up. —Ecclesiastes 4:9–10

In the middle of the night, Pastor Samuel Baggaga received a call asking him to come to the home of a church member. When he arrived, he found a house engulfed by fire. The father, though burned himself, had reentered the home to rescue one of his children and emerged with an unconscious daughter. The hospital, in this rural Ugandan setting, was six miles away. With no transportation available, the pastor and the father started running to the hospital with the child. When one of them tired from carrying the injured girl, the other one took over. Together they made the journey; the father and his daughter were treated and then fully recovered.

In Exodus 17:8–13 the Lord orchestrated a great victory that included the efforts of Joshua, who led fighting men on the battlefield; and Moses, who kept his hands raised while holding the staff of God. When Moses's hands grew weary, Aaron and Hur assisted by each holding up one of his hands until the setting of the sun and the defeat of the enemy.

The value of interdependence can never be underestimated. God, in His kindness, graciously provides people as His agents for mutual good. Listening ears and helpful hands, as well as wise, comforting, and correcting words, along with other resources, come to us and through us to others. Together we win and God gets the glory! **Arthur Jackson**

Warning Lights

Joel 2:12–17

"Even now," declares the LORD, "return to me with all your heart, with fasting and weeping and mourning." —Joel 2:12

I didn't think the hesitation in my car engine and that little yellow "check engine" light on my dashboard really needed my immediate attention. I sang it away, saying that I would get to it tomorrow. However, the next morning when I turned the key to start my car, it wouldn't start. My first reaction was frustration, knowing that this would mean money, time, and inconvenience. My second thought was more of a resolution: *I need to pay attention to warning lights that are trying to get my attention—they can mean something is wrong.*

In Joel 2:12–17, we read that God used the prophet Joel to encourage His people to pay attention to the warning light on their spiritual dashboard. Prosperity had caused them to become complacent and negligent in their commitment to the Lord. Their faith had degenerated into empty formalism and their lives into moral bankruptcy. So, God sent a locust plague to ruin crops in order to get His people's attention, causing them to change their behavior and turn to Him with their whole heart.

What warning lights are flashing in your life? What needs to be tuned up or repaired through confession and repentance? **Marvin Williams**

Full Attention

1 Thessalonians 5:12–18

Rejoice always, pray continually, give thanks in all circumstances. —1 Thessalonians 5:16–18

Technology today seems to demand our constant attention. The modern "miracle" of the Internet (easily accessible via the smartphone) gives us the amazing capacity to access humanity's collective learning in the palm of our hand. But for many, such constant access can come at a cost.

Writer Linda Stone has coined the phrase "continual partial attention" to describe the modern impulse to always need to know what's happening "out there," to make sure we're not missing anything. If that sounds like it could produce chronic anxiety, you're right!

Although the apostle Paul struggled with different reasons for anxiety, he knew our souls are wired to find peace in God. Which is why, in a letter to new believers who had endured persecution (1 Thessalonians 2:14), Paul concluded by urging the believers to "rejoice always, pray continually, give thanks in all circumstances" (5:16–18).

Praying "continually" might seem pretty daunting. But then, how often do we check our phones? What if we instead let that urge be a prompt to talk to God? To say thank you, lift up a prayer request, or praise Him?

More important, what if we learned to exchange a need to always be in "the know" for continual, prayerful rest in God's presence? Through relying on Christ's Spirit, we can learn to give our heavenly Father our continual full attention as we make our way through each day. Adam Holz

NOVEMBER 9

Great Things!

Psalm 126

What, then, shall we say in response to these things? If God is for us, who can be against us? —Romans 8:31

On November 9, 1989, the world was astonished by the news of the fall of the Berlin Wall. The wall that had divided Berlin, Germany, was coming down; the city that had been divided for twenty-eight years would be united again. Though the epicenter of joy was Germany, an onlooking world shared in the excitement. Something great had taken place!

When Israel returned to her homeland in 538 BC after being exiled for almost seventy years, it was also momentous. Psalm 126 begins with an over-the-shoulder look at that joy-filled time in the history of Israel. The experience was marked by laughter, joyful singing, and international recognition that God had done great things for His people (v. 2). And what was the response of the recipients of His rescuing mercy? Great things from God prompted great gladness (v. 3). Furthermore, His works in the past became the basis for fresh prayers for the present and bright hope for the future (vv. 4–6).

You and I need not look far in our own experiences for examples of great things from God, especially if we believe in God through His Son, Jesus. Nineteenth-century hymn writer Fanny Crosby captured this sentiment when she wrote, "Great things He hath taught us, great things He hath done, and great our rejoicing through Jesus the Son." Yes, to God be the glory, great things He has done!

Arthur Jackson

Abandon It All

Romans 12:1–8

I urge you, brothers and sisters, in view of God's mercy, to offer your bodies as a living sacrifice. —Romans 12:1

When I played college basketball, I made a conscious decision at the beginning of each season to walk into that gym and dedicate myself totally to my coach—doing whatever he might ask me to do.

It would not have benefited my team for me to announce, "Hey, Coach! Here I am. I want to shoot baskets and dribble the ball, but don't ask me to run laps, play defense, and get all sweaty!"

Every successful athlete has to trust the coach enough to do whatever the coach asks them to do for the good of the team.

In Christ, we are to become God's "living sacrifice" (Romans 12:1). We say to our Savior and Lord: "I trust you. Whatever you want me to do, I am willing." Then He "transforms" us by renewing our minds to focus on the things that please Him.

It's helpful to know that God will never call on us to do something for which He has not already equipped us. As Paul reminds us, "We have different gifts, according to the grace given to each of us" (v. 6).

Knowing that we can trust God with our lives, we can abandon ourselves to Him, strengthened by the knowledge that He created us and is helping us to make this effort in Him. Dave Branon

Every Word Matters

Deuteronomy 4:1–10

Do not add to what I command you and do not subtract from it, but keep the commands of the LORD your God. —Deuteronomy 4:2

Kim Peek was a savant (a person with extraordinary memory) who memorized all of Shakespeare's plays. During a performance of *Twelfth Night*, Peek noticed that the actor had skipped a word from one of the lines. Peek suddenly stood up and shouted, "Stop!" The actor apologized and said he didn't think anyone would mind. Peek replied, "Shakespeare would."

Words matter. But especially when they are the very words of God. Moses warned Israel, "Do not add to what I command you and do not subtract from it, but keep the commands of the LORD your God" (Deuteronomy 4:2). Moses often reminded Israel of God's mercy and faithfulness to them in the past. But he also stressed the importance of obedience to God's commands as they prepared to enter the promised land. He told them that obedience would result in blessings of life and a rich inheritance (vv. 39–40). Every command and regulation mattered to God. The value His people placed on God's Word showed their view of Him.

Today, when we value God's Word, handle it with great care, and obey what it says, we give God the reverence He truly deserves. Marvin Williams

A Strong Heart

Psalm 73:21–28

My flesh and my heart may fail, but God is the strength of my heart and my portion forever. —Psalm 73:26

In his book *Fearfully and Wonderfully Made*, coauthored with Philip Yancey, Dr. Paul Brand observed, "A hummingbird heart weighs a fraction of an ounce and beats eight hundred times a minute; a blue whale's heart weighs half a ton, beats only ten times per minute, and can be heard two miles away. In contrast to either, the human heart seems dully functional, yet it does its job, beating 100,000 times a day [65–70 times a minute] with no time off for rest, to get most of us through seventy years or more."

The amazing heart so thoroughly powers us through life that it has become a metaphor for our overall inner well-being. Yet, both our literal and metaphorical hearts are prone to failure. What can we do?

The psalmist Asaph, a worship leader of Israel, acknowledged in Psalm 73 that true strength comes from somewhere—Someone—else. He wrote, "My flesh and my heart may fail, but God is the strength of my heart and my portion forever" (v. 26). Asaph was right. The living God is our ultimate and eternal strength. As the Maker of heaven and earth, He knows no such limitations to His perfect power.

In our times of difficulty and challenge, may we discover what Asaph learned through his own struggles: God is the true strength of our hearts. We can rest in that strength every day. **Bill Crowder**

A Cure for Burnout

Psalm 103:1–5

Praise the LORD . . . who satisfies your desires with good things. —Psalm 103:1, 5

Psychiatrist Robert Coles once noticed a pattern in those who burn out while serving others. The first warning sign is weariness. Next comes cynicism about things ever improving, then bitterness, despair, depression, and finally burnout.

After writing a book about recovering from broken dreams, I once entered a busy season of conference speaking. Helping people find hope after disappointment was richly rewarding, but it came at a cost. One day, about to step on stage, I thought I was going to faint. I hadn't slept well, a vacation hadn't fixed my weariness, and the thought of hearing another person's problems afterward filled me with dread. I was following Coles's pattern.

Scripture gives two strategies for beating burnout. In Isaiah 40, the weary soul is renewed when it hopes in the Lord (vv. 29–31). I needed to rest in God, trusting Him to work, rather than pushing on in my own dwindling strength. And Psalm 103 says God renews us by satisfying our desires with good things (v. 5). While this includes forgiveness and redemption (vv. 3–4), provisions of joy and play come from Him too. When I reworked my schedule to include more prayer, rest, and hobbies like photography, I began to feel healthy again.

Burnout begins with weariness. Let's stop it from going further. We serve others best when our lives include both worship and rest. **Sheridan Voysey**

Just a Spark

James 3:1–6

The tongue is a small part of the body, but it makes great boasts. —James 3:5

"We're in the library, and we can see the flames right outside!" She was scared. We could hear it in her voice. We know her voice—the voice of our daughter. At the same time, we knew her college campus was the safest place for her and her almost three thousand fellow students.

The 2018 Woolsey Fire spread more quickly than anyone anticipated—including fire personnel. The record heat and dry conditions in the California canyon, along with the legendary Santa Ana winds, were all the rather small sparks needed to start a fire that ultimately burned 97,000 acres, destroyed more than 1,600 structures, and killed three people. After the fire was contained, the usual lush coastline resembled the barren surface of the moon.

In the book of James, the author names some small but powerful things: a bit in a horse's mouth and the rudder of a ship (3:3–4). And while familiar, these examples may be somewhat removed from us. But then he names something a little closer to home, something small that every human being possesses—a tongue. And while this chapter is first directed specifically to teachers (v. 1), the application quickly spreads to each of us. The tongue, small as it is, can lead to disastrous results when it runs out of control.

Our small tongues are powerful, but our big God is more powerful. His daily help of the Holy Spirit provides the strength we need to rein in our tongue and guide our words. **John Blase**

Going, Going, Gone

Proverbs 23:1–5

Cast but a glance at riches,
and they are gone. —Proverbs 23:5

The mischievous artist Banksy pulled off another practical joke. His painting *Girl with Balloon* sold for one million pounds at Sotheby's auction house in London. Moments after the auctioneer yelled "Sold," an alarm sounded, and the painting slipped halfway through a shredder mounted inside the bottom of the frame. Banksy tweeted a picture of bidders gasping at his ruined masterpiece, with the caption, "Going, going, gone."

Banksy relished pulling one over on the wealthy, but he need not have bothered. Wealth itself has plenty of pranks up its sleeve. God says, "Do not wear yourself out to get rich . . . . Cast but a glance at riches, and they are gone, for they will surely sprout wings and fly off to the sky like an eagle" (Proverbs 23:4–5).

Few things are less secure than money. We work hard to earn it, yet there are many ways to lose it. Investments go sour, inflation erodes, bills come, thieves steal, and fire and flood destroy. Even if we manage to keep our money, the time we have to spend it continually flies past. Blink, and your life is going, going, gone.

What to do? God tells us a few verses later: "always be zealous for the fear of the Lord. There is surely a future hope for you, and your hope will not be cut off" (vv. 17–18). Invest your life in Jesus; He alone will keep you forever. Mike Wittmer

Heeding the Warnings

Matthew 10:1–7, 32–33

Whoever disowns me before others, I will disown before my Father in heaven. —Matthew 10:33

When a pickpocket tried to pilfer my property while I was on vacation in another country, it wasn't a surprise. I'd read warnings about the danger of subway thieves, so I knew what to do to protect my wallet. But I never expected it to happen.

Fortunately, the young man who grabbed my wallet had slippery fingers, so it fell to the floor where I could retrieve it. But the incident reminded me that I should have heeded the warnings.

We don't like to dwell on warnings because we think they'll get in the way of enjoying life, but it's imperative to pay attention to them. For instance, Jesus gave us a clear warning while sending out His disciples to proclaim God's coming kingdom (Matthew 10:7). He said, "Whoever acknowledges me before others, I will also acknowledge before my Father in heaven. But whoever disowns me before others, I will disown before my Father in heaven" (vv. 32–33).

We have a choice. In love, God provided a Savior and a plan for us to be in His presence for eternity. But if we turn away from God and choose to reject His message of salvation and the real life He offers for both now and forever, we lose out on the opportunity to be with Him.

May we trust in Jesus, the one who chose to save us from being eternally separated from the one who loves and made us. Dave Branon

NOVEMBER 17

Poor Example

Matthew 23:1–3

Whatever they tell you to observe, that observe and do, but do not do according to their works; for they say, and do not do. —Matthew 23:3 NKJV

A woman in Oregon was caught driving 103 miles per hour with her ten-year-old grandson in the car. When she was stopped by the police, she told them that she was only trying to teach him never to drive that fast. I suppose she wanted him to do as she said, not as she did.

The Pharisees and teachers of the law seemed to have a similar problem. Jesus had a scathing assessment of them: They were spiritually bankrupt. He held these two groups directly responsible for this sad spiritual condition. As the successors of the lawgiver Moses, they were responsible for expounding the law so that people would walk in God's ways and have a genuine and vibrant relationship with the Lord (Deuteronomy 10:12–13). But their personal interpretation and application of the law became more important than God's law. They did not practice what they preached. What they did observe was done not to bring glory to God but to honor themselves. Jesus exposed who they were—image managers, posers, and hypocrites.

The test of the effectiveness of following Jesus is not just in what we say but in how we live. Are we telling others God's Word and doing what it says? Let's model by words and actions what it means to follow Him. **Marvin Williams**

Life to the Full

John 10:7–15

The thief comes only to steal and kill and destroy; I have come that they may have life, and have it to the full. —John 10:10

The year was 1918, near the end of World War I, and photographer Eric Enstrom was putting together a portfolio of his work. He wanted to include one that communicated a sense of fullness in a time that felt quite empty to so many people. In his now much-loved photo, a bearded old man sits at a table with his head bowed and his hands clasped in prayer. On the surface before him there is only a book, spectacles, a bowl of gruel, a loaf of bread, and a knife. Nothing more, but also nothing less.

Some might say the photograph reveals scarcity. But Enstrom's point was quite the opposite: Here is a full life, one lived in gratitude, one you and I can experience as well—regardless of our circumstances. Jesus announces the good news in John 10: "life . . . to the full" (v. 10). We do a grave disservice to such good news when we equate full with "many things." The fullness Jesus speaks of isn't measured in worldly categories like riches or real estate but rather a heart, mind, soul, and strength brimming in gratitude that the Good Shepherd gave "his life for the sheep" (v. 11), and cares for us and our daily needs.

This is a full life—enjoying a relationship with God. That is possible for every one of us. **John Blase**

NOVEMBER 19

Facing the Battle

1 Chronicles 16:1–11

Look to the LORD and his strength;
seek his face always. —1 Chronicles 16:11

Not long ago I met up with a group of friends. As I listened to the conversation, it seemed as if everyone in the room was facing some significant battle. Two of us had parents fighting cancer, one had a child with an eating disorder, another friend was experiencing chronic pain, and another was facing major surgery. It seemed a lot for a bunch of people in their thirties and forties.

First Chronicles 16 recounts a key moment in Israel's history when the ark of the covenant was brought into the city of David (Jerusalem). Samuel tells us it happened in a moment of peace between battles (2 Samuel 7:1). When the ark was in place, symbolizing God's presence, David led the people in a song (1 Chronicles 16:8–36). Together the nation sang of God's wonder-working power, His promise-keeping ways, and His past protection (vv. 12–22). "Look to the LORD and his strength," they cried out; "seek his face always" (v. 11). They'd need to, because more battles were coming.

Look to the Lord and His strength. Seek His face. That's not bad advice to follow when illness, family concerns, and other battles confront us, because we haven't been left to fight in our own dwindling energies. God is present; God is strong; He has looked after us in the past, and He will do so again. Together, we can face the battle.

Our God will get us through. **Sheridan Voysey**

He's Got This

2 Peter 3:14–18

But grow in the grace and knowledge of our LORD and Savior Jesus Christ. —2 Peter 3:18

Pastor Watson Jones remembers learning to ride a bike. His father was walking alongside when little Watson saw some girls sitting on a porch. "Daddy, I got this!" he said. He didn't. He realized too late he hadn't learned to balance without his father's steadying grip. He wasn't as grown up as he thought.

Our heavenly Father longs for us to grow up and "become mature, attaining to the whole measure of the fullness of Christ" (Ephesians 4:13). But spiritual maturity is different from natural maturity. Parents raise their children to become independent, to no longer need them. Our divine Father raises us to daily depend on Him more and more.

Peter begins the letter we call 2 Peter by promising "grace and peace . . . through the knowledge of God and of Jesus our Lord," and he ends by urging us to "grow in" that same "grace and knowledge of our Lord and Savior Jesus Christ" (2 Peter 1:2; 3:18). Mature Christians never outgrow their need for Jesus.

Pastor Watson warns, "Some of us are busy slapping Jesus's hands off the handlebars of our life." As if we didn't need His strong hands to hold us, to pick us up, and to hug us when we wobble and flop. We can't grow beyond our dependence on Christ. We only grow by sinking our roots deeper in the grace and knowledge of Him. **Mike Wittmer**

NOVEMBER 21

Words and Actions

Matthew 21:28–32

Let us not love with words or speech but with actions and in truth. —1 John 3:18

The email from the student in my college writing class expressed urgency. It was the end of the semester, and he realized he needed a better grade to participate in sports. What could he do? He had missed some assignments, so I gave him two days to complete those papers and improve his grade. His response: "Thank you. I'll do it."

Two days—and the deadline—passed, and no papers appeared. He didn't back up his words with action.

Jesus told about a young man who did something similar. The boy's dad asked him to do some work in the vineyard. The son said, "I will, sir" (Matthew 21:30). But he was all talk and no action.

In commenting on this parable, Matthew Henry concluded: "Buds and blossoms are not fruit." The buds and blossoms of our words, which breed anticipation of what we might do, are empty without the fruit of our follow-through. Jesus's main application was to religious leaders who spoke of obedience yet refused to follow through with repentance. But the words apply to us as well. It is in following God "with actions and in truth" (1 John 3:18)—not in making empty promises—that we honor our Lord and Savior.

Our actions in obeying God show Him more love, honor, and praise than any empty words we might say to try to appear good. **Dave Branon**

The Babushka Lady

Acts 2:22–36

Let all Israel be assured of this: God has made this Jesus, whom you crucified, both Lord and Messiah. —Acts 2:36

The "Babushka Lady" is one of the mysteries surrounding the 1963 assassination of US President John F. Kennedy. Captured on film recording the events with a movie camera, she has proven to be elusive. This mystery woman, wearing an overcoat and scarf (resembling a Russian *babushka*), has never been identified and her film has never been seen. For decades, historians and scholars have speculated that fear has caused the "Babushka Lady" to hide from the public.

No speculation is needed to understand why Jesus's disciples hid. They cowered in fear because of the authorities who had killed their teacher (John 20:19)—reluctant to come forward and declare their experience. But then Jesus rose from the grave. The Holy Spirit soon arrived, and you couldn't keep those once-timid followers of Christ quiet! On the day of Pentecost, a Spirit-empowered Simon Peter declared, "Let all Israel be assured of this: God has made this Jesus, whom you crucified, both Lord and Messiah" (Acts 2:36).

The opportunity to boldly speak in Jesus's name is not limited to those with daring personalities or career ministry training. It is the indwelling Spirit who enables us to tell the good news of Jesus. By His strength, we can experience the courage to share our Savior with others.

Bill Crowder

NOVEMBER 23

Asking God

Psalm 37:3–7, 23–24

Take delight in the Lord, and he will give you the desires of your heart. —Psalm 37:4

Early in our marriage, I struggled to figure out my wife's preferences. Did she want a quiet dinner at home or a meal at a fancy restaurant? Was it okay for me to hang out with the guys, or did she expect me to keep the weekend free for her? Once, instead of guessing and deciding first, I asked her, "What do you want?"

"I'm fine with either," she replied with a warm smile. "I'm just happy you thought of me."

At times I've wanted desperately to know exactly what God wanted me to do—such as which job to take. Praying for guidance and reading the Bible didn't reveal any specific answers. But one answer was clear: I was to trust in the Lord, take delight in Him, and commit my way to Him (Psalm 37:3–5).

That's when I realized that God usually gives us the freedom of choice—if we first seek to put His ways before our own. That means dropping choices that are plainly wrong or would not please Him. It might be something immoral, ungodly, or unhelpful toward our relationship with Him. If the remaining options please God, then we're free to choose from them. Our loving Father wants to give us the desires of our hearts—as long as our hearts take delight in Him (v. 4). **Leslie Koh**

Stop to Help

Luke 10:30–37

Love your neighbor as yourself. —Luke 10:27

Dr. Scott Kurtzman, chief of surgery at Waterbury Hospital in Connecticut, was on his way to deliver a lecture when he witnessed a horrible crash involving twenty vehicles. The doctor shifted into trauma mode, worked his way through the mess of metal, and called out, "Who needs help?" After ninety minutes of assisting, and the victims were taken to area hospitals, Dr. Kurtzman commented, "A person with my skills simply can't drive by someone who is injured. I refuse to live my life that way."

Jesus told a parable about a man who stopped to help another (Luke 10:30–37). A Jewish man had been ambushed, stripped, robbed, and left for dead. A Jewish priest and a temple assistant passed by, saw the man, and crossed over to the other side. Then a despised Samaritan came by, saw the man, and was filled with compassion. His compassion was translated into action: He soothed and bandaged the man's wounds, took him to an inn, cared for him while he could, paid for all his medical expenses, and then promised the innkeeper he would return to pay any additional expenses.

There are people around us who are suffering. Moved with compassion for their pain, let's be those who stop to help. Marvin Williams

NOVEMBER 25

Active Faith

James 2:14–16

Religion that God our Father accepts as pure and faultless is this: to look after orphans and widows in their distress. —James 1:27

Sam's father had to flee for his life during a military coup. With the sudden loss of income, the family could no longer afford the crucial medicine that kept Sam's brother alive. Seething at God, Sam thought, *What have we done to deserve this?*

A follower of Jesus heard about the family's troubles. Finding that he had enough money to cover the medicine, he bought a supply and took it to them. The life saving gift from a stranger had a profound impact. "This Sunday, we will go to this man's church," his mother declared. Sam's anger began to subside. And eventually, one by one, each member of the family put their faith in Jesus.

When James wrote about the necessity of a lifestyle of integrity accompanying a profession of faith in Christ, he singled out the need to care for others. "Suppose a brother or a sister is without clothes and daily food," James wrote. "If one of you says to them, 'Go in peace; keep warm and well fed,' but does nothing about their physical needs, what good is it?" (2:15–16).

Our actions demonstrate the genuineness of our faith. Significantly, those actions can influence the faith choices of others. In Sam's case, he became a pastor and sought to start churches where they were needed. Eventually he would call the man who helped his family "Papa Mapes." He now knew him as his spiritual father—the one who showed them the love of Jesus. **Tim Gustafson**

The Savior Who Knows Us

John 1:43–51

"How do you know me?" Nathanael asked. —John 1:48

"Dad, what time is it?" my son asked from the back seat. "It's 5:30." I knew exactly what he'd say next. "No, it's 5:28!" I watched his face light up. Gotcha! his beaming smile said. I felt delight too—the kind that comes from knowing your child the way only a parent can.

Like any attentive parent, I know my children. I know how they'll respond when I wake them up. I know what they'll want in their lunches. I know countless interests, desires, and preferences.

But for all that, I'll never know them perfectly, inside and out, the way our Lord knows us.

We catch a glimpse of the kind of intimate knowledge Jesus has of His people in John 1. As Nathanael, who Philip had urged to meet Jesus, moved toward Him, Jesus pronounced, "Here truly is an Israelite in whom there is no deceit" (v. 47). Startled, Nathanael responded, "How do you know me?" Somewhat mysteriously, Jesus replied that He'd seen him under the fig tree (v. 48).

We may not know why Jesus chose to share this detail, but Nathanael did! Overwhelmed, he responded, "Rabbi, you are the Son of God" (v. 49).

Jesus knows each of us like this: intimately, completely, and perfectly—the way we long to be known. And He accepts us completely—inviting us to be not only His followers but His beloved friends (John 15:15). **Adam Holz**

NOVEMBER 27

A Friend in Failure

Acts 15:36–16:5

Paul did not think it wise to take him, because he had deserted them. —Acts 15:38

On November 27, 1939, three treasure hunters accompanied by film crews dug through the asphalt outside of the Hollywood Bowl amphitheater in Southern California. They were looking for the Cahuenga Pass treasure, which allegedly contained gold, diamonds, and pearls that were rumored to have been buried there seventy-five years earlier.

They never found it. After twenty-four days of digging, they struck a boulder and stopped. All they accomplished was a nine-foot-wide, forty-two-foot-deep hole in the ground. They walked away dejected.

We all fail sometimes. Scripture tells us that young Mark walked away from Paul and Barnabas on a missionary trip "and had not continued with them in the work." Because of this, "Paul did not think it wise to take him" on his next trip (Acts 15:38), which resulted in a strong disagreement with Barnabas. But despite his initial failings, Mark shows up years later in surprising ways. When Paul was lonely and in prison toward the end of his life, he asked for Mark and called him "helpful to me in my ministry" (2 Timothy 4:11). And God even inspired Mark to write the gospel that bears his name.

Mark's life shows us that God won't leave us to face our errors and failures alone. We have a friend who's greater than every mistake. As we follow our Savior, He'll provide the help and strength we need. **James Banks**

Give It All You've Got

2 Corinthians 9:6–11

Each of you should give what you have decided in your heart to give, not reluctantly or under compulsion, for God loves a cheerful giver. —2 Corinthians 9:7

Scaling. It's a term used in the world of fitness that allows room for anyone to participate. If the specific exercise is a push-up, for example, then maybe you can do ten in a row, but I can only do four. The instructor's encouragement to me would be to scale back the push-ups according to my fitness level at the time. We're not all at the same level, but we can all move in the same direction. In other words, he would say, "Do your four push-ups with all the strength you have. Don't compare yourself with anyone else. Scale the movement for now, keep doing what you can do, and you may be amazed in time you're doing seven, and even one day, ten."

When it comes to giving, the apostle Paul was clear: "God loves a cheerful giver" (2 Corinthians 9:7). But his encouragement to the believers in Corinth, and to us, is a variation of scaling. "Each of you should give what you have decided in your heart to give" (v. 7). We each find ourselves at different giving levels, and sometimes those levels change over time. Comparison is not beneficial, but attitude is. Based on where you are, give generously (v. 6). Our God has promised that the disciplined practice of such cheerful giving brings enrichment in every way with a blessed life that results in "thanksgiving to God" (v. 11).

John Blase

NOVEMBER 29

Help Needed

Hebrews 4:9–16

Let us then approach God's throne of grace with confidence, so that we may receive mercy and find grace to help us in our time of need. —Hebrews 4:16

During World War II, the British Isles represented the last line of resistance against the sweep of Nazi oppression in Europe. Under relentless attack and in danger of collapse, however, Britain lacked the resources to see the conflict through to victory. For that reason, British Prime Minister Winston Churchill went on BBC radio and appealed to the world: "Give us the tools, and we will finish the job." He knew that without help from the outside, they could not endure the assault they were facing.

Life is like that. Often, we are inadequate for the troubles life throws at us, and we need help from outside of ourselves. As members of the body of Christ, that help can come at times from our Christian brothers and sisters (Romans 12:10–13)—and that is a wonderful thing. Ultimately, however, we seek help from our heavenly Father. The good and great news is that our God has invited us to come confidently before Him: "Let us then approach God's throne of grace with confidence, so that we may receive mercy and find grace to help us in our time of need" (Hebrews 4:16).

At such times, our greatest resource is prayer—for it brings us into the very presence of God. There we find, in His mercy and grace, the help we need. **Bill Crowder**

Call for Help

Acts 2:14–21

Everyone who calls on the name of the Lord will be saved. —Acts 2:21

After five deaths and fifty-one injuries in elevator accidents in a recent year, New York City launched an ad campaign to educate people on how to stay calm and be safe. The worst cases were people who tried to save themselves when something went wrong. The best plan of action, authorities say, is simply, "Ring, relax, and wait." New York building authorities made a commitment to respond promptly to protect people from injury and extract them from their predicament.

In the book of Acts, Peter preached a sermon that addressed the error of trying to save ourselves. Luke, who wrote the book, records some remarkable events in which believers in Christ were speaking in languages they did not know (Acts 2:1–12). Peter got up to explain to his Jewish brothers and sisters that what they were witnessing was the fulfillment of an ancient prophecy (Joel 2:28–32)—the outpouring of the Spirit and a day of salvation. The blessing of the Holy Spirit was now visibly seen in those who called on Jesus for rescue from sin and its effects. Then Peter told them how this salvation is available for anyone (v. 21). Our access to God comes not through keeping the Law but through trusting Jesus as Lord and Messiah.

If we are trapped in sin, we cannot save ourselves. Our only hope for being rescued is acknowledging and trusting Jesus as Lord and Messiah. Marvin Williams

DECEMBER 1

Your Eulogy

Ecclesiastes 7:1–6

Death is the destiny of everyone; the living should take this to heart. —Ecclesiastes 7:2

My heart is full from attending the funeral of a faithful woman. Her life wasn't spectacular. She wasn't known widely outside her church, neighbors, and friends. But she loved Jesus, her seven children, and her twenty-five grandchildren. She laughed easily, served generously, and could hit a softball a long way.

Ecclesiastes says, "It is better to go to a house of mourning than to go to a house of feasting" (7:2). "The heart of the wise is in the house of mourning" because there we learn what matters most (7:4). *New York Times* columnist David Brooks says there are two kinds of virtues: those that look good on a résumé and those you want said at your funeral. Sometimes these overlap, though often they seem to compete. When in doubt, always choose the eulogy virtues.

The woman in the casket didn't have a résumé, but her children testified that "she rocked Proverbs 31" and its description of a godly woman. She inspired them to love Jesus and care for others. As Paul said, "Follow my example, as I follow the example of Christ" (1 Corinthians 11:1), so they challenged us to imitate their mother's life as she imitated Jesus.

What will be said at your funeral? What do you want said? Now is the time to develop eulogy virtues. Trust in Jesus. His salvation frees us to live for what matters most.
Mike Wittmer

Rescued

Colossians 1:12–22

He has rescued us from the dominion of darkness and brought us into the kingdom of the Son he loves. —Colossians 1:13

A South African man surprised nine men robbing his home. Seven of the robbers ran away, but the homeowner managed to shove two into his backyard pool. After realizing that one of the robbers couldn't swim, the homeowner jumped in to save him. *The Cape Times* reports that once out of the pool, the wet thief called to his friends to come back. Then he pulled a knife and threatened the man who had just rescued him. The homeowner said, "We were still standing near the pool, and when I saw the knife I just threw him back in. But he was gasping for air and was drowning. So I rescued him again."

In his letter to the Colossians, the apostle Paul wrote of another rescue: God the Father had saved them from the domain of darkness. This rescue occurred at the death of Christ and also at the Colossians' conversion. The imagery Paul used (1:12–13) suggests that believers have been rescued from the dark reign of Satan by being transferred as free people into the peaceable rule of Christ. By Jesus's death, believers become free citizens in the kingdom of light.

The appropriate response to such amazing grace is to show joyous gratitude by offering God acceptable service with reverence and awe (Hebrews 12:28). Marvin Williams

DECEMBER 3

Christmas Awe

Hebrews 1:1–9

Let all God's angels worship him. —Hebrews 1:6

I was in London one night for a meeting. It was pouring rain, and I was late. I rushed through the streets, turned a corner, and then stopped still. Dozens of angels hovered above Regent Street, their giant shimmering wings stretching across the traffic. Made of thousands of pulsing lights, it was the most amazing Christmas display I'd ever seen. I wasn't the only one captivated. Hundreds lined the street, gazing up in awe.

Awe is central to the Christmas story. When the angel appeared to Mary explaining she would miraculously conceive (Luke 1:26–38), and when a host of angels appeared to the shepherds announcing Jesus's birth (2:8–20), each reacted with fear, wonder—and awe. Looking around at that Regent Street crowd, I wondered if we were experiencing in small part what those first angelic encounters felt like.

A moment later, I noticed something else. Some of the angels had their arms raised, as if they too were gazing up at something. Like the angelic choir that burst into praise at the mention of Jesus (vv. 13–14), it seems angels too can be caught up in awe—as they gaze on Him.

"The Son is the radiance of God's glory and the exact representation of his being" (Hebrews 1:3). Bright and luminous, Jesus is the focus of every angel's gaze (v. 6). If an angel-themed Christmas display can stop busy Londoners in their tracks, just imagine the moment when we see Him face-to-face. **Sheridan Voysey**

Dad, Where Are You?

Deuteronomy 31:1–8

The LORD himself goes before you and will be with you; he will never leave you nor forsake you. Do not be afraid; do not be discouraged. —Deuteronomy 31:8

"Dad! Where are you?"

I was pulling into our driveway when my daughter, panicking, called me on my cell phone. I'd needed to be home by 6:00 to get her to play practice; I was on time. My daughter's voice, however, betrayed her lack of trust. Reflexively, I responded: "I'm here. Why don't you trust me?"

As I spoke those words, I wondered, *How often could my heavenly Father ask that of me?* In stressful moments, I too am impatient and struggle to trust, to believe that God will keep His promises. I cry out: "Father, where are you?"

Amid stress and uncertainty, I sometimes doubt God's presence, or even His goodness and purposes for me. The Israelites did too. In Deuteronomy 31, they were preparing to enter the promised land, knowing their leader, Moses, would stay behind. Moses sought to reassure God's people by reminding them, "The LORD himself goes before you and will be with you; he will never leave you nor forsake you. Do not be afraid; do not be discouraged" (v. 8).

That promise—that God is always with us—remains a cornerstone of our faith (see Hebrews 13:5). Indeed, Revelation 21:3 culminates with these words: "God's dwelling place is now among the people, and he will dwell with them."

Where is God? He is right here, right now, right with us—always ready to hear our prayers. **Adam Holz**

Officer Waxworks

John 14:15–24

If you love me, keep my commands. —John 14:15

For several years, our family lived in southern California while I was pastoring a church there. The community in which we lived didn't have the resources to fully patrol the streets with police. So, there was a genuine concern about the lack of safety as a result of reckless driving.

In response to the situation, city officials came up with a solution they called Officer Waxworks. These uniformed mannequins were placed in patrol cars alongside the road. Obviously, these "officers" couldn't pursue lawbreakers or write tickets, but just the appearance of "manned" patrol cars was enough to make people slow down. It was a creative way to trick people into obeying the law.

As believers in Christ, we shouldn't have to be forced or tricked into doing what's right. In fact, obedience can be drained of its significance if we obey only out of obligation or duty. Our desire should be to do what is pleasing to our Lord because we love Him. Jesus said, "He who has My commandments and keeps them, it is he who loves Me" (John 14:21 NKJV). We should "make it our aim . . . to be well pleasing to Him" (2 Corinthians 5:9 NKJV).

Let's do what's right out of a heart of gratitude for His grace to us. Bill Crowder

Despised for All of This

Isaiah 53:3–12

He bore the sin of many, and made intercession for the transgressors. —Isaiah 53:12

Susannah Cibber gained fame in the eighteenth century for her talent as a singer. However, she was equally well known for her scandalous marital problems. That's why when Handel's *Messiah* was first performed in Dublin in April 1742, many in the audience did not approve of her role as a featured soloist.

During that inaugural performance, Cibber sang of the Messiah: "He is despised and rejected of men; a man of sorrows, and acquainted with grief" (Isaiah 53:3 KJV). Those words so moved Rev. Patrick Delany that he jumped to his feet and said, "Woman, for this be all thy sins forgiven thee!"

The connection between Susannah Cibber and the theme of Handel's *Messiah* is evident. The "man of sorrows"—Jesus the Messiah—was "despised and rejected" because of *sin*. The prophet Isaiah said, "My righteous servant will justify many, and he will bear their iniquities" (v. 11).

The connection between Messiah and us is no less apparent. Whether we stand with the judgmental audience members, with Susannah Cibber, or somewhere in between, we all need to repent and receive God's forgiveness. Jesus, by His life, death, and resurrection, restored our relationship with God our Father.

For this—for all *Jesus* did—be all our sins forgiven.

Tim Gustafson

DECEMBER 7

His Presence

Exodus 3:7–12

The LORD replied, "My Presence will go with you, and I will give you rest." —Exodus 33:14

The anxious father and his teenage son sat before the psychic. "How far is your son traveling?" the psychic asked. "To the big city," the man replied, "and he will be gone for a long time." Handing the father a talisman (a kind of good-luck charm), he said, "This will protect him wherever he goes."

I was that boy. However, that psychic and that talisman could do nothing for me. While in that city, I put my faith in Jesus. I threw away the talisman and clung to Christ. Having Jesus in my life guaranteed God's presence.

Thirty years later, my father, now a believer, said to me as we rushed my brother to the hospital, "Let us first pray; the Spirit of God goes with you and will be with you all the way!" We had learned that God's presence and power is our only security.

Moses learned a similar lesson. He had a challenging task from God—to lead the people out of bondage in Egypt and into the promised land (Exodus 3:10). But God assured him, "I will be with you" (v. 12).

Our journey too is not without challenges, but we're assured of God's presence. As Jesus told His disciples, "I am with you always, to the very end of the age" (Matthew 28:20). Lawrence Darmani

Remember and Celebrate

Luke 22:14–23

[Jesus] took bread, gave thanks and broke it, and gave it to them, saying, "This is my body given for you." —Luke 22:19

In December 1907, explosions rocked a small community in West Virginia, producing one of the worst disasters in the history of the coal-mining industry. Some 360 miners were killed, and it's been estimated that this horrific tragedy left behind about 250 widows and 1,000 children without fathers. Historians maintain that the memorial service became the seedbed from which the celebration of Father's Day in the US would eventually grow. Out of great loss came remembrance and—eventually—celebration.

The greatest tragedy in human history occurred two thousand years ago when human beings crucified their Creator. Yet that dark moment also produced both remembrance and celebration. The night before He would go to the cross, Jesus took the elements of Israel's Passover and created His own memorial celebration. Luke's record describes the scene this way: "And he took bread, gave thanks and broke it, and gave it to them, saying, 'This is my body given for you; do this in remembrance of me'" (Luke 22:19).

Still today, whenever we take communion, we honor His great, unflinching love for us—remembering the cost of our rescue and celebrating the gift of life His sacrifice produced. As Charles Wesley said in his great hymn, "Amazing love! How can it be that Thou, my God, shouldst die for me?" **Bill Crowder**

DECEMBER 9

Pay Close Attention

Nehemiah 8:2–6, Acts 8:4–8

All the people listened attentively to the Book of the Law. —Nehemiah 8:3

As I sat in the auditorium, I faced the pastor with my eyes fixed on him. My posture suggested I was absorbing everything he was saying. Suddenly I heard everybody laughing and clapping. Surprised, I looked about. The preacher had apparently said something humorous, but I had no clue what it might have been. From all appearances I had been listening carefully, but in reality my mind was far away.

It's possible to hear what is being said but not listen, to watch but not see, to be present and yet absent. In such a condition, we may miss important messages meant for us.

As Ezra read God's instructions to the people of Judah, "All the people listened attentively to the Book of the Law" (Nehemiah 8:3). Their attention to the explanation produced understanding (v. 8), which resulted in their repentance and revival. In another situation in Samaria, Philip, after persecution of the believers broke out in Jerusalem (Acts 8:1), reached out to the Samaritan people. The crowd not only observed the miraculous signs he did but they also "paid close attention to what he said" (v. 6). "So there was great joy in that city" (v. 8).

The mind can be like a wandering adventurer that misses a lot of excitement close by. Nothing deserves more attention than words that help us discover the joy and wonder of our Father in heaven. Lawrence Darmani

Adopted

Galatians 4:1–7

God sent his Son . . . that we might receive adoption to sonship. —Galatians 4:4–5

I'm glad when a philanthropist builds an orphanage for homeless children. I'm thrilled when that person gives even more and adopts one of them. Most orphans would be delighted merely to have a patron. But then to learn that the sponsor isn't content merely to help me but also wants me. How must that feel?

If you're a child of God you already know, because it's happened to you. We couldn't complain if God had merely loved us enough to send His Son that we might "not perish but have eternal life" (John 3:16). It would be enough for us. But not for God. He "sent his Son . . . to redeem" us, not as an end in itself but "that we might receive adoption to sonship" (Galatians 4:4–5).

The apostle Paul refers to us as "sons" because in his day it was common for sons to inherit their father's wealth. His point is that now everyone who puts their faith in Jesus, whether man or woman, becomes a "son" of God with equal and full rights of inheritance (v. 7).

God does not merely want to save you. He wants you. He has adopted you into His family, given you His name (Revelation 3:12), and proudly calls you His child. You could not possibly be loved more, or by anyone more important. You aren't merely blessed by God. You are the child of God. Your Father loves you. **Mike Wittmer**

DECEMBER 11

Making Peace with Trouble

James 1:2–4

Consider it pure joy, my brothers and sisters,
whenever you face trials of many kinds. —James 1:2

We were almost home when I noticed it: the needle of our car's temperature gauge was rocketing up. As we pulled in, I killed the engine and hopped out. Smoke wafted from the hood. The engine sizzled like bacon. I backed the car up a few feet and found a puddle beneath: oil. Instantly, I knew what had happened: The head gasket had blown.

I groaned. We'd just sunk money into other expensive repairs. Why can't things just work? I grumbled bitterly. Why can't things just stop breaking?

Can you relate? Sometimes we avert one crisis, solve one problem, pay off one big bill, only to face another. Sometimes those troubles are much bigger than an engine self-destructing—an unexpected diagnosis, an untimely death, a terrible loss.

In those moments, we yearn for a world less broken, less full of trouble. That world, Jesus promised, is coming. But not yet: "In this world you will have trouble," He reminded His disciples in John 16. "But take heart! I have overcome the world" (v. 33). Jesus spoke in that chapter about grave troubles, such as persecution for your faith. But such trouble, He taught, would never have the last word for those who hope in Him.

Troubles small and large may dog our days. But Jesus's promise of a better tomorrow with Him encourages us not to let our troubles define our lives today. Adam Holz

God's Sure Pursuit

Psalm 23

Surely your goodness and love will follow me
all the days of my life. —Psalm 23:6

Some years ago, a man walked about a block ahead of me. I could clearly see his arms were full of packages. All of a sudden, he tripped, dropping everything. A couple of people helped him to his feet, assisting him in collecting what he'd dropped. But they missed something—his wallet. I picked it up and took off in hot pursuit of the stranger, hoping to return that important item. I yelled "Sir, sir!" and finally got his attention. He turned just as I reached him. As I held out the wallet, I'll never forget his look of surprised relief and immense gratitude.

What began as following along after that man turned into something quite different. Most English translations use the word *follow* in the final verse of the familiar Psalm 23: "Surely your goodness and love will follow me" (v. 6). And while *follow* fits, the actual Hebrew word used is more forceful, aggressive even. The word literally means "to pursue or chase," much like a predator pursues his prey (think of a wolf pursuing sheep).

God's goodness and love don't merely follow along after us at a casual pace, in no real hurry, like a pet might leisurely follow you home. No, "surely" we are being pursued—chased even—with intention. Much like pursuing a man to return his wallet, we're pursued by the Good Shepherd who loves us with an everlasting love (v. 1). **John Blase**

DECEMBER 13

For Others' Sake

Romans 14:13–21

Do not destroy the work of God for the sake of food. —Romans 14:20

During the COVID-19 pandemic, many Singaporeans stayed home to avoid being infected. But I blissfully continued swimming, believing it was safe. My wife, however, feared that I might pick up an infection at the public pool and pass it on to her aged mother—who, like other seniors, was more vulnerable to the virus. "Can you just avoid swimming for some time, for my sake?" she asked.

At first, I wanted to argue that there was little risk. Then I realized that this mattered less than her feelings. Why would I insist on swimming—hardly an essential thing—when it made her worry unnecessarily?

In Romans 14, Paul addressed issues like whether believers in Christ should eat certain foods or celebrate certain festivals. He was concerned that some people were imposing their views on others.

Paul reminded the church in Rome, and us, that believers in Jesus may view situations differently. We also have diverse backgrounds that color our attitudes and practices. He wrote, "Let us stop passing judgment on one another. Instead, make up your mind not to put any stumbling block or obstacle in the way of a brother or sister" (v. 13).

God's grace gives us great freedom even as it helps us express His love to fellow believers. We can use that freedom to put the spiritual needs of others above our own convictions about rules and practices that don't contradict the essential truths found in the gospel (v. 20). **Leslie Koh**

Let Freedom Ring

Isaiah 58:1–12

Is not this the kind of fasting I have chosen: to loose the chains of injustice . . . to set the oppressed free? —Isaiah 58:6

In 1963, during a peaceful march on Washington, DC, Martin Luther King, Jr., delivered his now famous "I Have a Dream" speech. He eloquently called for freedom to ring from every mountaintop across the nation. The cost to him personally and to those who joined his peaceful resistance movement was steep, but real change soon began. God used that speech to awaken the conscience of the US to fight for the freedom of the oppressed and downtrodden.

In the eighth century BC, amid personal and national injustice, the prophet Isaiah was used by God to awaken the conscience of His people. Their convenient spirituality had led them to violence and insensitivity toward their fellow humans. God's people were oppressing the poor and substituting religious practices for genuine righteous living (vv. 1–5). God indicted them (v. 1) and prescribed spiritual living that would be expressed through turning to God in genuine repentance and setting people free (vv. 6–12).

Like Isaiah, we have been sent to let freedom ring. By the power of the Holy Spirit, we must proclaim that the captives can be released, that the downtrodden can be freed from their oppressors, and that the time of the Lord's favor has come. Marvin Williams

DECEMBER 15

Wiping Away the Guilt

Romans 2:12–16

They show that the requirements of the law are written on their hearts. —Romans 2:15

In his book *Human Universals*, anthropologist Donald Brown lists more than four hundred behaviors that he considers common across humanity. He includes such things as toys, jokes, dances, and proverbs, wariness of snakes, and tying things with string! Likewise, he believes all cultures have concepts of right and wrong, where generosity is praised, promises are valued, and things like meanness and murder are understood to be wrong. We all have a sense of conscience, wherever we're from.

The apostle Paul made a similar point many centuries ago. While God gave the Jewish people the Ten Commandments to clarify right from wrong, Paul noted that since gentiles could do right by obeying their conscience, God's laws were evidently written on their hearts (Romans 2:14–15). But that didn't mean people always did what was right. The gentiles rebelled against their conscience (1:32) and the Jews broke the Law (2:17–24), leaving both guilty. But through faith in Jesus, God removes the death penalty from all our rule-breaking (3:23–26; 6:23).

Since God created all humans with a sense of right and wrong, each of us will feel some guilt over a bad thing we've done or a good thing we failed to do. When we confess those sins, God wipes away the guilt like a whiteboard wiped clean. All we have to do is ask Him—whoever we are, wherever we're from. Sheridan Voysey

Bold Faith

Acts 4:8–13

Salvation is found in no one else, for there is no other name under heaven given to mankind by which we must be saved. —Acts 4:12

After Prem Pradhan's plane was shot down during World War II, he was wounded while parachuting to safety. As a result, he walked with a limp for the rest of his life. He once noted, "I have a lame leg. Isn't it strange of God that He called [me] to preach the gospel in the Himalaya Mountains?" And preach in Nepal he did—but not without opposition that included imprisonment in "dungeons of death" where prisoners faced extreme conditions. In a span of fifteen years, Prem spent ten years in fourteen different prisons. His bold witness, however, bore the fruit of changed lives for Christ, which included guards and prisoners who took the message of Jesus to their own people.

The apostle Peter faced opposition because of his faith in Jesus and for being used by God to heal a "man who was lame" (Acts 4:9). But he used the opportunity to boldly speak for Christ (vv. 8–13).

Today, like Peter, we too may face opposition (v. 3), yet we have family members, co-workers, fellow students, and others we know who desperately need to hear about the One in whom "salvation is found" (v. 12), who died as payment for our sins and was raised from the dead as proof of His power to forgive (v. 10). Let's make sure they hear us as we prayerfully and boldly proclaim this good news of salvation found in Jesus. **Arthur Jackson**

DECEMBER 17

Living God's Story

Romans 13:8–14

The night is nearly over; the day is almost here. —Romans 13:12

The great novelist Ernest Hemingway was asked if he could write a compelling story in six words. His response: "For sale: Baby shoes. Never worn." Hemingway's story is powerful because it inspires us to fill in the details. Were the shoes simply not needed by a healthy child? Or was there a tragic loss—something requiring God's deep love and comfort?

The best stories pique our imagination, so it's no surprise that the greatest story ever told stokes the fires of our creativity. God's story has a central plot: He created all things; we (the human race) fell into sin; Jesus came to earth and died and rose again to save us from our sins; and we now await His return and the restoration of all things.

Knowing what has come before and what lies ahead, how should we live now? If Jesus is restoring His entire creation from the clutches of evil, we must "put aside the deeds of darkness and put on the armor of light" (Romans 13:12). This includes turning from sin by God's power and choosing to love Him and others well (vv. 8–10).

The specific ways we fight with Jesus against evil will depend on what gifts we have and what needs we see. Let's use our imagination and look around us. Let's seek out the wounded and weeping, and extend God's justice, love, and comfort as He guides us to live His story. **Mike Wittmer**

Don't Forget the Giver

Deuteronomy 6:4–12

Be careful that you do not forget the LORD. —Deuteronomy 6:12

It was just before Christmas, and his kids were having a difficult time with gratitude. Dad knew how easy it was to slip into that kind of thinking, but he also knew he wanted something better for the hearts of his children. So he went through the house and placed red bows on light switches, the pantry and refrigerator doors, the washing machine and dryer, and the water faucets. Each bow was accompanied by a handwritten note: "Some of the gifts God gives us are easy to overlook, so I've put a bow on them. He is so good to our family. Let's not forget where the gifts come from."

In Deuteronomy 6, we see that the future of the nation of Israel involved the conquest of existing places. So, they would move into large flourishing cities they did not build (v. 10), occupy houses filled with good things they didn't provide, and benefit from wells and vineyards and olive groves they didn't dig or plant (v. 11). All these blessings could be easily traced back to a single source—"the LORD your God" (v. 10). And while God lovingly provided these things and more, Moses wanted to make sure the people were careful not to forget (v. 12).

During certain seasons of life it's easy to forget. But let's not lose sight of God's goodness, the source of all our blessings. **John Blase**

DECEMBER 19

Situational Awareness

Philippians 1:3–11

This is my prayer: that your love may abound more and more in knowledge and depth of insight. —Philippians 1:9

My family, all five of us, was visiting Rome over the Christmas holidays. I don't know when I've ever seen more people jammed together in one place. As we snaked our way through crowds to see sights like the Vatican and the Coliseum, I repeatedly emphasized to my kids the practice of "situational awareness"—pay attention to where you are, who's around you, and what's going on. We live in a day when the world, at home and abroad, isn't a safe place. And with the use of cell phones and earbuds, kids (and adults for that matter) don't always practice an awareness of surroundings.

Situational awareness. This is an aspect of Paul's prayer for the believers in Philippi recorded in Philippians 1:9–11. His desire for them was an ever-increasing discernment as to the who/what/where of their situations. But rather than some goal of personal safety, Paul prayed with a grander purpose: That God's holy people might be good stewards of the love of Christ they'd received, that they would discern "what is best," live "pure and blameless," and that they would be filled with good qualities only Jesus can produce.

This kind of living springs from an awareness that God is the "who" in our lives, and our increasing reliance on Him is what brings Him pleasure. In any and all situations we can share from the overflow of His great love.

John Blase

Home for Christmas

Genesis 28:10–17

I am with you and will watch over you wherever you go, and I will bring you back to this land. —Genesis 28:15

One year Christmas found me on assignment in a place many of my friends couldn't locate on a map. Trudging from my work site back to my room, I braced against the chill wind blowing off the bleak Black Sea. I missed home.

When I arrived at my room, I opened the door to a magical moment. My artistic roommate had completed his latest project—a nineteen-inch ceramic Christmas tree that now illuminated our darkened room with sparkling dots of color. If only for a moment, I was home again!

As Jacob fled from his brother Esau, he found himself in a strange and lonely place too. Asleep on the hard ground, he met God in a dream. And God promised Jacob a home. "I will give you and your descendants the land on which you are lying," He told him. "All peoples on earth will be blessed through you and your offspring" (Genesis 28:13–14).

From Jacob, of course, would come the promised Messiah, the one who left His home to draw us to himself. "I will come back and take you to be with me that you also may be where I am," Jesus told His disciples (John 14:3).

That December night I sat in the darkness of my room and gazed at that Christmas tree. Perhaps it was inevitable that it made me think of the Light that entered the world to show us the way home. Tim Gustafson

DECEMBER 21

Prayer of the Broken-Down

Psalm 109:21–27

Help me, LORD my God. —Psalm 109:26

"Dear Father in heaven, I'm not a praying man, but if you're up there, and you can hear me, show me the way. I'm at the end of my rope." That prayer is whispered by a broken-down George Bailey, the character played by James Stewart in the classic film *It's a Wonderful Life*. In the now iconic scene, Bailey's eyes fill with tears. They weren't part of the script, but as he spoke that prayer Stewart said he "felt the loneliness, the hopelessness of people who had nowhere to turn." It broke him.

Bailey's prayer, boiled down, is simply "Help me." And this is exactly what's voiced in Psalm 109. David was at the end of his rope: "poor and needy," his "heart . . . wounded" (v. 22), and his body "thin and gaunt" (v. 24). He was fading "like an evening shadow" (v. 23), and he sensed himself to be an "object of scorn" in the eyes of his accusers (v. 25). In his extreme brokenness, he had nowhere else to turn. He cried out for the Sovereign Lord to show him the way: "Help me, LORD my God" (v. 26).

There are seasons in our lives when "broken-down" says it all. In such times it can be hard to know what to pray. Pray anyway. Our loving God will respond to our simple prayer for help. **John Blase**

Lonely Christmas

Psalm 25:14–22

My eyes are ever on the Lord. —Psalm 25:15

The loneliest Christmas I ever spent was in my grandfather's cottage near Sakogu, northern Ghana. I was just fifteen, and my parents and siblings were a thousand kilometers away.

In previous years, when I'd been with them and my village friends, Christmas was always big and memorable. But this Christmas was quiet and lonely. As I lay on my floor mat early Christmas morning, I remembered the words to a local song: "The year has ended; Christmas has come; the Son of God is born; peace and joy to everybody." Mournfully, I sang it over and over.

My grandmother came and asked, "What song is that?" My grandparents didn't know about Christmas—or about Christ. So, I shared what I knew about Christmas with them. Those moments brightened my loneliness.

Alone in the fields with only sheep and occasional predators, the shepherd boy David experienced loneliness. It would not be the only time. Later in his life he wrote, "I am lonely and afflicted" (Psalm 25:16). But David didn't allow loneliness to cause him to be despondent. Instead, he sang: "My hope, Lord, is in you" (v. 21).

From time to time we all face loneliness. Wherever Christmas may find you this year, in loneliness or in companionship, you can enjoy the season with Christ.
Lawrence Darmani

DECEMBER 23

The Seventh Stanza

Luke 2:8–14

Today in the town of David a Savior has been born to you; he is the Messiah, the Lord. —Luke 2:11

In the summer of 1861, Henry Wadsworth Longfellow's wife, Frances, died tragically in a fire. That first Christmas without her, he wrote in his diary, "How inexpressibly sad are the holidays." The next year was no better, as he recorded, "'A merry Christmas,' say the children, but that is no more for me." In 1863, as the American Civil War was dragging on, Longfellow's son joined the army against his father's wishes and was critically injured. As church bells announced the arrival of another painful Christmas, Longfellow picked up his pen and began to write, "I Heard the Bells on Christmas Day."

The poem begins pleasantly, lyrically, but then it takes a dark turn. In the violent imagery of the pivotal fourth verse, "accursed" cannons "thundered," mocking the message of peace. By the fifth and sixth verses, Longfellow's desolation is nearly complete. "It was as if an earthquake rent the hearthstones of a continent," he wrote. The poet nearly gave up: "And in despair I bowed my head; 'There is no peace on earth,' I said." But then he wrote this seventh stanza: *Then pealed the bells more loud and deep: "God is not dead, nor doth He sleep! The wrong shall fail, the right prevail, with peace on earth, goodwill to men!"*

The war raged on and so did memories of his personal tragedies, but it could not stop Christmas. The Messiah is born! He promises, "I am making everything new!" (Revelation 21:5). **Tim Gustafson**

When Peace Breaks Out

Luke 2:8–20

Peace to those on whom [God's] favor rests. —Luke 2:14

On a cold Christmas Eve in Belgium in 1914, the sound of singing floated from the trenches where soldiers were dug in. Strains of the carol "Silent Night" rang out in German and then in English. Soldiers who earlier in the day had been shooting at each other laid down their weapons and emerged from their trenches to shake hands in the no-man's-land between them, exchanging Christmas greetings and spontaneous gifts from their rations. The ceasefire continued through the next day as the soldiers talked and laughed and even organized soccer matches together.

The Christmas Truce of 1914 that occurred along World War I's Western Front offered a brief glimpse of the peace the angels proclaimed on the first Christmas Eve long ago. An angel spoke to terrified shepherds with these reassuring words: "Do not be afraid. I bring you good news that will cause great joy for all the people. Today in the town of David a Savior has been born to you" (Luke 2:10–11). Then a multitude of angels appeared, "praising God and saying, 'Glory to God in the highest heaven, and on earth peace to those on whom his favor rests'" (vv. 13–14).

Jesus is the "Prince of Peace" who saves us from our sins (Isaiah 9:6). Through His sacrifice on the cross He offers forgiveness and peace with God to all who trust in Him. James Banks

DECEMBER 25

Christmas Child

Philippians 2:6–11

He made himself nothing by taking the very nature of a servant, being made in human likeness. —Philippians 2:7

Imagine the one who caused cedars to spring from seeds starting life over as an embryo; the one who made the stars submitting himself to a womb; the one who fills the heavens becoming what would be in our day a mere dot on an ultrasound. Jesus, in very nature God, making himself nothing (Philippians 2:6–7). What an astonishing thought!

Imagine the scene as He's born in a plain peasant village, among shepherds. Angels, and bright lights in the sky, with the bleating of animals His first lullabies. Watch as He grows in favor and stature: as a youngster, astounding teachers with answers to grand questions; as a young man at the Jordan, getting His Father's approval from heaven; and in the wilderness, as He wrestles in hunger and prayer.

Watch next as He launches His world-changing mission—healing the sick, touching lepers, forgiving the impure. Watch as He kneels in a garden in anguish and as they arrest Him while His closest friends flee. Watch as He is spat on and nailed to two wooden posts, the world's sins on His shoulders. But watch, yes watch, as the stone rolls away, an empty tomb ringing hollow, because He is alive!

Watch as He is lifted to the highest place (v. 9). Watch as His name fills heaven and earth (vv. 10–11).

This Maker of the stars who became a dot on an ultrasound. This, our Christmas Child. **Sheridan Voysey**

Never Enough

Ecclesiastes 1:1–11

The eye never has enough of seeing. —Ecclesiastes 1:8

Frank Borman commanded the first space mission that circled the moon. He wasn't impressed. The trip took two days both ways. Frank got motion sickness and threw up. He said being weightless was cool—for thirty seconds. Then he got used to it. Up close he found the moon drab and pockmarked with craters. His crew took pictures of the gray wasteland, then became bored.

Frank went where no one had gone before. It wasn't enough. If he quickly tired of an experience that was out of this world, perhaps we should lower our expectations for what lies in this one. The teacher of Ecclesiastes observed that no earthly experience delivers ultimate joy. "The eye never has enough of seeing, nor the ear its fill of hearing" (1:8). We may feel moments of ecstasy, but our elation soon wears off and we seek the next thrill.

Frank had one exhilarating moment, when he saw the earth rise from the darkness behind the moon. Like a blue and white swirled marble, our world sparkled in the sun's light. Similarly, our truest joy comes from the Son shining on us. Jesus is our life, the only ultimate source of meaning, love, and beauty. Our deepest satisfaction comes from out of this world. Our problem? We can go all the way to the moon, yet still not go far enough. **Mike Wittmer**

DECEMBER 27

Your Children Will Ask

Exodus 12:13–17, 25

When your children ask you, "What does this ceremony mean to you?" then tell them, "It is the Passover sacrifice of the LORD." —Exodus 12:26–27

One of the most important events in Jewish history is the exodus, when God freed His people from the bondage of Egypt. Prior to leaving Egypt, the Israelites were commanded to eat a special meal called the Passover. As an act of judgment upon the Egyptians, God said that He would strike down every firstborn son, but He would pass over the houses that had the blood of a lamb on the top and sides of the door frame (Exodus 12).

To commemorate this act of judgment and grace, God's people would share in the Passover meal. God said that one day their children would ask: "What does this ceremony mean?" They were then responsible to retell the story of the exodus and God's salvation. God did not want the story of His great salvation to get lost in one generation.

When our children ask us about our values, lifestyle, prayer in decision-making, Bible reading, church attendance, and worship, we have a responsibility to answer them. We are followers of Jesus. We must retell the story of how He became our Passover Lamb. His blood is the marker over our lives. We are no longer slaves to sin but free to serve the eternal one of heaven.

What are you teaching the children? Marvin Williams

Good Riddance Day

Psalm 103:1–12

As far as the east is from the west, so far has he removed our transgressions from us. —Psalm 103:12

A new tradition has grown up around the New Year. It's called Good Riddance Day. Based on a Latin American tradition, individuals write down unpleasant, embarrassing memories and bad issues from the past year and throw them into an industrial-strength shredder. Or some take a sledgehammer to their good riddance item.

The writer of Psalm 103 goes beyond suggesting that people say good riddance to unpleasant memories. He reminded us that God bids good riddance to our sins. In his attempt to express God's vast love for His people, the psalmist used word pictures. He compared the vastness of God's love to the distance between the heavens and the earth (v. 11). Then the psalmist talked about His forgiveness in spatial terms. As far as the place where the sun rises is from the place where the sun sets, so the Lord has removed His people's sins from them (v. 12). The psalmist wanted God's people to know that His love and forgiveness were infinite and complete. God freed His people from the power of their transgressions by fully pardoning them.

Good news! We don't have to wait until the New Year to experience Good Riddance Day. Through our faith in Jesus, when we confess and turn from our sins, He bids good riddance to them and casts them into the depths of the sea. Today can be a Good Riddance Day! Marvin Williams

DECEMBER 29

What You're Worth

Zechariah 11:4–13

The LORD said to me, "Throw it to the potter!" —Zechariah 11:13

Now an accomplished writer, Caitlin describes the depression she battled after fighting off an assault. The emotional violence cut deeper than her physical struggle, for she felt it proved "how undesirable I was. I was not the kind of girl you wanted to get to know." She felt unworthy of love, the kind of person others use and toss aside.

God understands. He lovingly shepherded Israel, but when He asked them what He was worth, "they paid me thirty pieces of silver" (Zechariah 11:12). This was the price of a slave; what masters must be reimbursed should their slave be accidentally killed (Exodus 21:32). God was insulted to be offered the lowest possible value—look at "the handsome price at which they valued me!" He said sarcastically (Zechariah 11:13). And He had Zechariah throw the money away.

Jesus understands. He wasn't merely betrayed by His friend; He was betrayed with contempt. The Jewish leaders despised Christ, so they offered Judas thirty pieces of silver—the lowest price you could put on a person—and he took it (Matthew 26:14–15; 27:9). Judas thought so little of Jesus that he sold Him for nearly nothing.

If people undervalued Jesus, don't be surprised when they undervalue you. Your value isn't what others say it is. It's not even what you say. It's entirely and only what God says. And He thinks you are worth dying for. Mike Wittmer

Just a Second

Psalm 39:4–6

How fleeting my life is. —Psalm 39:4

Scientists are pretty fussy about time. At the end of 2016, the folks at Goddard Space Flight Center in Maryland added an extra second to the year. So if you felt that year dragged on a bit longer than normal, you were right.

Why did they do that? Because the rotation of the earth slows down over time, and sometimes the years get just a tiny bit longer. When scientists track man-made objects launched into space, they must have accuracy down to the millisecond. This is "to make sure our collision avoidance programs are accurate," according to one scientist.

For most of us, a second gained or lost doesn't make much difference. Yet according to Scripture, our time and how we use it is important. For instance, Paul reminded us in 1 Corinthians 7:29 that "time is short." The time we are given in which to do God's work is limited, so we must use it wisely. Paul urged us to "[make] the best use of the time, because the days are evil" (Ephesians 5:16 ESV).

This doesn't mean we have to count each second as do the scientists, but when we consider the fleeting nature of life (Psalm 39:4), we can be reminded of the importance of using our time wisely. Dave Branon

Where Are You Headed?

Psalm 54

Where does my help come from? My help comes from the LORD. —Psalm 121:1–2

What determines our direction in life? I once heard an answer to that question in a surprising place: a motorcycle training course. Some friends and I wanted to ride, so we took a class to learn how. Part of our training dealt with something called target fixation.

"Eventually," our instructor said, "you're going to face an unexpected obstacle. If you stare at it—if you target fixate—you'll steer right into it. But if you look above and past it to where you need to go, you can usually avoid it." Then he added, "Where you're looking is the direction you're going to go."

That simple-but-profound principle applies to our spiritual lives too. When we "target fixate," focusing on our problems or struggles, we almost automatically orient our lives around them.

However, Scripture encourages us to look past our problems to the One who can help us with them. In Psalm 54:4, we read, "Surely God is my help; the Lord is the one who sustains me." The psalmist goes on: "You have delivered me from all my troubles" (v. 7). "Where does my help come from?" we ask with the psalm-writer. And he answers: "My help comes from the LORD" (121:1–2).

Sometimes our obstacles can seem insurmountable. But God invites us to look to Him to help us see beyond our troubles instead of letting them dominate our perspective. **Adam Holz**

THE WRITERS

James Banks, pastor of Peace Church in Durham, North Carolina, often enjoys a three-mile workout he does with his dog Max. Back at the house, James enjoys tinkering with old diesel engines with the goal of keeping them running for hundreds of thousands of miles. James is the author of several books, including *Praying Together, Praying the Prayers of the Bible*, and *Prayers for Prodigals*. He and his wife, Cari, have two adult children.

John Blase is a poet, adjunct seminary professor, literary agent, and part-time UPS employee. John and his wife live in Hot Springs, Arkansas. His books include *The Jubilee: Poems*; *Know When to Hold 'Em: The High Stakes Game of Fatherhood*; *Touching Wonder: Recapturing the Awe of Christmas*; and *All Is Grace: A Ragamuffin Memoir*. He says he's a fortunate man with a beautiful wife and three kids who look like their mother.

Dave Branon was for several years a high school English teacher and basketball coach before entering the publishing world at Our Daily Bread Ministries as an assistant editor for *Our Daily Bread*. Later, Dave spent eighteen years as managing editor of *Sports Spectrum* magazine, which features top Christian athletes and their testimony of faith. Dave has written twenty books, including Zondervan's *Sports Devotional Bible*, *The Lands of the Bible Today*, and *Beyond the Valley*. Dave and his wife, Sue, have four children and eight grandchildren and live in Grand Rapids, Michigan.

Winn Collier and his family live in Holland, Michigan, where Winn teaches at Western Theological Seminary and directs the Eugene Peterson Center for Christian Imagination. Winn writes for magazines and is the author of five books: *Restless Faith*, *Let God: The Transforming Wisdom of François Fénelon*, *Holy Curiosity*, the epistolary novel *Love Big, Be Well*, and *A Burning in My Bones: The Authorized Biography of Eugene H. Peterson*. Winn and his wife, Miska, have two sons.

Bill Crowder is a Bible teacher and writer with a deep love of sports. He played intercollegiate soccer (goalkeeper) followed by decades of slow-pitch softball, and now he plays golf. He also follows college and professional sports—especially Liverpool Football Club of the English Premier League. He and his wife, Marlene, live in North Carolina and have five adult children and a growing number of grandchildren. Bill has written several books, including *One Thing Is Necessary*, *For This He Came*, *My Hope Is in You*, and *Windows on Christmas*.

Lawrence Darmani has enjoyed bird-watching since he was a kid growing up in Ghana. Lawrence also loves to drop a line in the water and see what is biting. Over the years, Lawrence has established himself as an award-winning author. His first novel, *Grief Child*, won a British

Commonwealth Writers Prize. His books include *One for the Road*, *Strength for the Journey*, and *Palm-Tree Parables.* Lawrence and his wife, Comfort, have two daughters. The family lives in Accra, Ghana, where Lawrence is editor of *Step* magazine and CEO of Step Publishers.

Tim Gustafson had the special privilege of growing up as a missionary kid in Ghana. Tim would accompany his dad on hunts in Ghana, where Pop would carry a .308 and an eight-gauge shotgun ("Hey, the critters could be large," Tim says). Back stateside, Tim graduated from Michigan State University before serving in the US military (Active Army plus Army and Navy Reserves for many years). He served in places such as the Philippines, Turkey, Singapore, and the Caribbean. Tim is currently a senior content editor and writer for Our Daily Bread Ministries. He and his wife, Leisa, have eight children.

Adam Holz is the director of Focus on the Family's media review website, Plugged In. He has also served as associate editor at *Discipleship Journal.* He's the author of the NavPress Bible study *Beating Busyness.* Adam is married to Jennifer, and they have three children whose passions include swimming, gymnastics, drama, piano, and asking dad what's for dessert. In his free time, he enjoys playing electric guitar.

Arthur Jackson served as a pastor in the Chicago area for nearly thirty years. In addition to being an *Our Daily Bread* author since 2016, he has also been on staff at PastorServe, where he assists pastors and churches through coaching, consulting, and crisis care. Arthur and Shirley (his wife of over fifty years) reside in Kansas City, Kansas. They're the parents of five adult children and the grandparents of seven grandsons.

Leslie Koh was born and raised in Singapore. Leslie spent more than fifteen years as a journalist in the busy newsroom of local newspaper *The Straits Times* before moving to Our Daily Bread Ministries. Switching from bad news to good news has been most rewarding, and he still believes that nothing reaches out to people better than a good, compelling story. He currently serves as an editor for the Our Daily Bread Ministries Singapore office.

Albert Lee served admirably in the Singapore Armed Forces, earning the Best Recruit and Best Non-Commissioned Officer awards while completing his national service. In his youth, he was also a rugby player. Among Albert's other interests are swimming, art, and photography. Albert has been the national director of Singapore Youth for Christ and the director of international ministries for Our Daily Bread Ministries. He and his wife, Catherine, have two children.

Sheridan Voysey is an author and broadcaster on the subjects of faith and spirituality. His books include *Resilient: Your Invitation to a Jesus-Shaped Life*; *Resurrection Year: Turning Broken Dreams into New Beginnings*; and the award-winning *Unseen Footprints: Encountering the Divine Along the Journey of Life*. He is a regular contributor to Britain's largest national network BBC Radio 2. He also speaks at conferences and events around the world. Although born in Australia and living in England, he never did get the cricket bug. But he keeps that a secret from the neighbors. Sheridan is married to Merryn, a medical researcher, and they reside in Oxford, United Kingdom.

Marvin Williams should write an autobiography called *My Life at 11,000 Feet*. That number seems rather significant, since he has jumped out of an airplane at that height (and survived), and he has climbed to the height of 11,000 on Mt. Kenya, the highest mountain in Kenya. Earlier in his life, he was a martial arts champion. Marvin is senior teaching pastor of Trinity Church in Lansing, Michigan. He and his wife, Tonia, have three children.

Mike Wittmer's down-to-earth writing style and his sense of humor as a speaker belie his position as a noted Bible scholar. Mike did his undergraduate work at Cedarville University, and he received his doctorate at Calvin College. He is a longtime professor at Grand Rapids Theological Seminary, and he is pastor of Cedar Springs Baptist Church near Grand Rapids. He likes to cross-country ski, ride his mountain bike, kayak, and play backyard whiffle ball. Mike has written several books, including *The Last Enemy*, *Despite Doubt*, *Becoming Worldly Saints*, and *Heaven Is a Place on Earth*. Mike and Julie have three children.

More devotionals for men from Our Daily Bread

Help us get the word out!

Our Daily Bread Publishing exists to feed the soul with the Word of God.

If you appreciated this book, please let others know.

- Pick up another copy to give as a gift.
- Share a link to the book or mention it on social media.
- Write a review on your blog, on a book-seller's website, or at our own site (odb.org/store).
- Recommend this book for your church, book club, or small group.

Connect with us:

@ourdailybread

@ourdailybread

@ourdailybread

Our Daily Bread Publishing
PO Box 3566
Grand Rapids, Michigan 49501 USA

books@odb.org